T0251419

Cybersecurity

Public Sector Threats and Responses

Cybersecurity

Public Sector Threats and Responses

Kim Andreasson

CRC Press
Taylor & Francis Group
Boca Raton London New York

CRC Press is an imprint of the
Taylor & Francis Group, an **informa** business

CRC Press
Taylor & Francis Group
6000 Broken Sound Parkway NW, Suite 300
Boca Raton, FL 33487-2742

Version Date: 20111027

International Standard Book Number: 978-1-4398-4663-6 (Paperback)

Library of Congress Cataloging-in-Publication Data

Cybersecurity : public sector threats and responses / editor, Kim J. Andreasson.
    p. cm. -- (Public administration and public policy)
  Includes bibliographical references and index.
  ISBN 978-1-4398-4663-6 (pbk.)
   1. Computer networks--Security measures--Government policy. 2. Government information--Security measures. 3. Computer crimes--Prevention. I. Andreasson, Kim J.

TK5105.59.C927 2011
352.3'79--dc23   2011038756

Visit the Taylor & Francis Web site at
http://www.taylorandfrancis.com

and the CRC Press Web site at
http://www.crcpress.com

To those without whom this book would not have been possible. My wife, Diane, my parents, Kenth and Gullvi, and my friend, Meital, all of whom provided ongoing support. All book chapter authors and the publisher, of course, provided editorial contributions. I am grateful to all.

Contents

Preface

KAREN S. EVANS

"When we first started this process...agencies didn't know what they didn't know."

Karen S. Evans
*Administrator for E-Government and Information Technology,
Office of Management and Budget, In testimony before the
House Committee on Homeland Security, February 28, 2008*

In the fast-paced and ever-changing world of cybersecurity, no one can afford to miss a learning opportunity. So no matter where or when such an opportunity arises, you and your team had best be ready, because how you handle it may play a critical role in how successfully you manage risk and protect your enterprise now and into the future.

Just such a learning opportunity presented itself to me in 1996. It profoundly affected not only my own perspective but also my team's performance in managing information technology resources and services. At the time, all federal departments and agencies were asked to create a website to make services available to the public online. It was when e-mail was becoming the norm and the World Wide Web was bursting onto the scene. Our team was to take the "basement" operation of the Department of Justice's (DOJ's) Internet services and move them into a production environment.

The weekend before the move, however, the DOJ website was hacked. As we worked to restore services, we had to brief top leaders, provide information to law enforcement, and figure out what had gone wrong and how we would fix it. The events shaped my views on risk management, policies, certification, and accreditation, as well as the ability of an agency to "respond" versus "react." In that one weekend, I learned the importance of backup, communications, response plans, configuration management, and policies.

Policies should actually carry a capital "P," because I learned the importance of effective policies on a practical level cannot be underestimated. The DOJ had policies in place and we were duly pushing the necessary documents out in support of them. But we were essentially producing drafts, not final documents, because we focused on the technology often to the exclusion of other critical elements of risk assessment. I learned that in order to develop policies that effectively and constantly assess risk, you have to use a more holistic approach that simultaneously studies all of the elements involved, including production, technology, and risk associated with the services being provided.

All of this then begs the question: "What is risk"? What amount of security controls is senior leadership willing to live with in the process of providing services? Is there a compensating control? How will you respond when an incident occurs? For me—as the Office of Management and Budget's (OMB's) Administrator for E-Government and Information Technology and as a manager and chief information officer—these questions were critical in evaluating potential services, programs, investments, policies, and statutes. Being able to articulate the technical risk to senior leadership is critical to success, whether you are talking to a department head in the federal government or the chief executive officer (CEO) of a company. They need to know that the risk has been identified, how you intend to manage it, and what plans you have in place if services are compromised.

The federal government has statutes that govern the development of information resources management, such as the Computer Security Act of 1987, the Government Information Resources Security Act (which later became the Federal Information Security Management

Act, FISMA), and the E-Government Act of 2002. These statutes have led to policies such as OMB circulars, memoranda, and guidelines, including National Institute of Standards and Technology (NIST) guidelines and publications. So there are enough policies out there to make your head pop, but the basic questions to guide us remain the same:

- What is the risk?
- Is there a control?
- Can you live with the residual risk?
- What is your response plan when services become compromised?

Depending on your environment, the answers can become complicated and complex. But regardless of the enterprise or the environment, the service owner must sign off on the responses and strategies. In the certification and accreditation (C&A) world, this is known as the designated authorizing official who grants the authority to operate. Many have criticized the C&A process as a paperwork exercise. I have to admit, until I experienced my own "learning opportunity" event described above and saw my project on the front pages of newspapers, I did not have a true appreciation for that process. I was complying with the rules but not truly understanding the objective to reduce risk to a manageable level. Hopefully not everyone will have to experience a crisis weekend like the one we did in order to be able to apply their knowledge to their own situation. I believe that regardless of whether the risk affects the public or private sector, risk management is the key to success.

There are other factors to consider in risk management such as scale and time to implement systems. I do not directly address funding, although this affects your plans and can obviously affect your ability to reduce the risk associated with services. However, you could have all the funding you need yet have a design solution so complex that the time it takes to implement it leaves you vulnerable.

In the public sector, you have to implement services that minimize the cost and provide the greatest amount of value to the taxpayer. The catch-as-catch-can information security model of the 20th century where everyone fended for himself or herself is over. Each department, agency, or program at the federal, state, and local levels can no longer work in a vacuum, trying to create a perimeter is difficult at best, and the idea of preventing and stopping services is also fruitless. In today's world, you are no longer dealing with stopgap measures—rather, you are trying to create an environment that attracts a computer-savvy workforce and ensures the integrity of your information and data.

During our major drive to implement the e-government initiatives, the issues were not ones of technology but of trust and accountability, of using the authority of your position to achieve maximum results. We used to say, "you will get the same level of service if not better, at the same price if not lower, while ensuring privacy and security." The basic goal of providing that level of service has not changed.

In closing, I return to the most fundamental of the basic issues: risk. Do I know who is who on my network accessing services and whether they should they really have access to all the services and data? Understanding and categorizing systems is a critical part of the planning for your enterprise. Using tools such as enterprise architecture and the associated activities that support it can help you understand the risk-management landscape and develop the necessary transition plans to put an effective system in place. Coupling this with your capital planning activities then helps you to decide the investment strategy that best supports a risk management system that will provide the security your enterprise needs today and into the future.

Karen S. Evans

Introduction

Global interconnectivity is spreading. The International Telecommunications Union (ITU), a specialized agency of the United Nations (UN), estimated that two billion people were online by the end of 2010; by 2015, the number will reach five billion. The ITU also reckons that 143 countries currently offer 3G services, potentially providing Internet access through smart phones to a growing portion of the estimated 5.3 billion people with mobile subscriptions, 3.8 billion of which are in the developing world.

Unfortunately, the more we move online, the more vulnerable we become to cyber threats. This book examines trends and strategies from around the world in order to raise awareness and offer a primer of cybersecurity in the public sector, which can be defined broadly as the vulnerability of computer systems, including Internet websites, against unauthorized access or attack, or the policy measures taken to protect them.

To understand cybersecurity in the public sector one has to recognize the convergence of three underlying forces: globalization, connectivity, and the movement of public sector functions online, commonly referred to as electronic government (e-government).

The Internet offers a common platform through which anyone can virtually take part in globalization. It's as easy to access a website in one country as in another, and people around the world are jumping at the opportunity to do so. According to data in early 2011 from Internet World Stats, a website, the number of Internet users has increased by 445% over the past 10 years for a global penetration level of 29%. Given the benefits of information and communications technology (ICT), countries around the world are also working hard to get their remaining citizens online. According to a May 2011 report from the McKinsey Global Institute, a consultancy research arm, the Internet's share of GDP is 3.4% across the G8, South Korea, Sweden, Brazil, China, and India. Among mature economies, it has accounted for 21% of GDP growth in the last five years.

According to Eurostat, the European statistics office, 39% of households in the EU 15 had Internet access in 2002; by 2010 the equivalent figure was 68%. In 2000, 30% of South Korean households had broadband access; in 2009 the figure was 96%. In the United States, the figure rose from 4% to 64% in the same time frame, all according to the OECD, which also reports that the median broadband price for a monthly subscription in 2010 had fallen to about $40.

The time people spend online is also increasing. In 2010, according to comScore, a digital measurement consultancy, the *average* American spent 32 hours per month on the Internet, despite the fact that about a fifth of the population remains completely offline.

Our reliance on the Internet is likely to increase. Development of radio frequency identification (RFID) technology combined with the introduction of Internet Protocol Version 6 (IPv6), for example, has enabled a platform to create "The Internet of Things," tech speak for connecting everything to the Internet, including everyday objects such as cars. And why not be able to unlock your car remotely in case of an emergency or install it with wireless technology for improved communication services?

Because of its benefits, the Internet is embraced by the public sector. A commonly cited example of increased efficiency is taxes. In 2011, the Swedish tax authority expected 65% of people to file online, saving time, effort, and money for the government while making the lives of its constituents easier. As the UN World Public Sector Report plainly stated in 2003, "Governments are increasingly becoming aware of the importance of employing e-government to improve the delivery of public services to the people" (p. 128). But the online environment also extends beyond simple services and provides governments at all levels with an opportunity to improve accountability, development, efficiency, and transparency.

Various international e-government benchmark surveys show great progress over the past decade, illustrated in part by the notion that most countries around the world are already "e-ready." Hence, measurement has moved from "readiness" to actual "development" in the case of the UN. The Economist Intelligence Unit, a consultancy, even changed the name of its 10-year-old report to reflect this trend, as its e-readiness rankings became the digital economy rankings in 2010. In an illustration of how rapid progress can be, the average availability of 20 important online public services in the EU27 increased from 69% in 2009 to 82% in 2010, according to Europe's ninth e-government benchmark report.

Although the demand for e-government (usage) has lagged availability (supply), governments everywhere are urging constituents to use their services and take advantage of online information. In the EU27, 42% of individuals between the ages of 16 and 74 currently use the Internet for interaction with public authorities. A key objective of the Digital Agenda, the EU strategy for using digital tools to develop the economy, is to increase that number by 2015 to half. Online inclusion, or e-inclusion, is also one of seven central pillars in the Digital Agenda, seeking to enhance digital literacy, skills, and inclusion. In the United States, 61% of all American adults looked for information or completed a transaction on a government website in the past 12 months, according to a 2010 survey by the Pew Internet and American Life Project.

Efforts to move government activities online, whether for external purposes to meet user demand for personalized offerings through a variety of channels, such as mobile government (m-government) and Web 2.0 tools, or for internal efficiency reasons, to share classified information or connect power plants to the Internet, are increasingly common at all levels of government and across the world. Although efficiency is certainly a driving force, the public sector is also under increasing pressure to use the Internet for transparency purposes.

The 2009 EU Ministerial Declaration on eGovernment in Malmö, Sweden, for example, called for the strengthening of online transparency as a way of promoting accountability and trust in government. In the United States, President Barack Obama promised "an unprecedented level of openness in government" only to find himself confronted with the WikiLeaks cables of sensitive government information being leaked, at which time, the White House Office of Management and Budget sent a memorandum, on December 3, 2010, according to CNN, prohibiting unauthorized federal government employees from accessing the website to read the classified documents, an illustration of cybersecurity issues to come.

American federal chief information officers (CIOs) are similarly excited about open government, but they too are concerned about cybersecurity, rating it as their greatest challenge, ahead of other concerns such as infrastructure, workforce, management, efficiency, accountability, and acquisition, according to an annual survey of federal CIOs in the United States in March 2010 conducted by TechAmerica, an information technology (IT) trade association.

Globalization and the Internet have given rise to new opportunities for the public sector to improve internal efficiency and better serve constituents in the form of e-government. But with an increasing user base and ever greater reliance on the Internet, digital tools are also exposing the public sector to great risks, hence the importance of cybersecurity.

Enter Cybersecurity

In an interconnected world, as Walter Wriston, the former Chairman of Citibank, once put it, information networks are vulnerable to attack by anyone at anytime. The numbers prove his point.

"Several CIOs say they see millions of malicious attempts per day to access their networks," according to the TechAmerica survey of federal CIOs, and participants alarmingly noted "growth in cyber attacks backed by countries looking for classified information or ways to control critical parts of our military and critical infrastructure" (p. 7).

According to the Fourth Quarter Threats Report from McAfee, a security company, 2010 "saw increases in targeted attacks, increases in sophistication, and increases in the number of attacks on the new classes of devices that seem to appear with regularity." By the end of the year, the report said, malicious software (malware) had reached its highest level ever. In 2010, McAfee identified about 55,000 such threats every day.

The 2010 state of enterprise security survey from Symantec, a security company, of 2,100 respondents across 27 countries found that three-quarters of all enterprises had experienced a cyber attack in the prior year and all of them had experienced a cyber loss, such as theft of information, lost productivity, or loss of customer trust.

A 2010 survey of 217 senior-level IT executives from U.S. federal organizations conducted by the Ponemon Institute, a consultancy, showed that 75% of respondents experienced one or more data breach incidents in the prior year. According to the same survey, 71% of respondents said cyber terrorism is on the rise.

Cyber threats can be categorized in several ways, one of which is to look at those politically motivated (such as cyber warfare, cyber terrorism, espionage, and hacktivism, the hacking for political purposes) compared with nonpolitical (typically financially motivated, such as cyber crime, intellectual property theft, and fraud, but also hacking for fun or retribution, for example, from a disgruntled employee). What is interesting about this classification is the realization that international cooperation is difficult regarding politically motivated threats as someone is likely to protect the perpetrators, whereas there tends to be broad agreement in combating cyber crime as most governments have an interest in doing so.

Politically Motivated Threats

The aim of politically motivated attacks is generally to disrupt services with or without the intention to also cause physical damage. A common approach is to use a botnet, a collection of infected computers (agents) that allows someone to control them remotely, to launch a distributed denial of service (DDoS) attack, which attempts to disrupt websites by overwhelming them with traffic. A commonly cited example is the attacks on Estonia during its diplomatic standoff with Russia in April 2007, when several government websites were made inaccessible for up to 3 weeks. The botnet problem is likely to increase as the rise in broadband devices that tend to be "always on" are increasingly targeted by bot networks. As early as December 2006, the most recent data available from the OECD as of this writing, an average of 1.7 computers per 100 broadband subscribers were infected by bots.

Attacks with physical consequences are rare given the needed sophistication; however, it is of increasing concern and likely to proliferate as more things become connected to the Internet. In 2010, for example, Stuxnet became the first malware specifically designed to attack critical infrastructure in the form of Iran's nuclear power reactors, which it succeeded in disrupting. Critical infrastructure, such as power plants, are often essential to government operations but in many cases it is owned or operated by the private sector, hence early and frequent calls for public–private partnerships (PPPs) in regard to the protection of such systems.

Politically motivated attacks can also seek to gain publicity in order to undermine the perception of the public. In 2010, a group called "Anonymous" successfully brought down the websites of various organizations, including the Swedish prosecution authority, and the private sector sites of MasterCard and Visa, in support of WikiLeaks, the whistle-blowing website. If sufficiently efficient, attacks on public sector websites can affect the trust of e-government to such a degree that public perception turns increasingly negative whereby people would be averse to make certain transactions online, be unwilling to share data, or be reluctant to believe the information provided. This is already a problem. According to Europe's Digital Agenda website, only 12% of European users feel completely safe in making transactions online.

Fake banking e-mails and websites that look like their real counterparts are common. It is likely only a matter of time before we witness their public sector equivalents, asking us for sensitive data or providing us with misleading information. To some extent this is already happening. The Internet was widely used in the 2010 to 2011 uprisings in the Middle East, and government websites often reported a different story than that from bloggers. On occasion, some governments, like Egypt, tried to shut down the Internet to stem the flow of information.

Politically motivated threats are also about the security of content and data, such as in cases of espionage or whistle blowing, both of which are increasingly common as a result of more information finding its way online.

Nonpolitically Motivated Threats

The motivation for nonpolitically motivated attacks is generally finan-cial, and most attacks will be considered cyber crimes. As such, they tend to focus on stealing data, such as credit card information, while keeping a low profile. A common approach is to use malware, either by designing it from scratch, repurposing existing malware, or buying it on the black market. Malware can be spread in a number of ways, including via e-mails or through websites, and accomplish a variety of things, such as installing applications that can track key strokes on individual devices. It can also hijack computers and make them part of botnets, which can be rented on the black market to conduct DDoS attacks, or be used as a platform to distribute spam e-mails.

A common spam technique is phishing, an attempt to solicit sensi-tive information from users by using an unsolicited e-mail that links to a malicious website. Even though people are commonly told not to provide such information, it remains a problem because of the sophis-tication of these e-mails. According to data from Cisco, about 3% of all users click on malware links. To raise awareness of phishing in the public sector, the Taiwan National Emergency Response Team (TWNCERT) sent 186,564 fake phishing e-mails to 31,094 pub-lic sector employees across 62 government agencies. Overall, 15,484 (8.30%) of those e-mails were opened and 7,836 (4.20%) links within them were clicked, potentially leaving thousands of unsuspecting pub-lic sector employees at risk as well as their employer, the government.

Yet another way to classify cyber attacks is whether the threat is external (as assumed in most cases above) or internal, such as current or former disgruntled employees. Again, WikiLeaks is an example where, purportedly, a soldier in the U.S. Army downloaded sensitive information to a USB drive only to later pass it on. But one could also use a memory stick to install a program or software on a computer for other various malicious purposes, such as monitoring keystrokes or installing a backdoor to access it remotely. In one instance, USB drives were blamed for the installation of Conficker, a highly advanced worm, on the Manchester City Council computers, an incident that cost it an estimated £1.5 million. The Council has since banned the use of such memory sticks and also disabled all USB ports. How to balance productivity against monitoring users and assigning them appropriate access levels is a topic of concern for public sector organizations around the world.

It is important to understand that every device connected to the Internet is a potential threat because it can be taken over and used as an agent by someone else, for example, as part of a botnet. Conficker is said to have taken over seven million computers around the world, including those of unsuspecting regular home users and those of the French Navy and the U.S. Air Force, among others.

Public Sector Responses

Because globalization, the Internet, and e-government will continue to flourish, the public sector must find a way to meet the cybersecurity challenge in an increasingly connected world. Every day, more people come online; every day, more things are connected to the Internet; every day, the public sector is increasingly leveraging ICTs; every day, the consequences of cyber attack are rising.

Cybersecurity is an organizational problem but also a global phenomenon. As such, it must be dealt with at all levels, from the international arena to the regional, national, and local levels. The threats may stay the same, but the response can vary. Consequently, that is how the book is organized: from global trends and current policy to local approaches and practical considerations.

Section I: Global Trends

Cybersecurity is ultimately a global challenge. As such, the first section discusses worldwide e-government trends and their unintended consequences, case studies of the types of cyber threats that are increasingly common, and a potential global solution from a global institution.

The first chapter illustrates some issues of moving public sector information online. In "The Global Rise of E-Government and Its Security Implications," Jeremy Millard at the Danish Technology Institute suggests we treat security and data protection as the most pressing technical challenge, but at the same time approach the issue incrementally and proportionally given that there is a trade-off between increased security and usage. The right approach, he argues, is to build in security and data protection from the start of any e-government initiative.

In "Understanding Cyber Threats," Deborah L. Wheeler at the U.S. Naval Academy provides the context for things to come by exemplifying cybersecurity issues globally through an assessment of emerging threats using two case studies: WikiLeaks and Stuxnet. She applies them to the new environment of IT for regime change and along the way identifies key vulnerabilities in this emerging, yet strategically important realm of engagement.

A well-known and highly debated cyber incident is the July 2009 DDoS attacks against American and South Korean websites. Motohiro Tsuchiya at Keio University illuminates them from a new perspective in "Cybersecurity in East Asia: Japan and the 2009 Attacks on South Korea and the United States." He analyzes how the Japanese government responded to the attacks, in particular the cooperation and competition between intelligence and law enforcement agencies. The chapter concludes with an outline of the current online security landscape in East Asia.

In "Toward a Global Approach to Cybersecurity," Marco Obiso and Gary Fowlie from the International Telecommunications Union (ITU) argue that a globally secure cyber environment is necessary to provide the more than five billion people who will be online by 2015 with a platform to bring about economic growth. Given the global nature of the threat, this is not a problem any one nation can solve alone. In order to accomplish this goal, therefore, the ITU created The Global Cybersecurity Agenda, the elements of which are outlined in this chapter.

Section II: National and Local Policy Approaches

Global trends feed into regional, national, and local initiatives. The second section begins by describing what makes policy organization so difficult in the area of cybersecurity, followed by an overview of the current policy environment in the United States and Europe.

Elaine C. Kamarck at Harvard University offers insights into why cybersecurity is difficult from an organizational perspective in "The Cybersecurity Policy Challenge: The Tyranny of Geography." The cyber challenge, she argues, is unlike anything government has encountered before. To help understand why, this chapter outlines the history of the U.S. federal government's steps in the area of cybersecurity and, along the way, details today's challenges as they relate to both the United States and Europe.

Daniel Castro at the Information Technology and Innovation Foundation illuminates the current federal government organization in "U.S. Federal Cybersecurity Policy" and also briefly compares it to Europe. The chapter describes various challenges and efforts at the federal level including threats, the evolution of the policy framework, and an overview of how human and financial cybersecurity resources are allocated across the federal government's civilian agencies. The chapter concludes with highlights of emerging policy challenges.

With its Digital Agenda, few places rely on ICTs as much as Europe. Yet, as if the challenge of cybersecurity was not difficult enough, imagine a community of over 600 million people in 27 different countries with various organizations and institutions at the national and regional levels trying to tackle the issue together. In "European Cybersecurity Policy," Neil Robinson at RAND Europe explains how it is currently done. The chapter first describes relevant European organizations involved in cybersecurity, followed by details on various EU laws and regulations.

International and national cybersecurity incidents often grab the headlines, but local governments frequently find themselves in the trenches, illustrating that there must be a holistic approach that is as much bottom up as it is top down. The second section ends with a case study on how this can be accomplished and a forward-looking chapter on how local Southern California government agencies are balancing security with emerging Government 2.0 policy.

Taking the Spanish region of Catalonia as an example, Ignacio Alamillo Domingo at Universitat Autònoma de Barcelona and Astrea La Infopista Jurídica SL, a consultancy, and Agustí Cerrillo-i-Martínez at the Universitat Oberta de Catalunya, show how a local cybersecurity plan can be created to supplement national (Spanish), regional (EU), and international (ITU) policies. "A Local Cybersecurity Approach: The Case of Catalonia" begins with an assessment of relevant policies, followed by an analysis of how the local Catalan plan supports them. The chapter concludes by discussing the role that subnational security policies can have within a global framework.

In "Securing Government Transparency: Cybersecurity Policy Issues in a Gov 2.0 Environment and Beyond," Gregory G. Curtin and Charity C. Tran at Civic Resource Group, a consultancy, argue that as more local government entities try to meet the growing expectation for Government 2.0—open data, transparency, increased information access and availability, and outlets for citizen feedback and interaction—they must also address the challenges of securing online information. To assess current trends at the local level, they present the findings of a micro-study from the innovative mega-region of Southern California.

Section III: Practical Considerations

The world has a long history of dealing with crime and war offline; it is likely we face the same challenge online. As the public sector must be prepared to respond to cyber attacks, the final section offers some practical considerations for doing so.

In "The Civilian Cyber Incident Response Policies of the U.S. Federal Government," Chris Bronk at Rice University provides an overview of relevant federal cyber incident response policies in order to help public sector managers gain a better understanding of the operational cyber environment. The focus is on federal cybersecurity regulations, including requirements from the Federal Information Security Management Act (FISMA) and guidance from the National Institute for Standards and Technology (NIST), and the chapter concludes with a discussion of the draft National Cyber Incident Response Plan (NCIRP).

In "Cybersecurity Health Check: A Framework to Enhance Organizational Security," Shih Ming Pan, Pei-Te Chen, and Pei Wen Liu of the Information and Communication Security Technology Service Center and Chii-Wen Wu at the Research, Development and Evaluation Commission, Executive Yuan, in Taiwan, Department of Information Management, Huafan University, describe a framework to assess organizational security. Based on business management theories but applied specifically to cybersecurity, the proposed framework contains quantifiable indicators that can help organizations track and monitor their ongoing efforts toward strengthening security while lowering cost.

A common response to the cybersecurity challenge is the formation of public–private partnerships (PPPs). But as Dave Sulek and Megan Doscher at Booz Allen Hamilton, a consultancy, point out in "Beyond Public–Private Partnerships: Leadership Strategies for Securing Cyberspace," these rarely work. The first part of their chapter describes the challenges for PPPs and outlines the emerging Cyber Domain before discussing the idea of overlapping vital interests. The second part identifies five key areas in which leaders from the public and private sectors, as well as civil society can take action to strengthen collaboration in cyberspace.

To conclude the volume, your editor takes a bleak view in "Is There a Conclusion to Cybersecurity?" Because it is an issue that is unlikely to go away, the first part of the chapter attempts to highlight some of the practical aspects to consider when thinking about cybersecurity from an organizational policy perspective. The second part provides an overview of two broad emerging trends that are likely to increasingly affect the public sector and hence its cybersecurity efforts: the movement to mobility and cyber warfare.

Kim Andreasson
Sài Gòn, May 2011

References

Addley, Esther, and Josh Halliday. December 8, 2010. Operation Payback cripples MasterCard site in revenge for WikiLeaks ban. guardian.co.uk

Cisco. 2010. Annual Security Report.

de Sola, David. December 3, 2010. U.S. agencies warn unauthorized employees not to look at WikiLeaks. CNN. http://articles.cnn.com/2010-12-03/us/wikileaks.access.warning_1_wikileaks-website-memo-documents?_s=PM:US

Economist Intelligence Unit. 2009. E-readiness rankings 2009: The usage imperative.

Economist Intelligence Unit. 2010. Digital economy rankings 2010: Beyond e-readiness.

European Commission. 2009. Ministerial Declaration on eGovernment. http://ec.europa.eu/information_society/activities/egovernment/events/past/malmo_2009/press/ministerial-declaration-on-egovernment.pdf

European Commission. 2010. Digitizing Public Services in Europe: Putting ambition into action. 9th Benchmark Measurement.

International Telecommunications Union. October 19, 2010. Media release. www.itu.int/net/pressoffice/pr ess_releases/2010/39.aspx#url

Internet World Stats. 2010. http://www.internet worldstats.com/stats.htm

Liu, Pei-Wen, Jia-Chyi Wu, and Pei-Ching Liu. 2008. TWNCERT Social Engineering Drill: The Best Practice to Protect against Social Engineering Attacks in E-mail Form. http://www.first.org/conference/2008/contest.html

McAfee. 2010. Threats Report: Fourth Quarter.

McKinsey Global Institute. May 2011. Internet matters: The Net's sweeping impact on growth, jobs, and prosperity. http://www.mckinsey.com/mgi/publications/internet_matters/pdfs/MGI_internet_matters_full_report.pdf

Obama, Barack. 2009. Memorandum for the Heads of Executive Departments and Agencies: Transparency and Open Government. http://www.whitehouse.gov/the_press_office/TransparencyandOpenGovernment/

OECD. 2008. Measuring Security and Trust in the Online Environment. A View Using Official Data.

OECD. Broadband data portal. http://www.oecd.org/sti/ict/broadband

Pew Internet and American Life Project. April 2010. Government Online: The Internet gives citizens new paths to government services and information. http://www.pewinternet.org/Reports/2010/Government-Online/Summary-of-Findings.aspx.

Ponemon Institute. 2009. Cyber Security Mega Trends: Study of IT leaders in the U.S. federal government.

Symantec. 2010. State of Enterprise Security.

TechAmerica. 2010. Twentieth Annual Survey of Federal Chief Information Officers (CIO).

Traynor, Ian. May 17, 2007. Russia accused of unleashing cyberwar to disable Estonia. *The Guardian*.

United Nations. 2003. World Public Sector Report: E-Government at the Crossroads.

Wriston, Walter B. September/October 1997. Bits, bytes, and diplomacy. *Foreign Affairs* 76(5): 174–175.

The Editor

Kim Andreasson has advised the United Nations on e-government since 2003, most recently in preparation for the global 2012 e-government survey, and is a managing director of DAKA advisory AB, a consultancy. He was previously an interim associate director and a senior editor at The Economist Group's Business Research division where he co-edited the annual report on the Digital Economy Rankings. Andreasson is an elected member of the International Institute of Strategic Studies and the Pacific Council of International Policy and is a John C. Whitehead Fellow at the Foreign Policy Association. He serves on the editorial board of the *Journal of Information Technology and Politics*.

Contributor Biographies (in Order of Appearance)

Karen Evans serves as the national director for the US Cyber Challenge, a nationwide program focused specifically on the cyber workforce. She is also an independent consultant in the areas of leadership, management, and the strategic use of information technology. She retired after nearly 28 years of federal government service with responsibilities ranging from a GS-2 to Presidential Appointee as the Administrator for E-Government and Information Technology at the Office of Management and Budget within the Executive Office of the President. Evans oversaw the federal information technology (IT) budget of nearly $71 billion which included implementation of IT throughout the federal government.

Kim Andreasson has advised the United Nations on e-government since 2003, most recently in preparation for the global 2012 e-government survey, and is a managing director of DAKA advisory AB, a consultancy. He was previously an associate director and a senior editor at *The Economist* Group's Business Research division where he coedited the annual report on the Digital Economy Rankings. Andreasson is an elected member of the International Institute of Strategic Studies and the Pacific Council of International Policy and is a John C. Whitehead Fellow at the Foreign Policy Association. Andreasson serves on the editorial board of the *Journal of Information Technology and Politics*.

Jeremy Millard has worked with governments, agencies, and the private and civil sectors in all parts of the world on information society and knowledge economy consultancy, including the European Commission, the United Nations, and the Organization for Economic Cooperation and Development (OECD). Recent assignments include the European eGovernment annual benchmark, leading an impact assessment of the European eGovernment 2010 Action Plan, leading a large-scale Europe-wide survey and analysis of eParticipation, and developing the eGovernment 2020 Vision Study on Future Directions of Public Service Delivery. He also recently prepared a paper for the OECD on back-office developments in support of user-centered eGovernment strategies.

Deborah L. Wheeler is an associate professor of political science at the U.S. Naval Academy. She is also visiting professor at American University in Kuwait. She holds a Ph.D. from the University of Chicago in Political Science. For the past 15 years she has specialized in the diffusion and impact of the Internet in the Muslim Middle East. Her work has been widely published and includes numerous articles, book chapters, and a book, *The Internet in the Middle East: Global Expectations and Local Imaginations in Kuwait* (Albany: State University of New York Press, 2006).

Motohiro Tsuchiya is a professor at the Graduate School of Media and Governance at Keio University in Japan. Prior to joining the Keio faculty, he was associate professor at Center for Global Communications (GLOCOM), International University of Japan. He was also a visiting scholar at University of Maryland, George Washington University, and Massachusetts Institute of Technology in the United States. He is interested in global governance and information technologies. Tsuchiya is a member of the editorial advisory board of *Info* (ISSN: 1463–6697). He earned his B.A. in political science, M.A. in international relations, and Ph.D. in media and governance from Keio University.

Marco Obiso has been working in the field of Information and Communication Technologies for the past 15 years. In 2000, Obiso moved to Geneva to start working at the International Telecommunication Union, the lead UN-specialized agency for ICTs, as an information technology (IT) expert and was involved in several areas including network infrastructure development, system integration, application cooperation, and IT service management. He subsequently moved to the ITU Corporate Strategy Division as Programme Manager, providing advice concerning technical developments and trends in the ICT sector, Internet and Cybersecurity related issues, and emerging ICT technologies. He is currently Coordinator of Intersectorial Activities on Cybersecurity, facilitating the work of the ITU in elaborating cybersecurity strategies for the benefit of the ITU member states as well as strengthening coordination and cooperation within the UN system.

Gary Fowlie is the head of the Liaison office of the International Telecommunication Union to the United Nations. Fowlie was responsible for communications and member relations for the UN World Summit on the Information Society and from 2005 until 2009 was the Chief of Media Liaison for the United Nations in New York. Fowlie is an economist and journalist. Prior to joining the International Telecommunication Union in 2000, he worked for Microsoft and the global consulting firm of Hill and Knowlton. He is a graduate of the University of Alberta and the London School of Economics.

Elaine C. Kamarck is a lecturer in Public Policy at the Harvard Kennedy School of Government. She teaches innovation in government and American politics. She is the author of two books, *The End of Government…As We Know It* and *Primary Politics: Presidential Candidates and the Making of the Modern Nominating System*. Prior to coming to Harvard, Kamarck was senior policy advisor to Vice President Al Gore and President Bill Clinton. In that capacity, she designed and led the National Performance Review, otherwise known as the reinventing government movement. Since leaving the government Kamarck has advised more than 20 governments around the world on innovation and reform.

Daniel Castro is a senior analyst with the Information Technology and Innovation Foundation (ITIF), a nonprofit think tank in Washington, DC. His research focuses on issues relating to technology and the information economy, including data privacy, information security, electronic voting, accessibility, e-government, and health information technology (IT). Before joining ITIF, Castro worked as an IT analyst at the U.S. Government Accountability Office (GAO) where he audited IT security and management controls at various government agencies, including the Securities and Exchange Commission (SEC) and the Federal Deposit Insurance Corporation (FDIC). He has a B.S. in foreign service from Georgetown University and an M.S. in information security technology and management from Carnegie Mellon University.

Neil Robinson is a senior analyst at RAND Europe, based in Brussels. Robinson has conducted public policy research into a variety of issues concerning risks and threats in cyberspace. He has led a number of research studies for various European Union institutions (Directorate General Home Affairs, Directorate General Information Society and Media of the European Commission, and ENISA) and has briefed the U.K. MoD, French Ecole Militaire, U.S. Congress, and North Atlantic Treaty Organization (NATO) on a variety of cybersecurity issues. He has written and presented extensively at a number of events across Europe on topics such as cloud computing, data protection, cyberdefense, and information risk.

Ignacio Alamillo Domingo is a researcher in risk governance at Universitat Autònoma de Barcelona, lawyer and general manager of Astrea La Infopista Jurídica SL. Formerly, he has been senior security consultant at Generalitat de Catalunya; research and consultancy manager at Agencia Catalana de Certificació; and legal trusted third party (TTP) manager at Agencia de Certificación Electrónica. He also has been a member of the European Electronic Signature Standardization Initiative Steering Committee; member of the European Network and Information Security Steering Committee; and member of the ETSI Electronic Signature Infrastructure Group. Ignacio has contributed to 14 books on electronic signature and network security, including legal and organizational issues.

Agustí Cerrillo-i-Martínez holds a Ph.D. in Law (Universitat de Barcelona, 2003) and a degree in Law (Universitat de Barcelona, 1994) and in Political Sciences (Universitat Autònoma de Barcelona, 1996). He is professor of Administrative Law at Universitat Oberta de Catalunya (September 2001 to present) and the Law and Political Sciences Department Director at the same university. He is also the e-government postgraduate academic director. He has researched and published articles and books on e-government and in particular on diffusion and re-use of public sector information through the Internet.

Gregory G. Curtin, Ph.D., J.D., is a member of the World Economic Forum's (WEF) Global Advisory Council on the Future of Government, and is the founder and principal of Civic Resource Group, a Gov 2.0 strategy and development firm.

Charity C. Tran is a Ph.D. candidate at Texas Tech University, and a digital communications consultant with Civic Resource Group.

Chris Bronk is the Baker Institute fellow in IT policy and a lecturer in Rice University's Department of Computer Science. He previously served as a career diplomat with the U.S. Department of State. Since arriving at Rice, Bronk divided his attentions among a number of areas including information security, technology for immigration management, broadband policy, Web 2.0 in government, and the militarization of cyberspace. Holding a Ph.D. from The Maxwell School of Syracuse University, Bronk also studied international relations at Oxford University and received a bachelor's degree from the University of Wisconsin–Madison.

Shih Ming Pan has 6 years experience in information security. He is now a manager of Information and Communication Security Technology Center (ICST). He has supported organizations or government measuring effectiveness of information security management and technical controls since 2005, including network infrastructure and perimeter security, system and end-point security, social engineering protection, information security incidents and human information security awareness. Shih Ming Pan had led a Cybersecurity

Health Check Team to support over 17 Taiwan government agencies to evaluate the information security level.

Chii-Wen Wu got his M.S. degree in computer science from San Diego State University in 1990. Currently, he is director of the government information and communication security working group of the National Information and Communication Security Taskforce, Executive Yuan. Chii-Wen Wu has engaged in information security related work since 1999, and he is responsible to Taiwan e-government information security issues at present.

Pei-Te Chen received his Ph.D. in Electrical Engineering from National Cheng Kung University in 2007. He is a certificated OSSTMM Professional Security Tester (OPST), and masters in information security, cryptology, and penetration testing. Chen is currently a section manager at the Information and Communication Security Technology Center (ICST), responsible for developing information security standards, building up a cybersecurity health check framework, and managing penetration testing services.

Yun Ting Lo is now an associate engineer of Information and Communication Security Technology Center (ICST). He has engaged in Taiwan government defense in-depth related works. Yun Ting serves as an expert of the penetration testing team and has provided professional pen-testing to secure over 15 Taiwan central government agencies. He has also been responsible for the "Information and Communication Security Service for Taiwan Local Government Agencies" project since 2008 and has improved the information security level of over 14 Taiwan local government agencies.

Pei Wen Liu, Ph.D., is the deputy general director of Project Resource Division, III, and he also serves as director of Information and Communication Security Technology Center (ICST) and Taiwan National Computer Emergency Response Team (TWNCERT) of the Taiwan government. During his career, Liu has been responsible for several important information security initiatives for the government of Taiwan, including the Government Security Operation Center (G-SOC) project, Incident Report and Response Mechanism, and ISMS directives and guidelines for government sectors. Devoting much of his time to IT security standards within the Asia-Pacific region, Liu is also the chair of AFACT Security Working Group and a member of Regional Asia Information Security Exchange (RAISE) Forum. Liu is also the honoree of 2008 (ISC)2 Information Security Leadership Achievements.

Dave Sulek is a principal at Booz Allen Hamilton with 20 years of strategy, public policy analysis, and general management consulting experience. Sulek leads a team of policy specialists who analyze cyber-security, public–private partnerships, homeland security, health, and defense issues for government and commercial clients. He received a master's degree in National Security Studies from the Edmund A. Walsh School of Foreign Affairs at Georgetown University and a bachelor's degree in political science from Syracuse University.

Megan Doscher has supported the Department of Homeland Security in multiple capacities with Booz Allen Hamilton for more than 6 years, focusing on communications and cybersecurity policy, and working extensively with public–private partnerships for critical infrastructure protection (CIP). Doscher has also supported cross-sector engagements with the National Cyber Security Division, and currently is a policy analyst for the Department of Defense's Internet Governance team. She spent the early years of her career writing and editing technology and business news for *The Wall Street Journal Online* before the events of September 11, 2001, inspired her interest in CIP. She received a master's degree in Criminal Justice/Security Management from George Washington University and a bachelor's degree in journalism from Syracuse University.

1

THE GLOBAL RISE OF E-GOVERNMENT AND ITS SECURITY IMPLICATIONS

JEREMY MILLARD

Contents

Introduction

The business of government is, at core, all about public sector data, information, and knowledge being created, altered, moved around, and deployed to meet the needs of society. E-government digitizes some or all of these processes and the outcomes produced, potentially transforming them in ways not always predicted or desired, whether

1

for the internal operations of the public sector or for the users of public services and facilities. These unintended consequences can be problematic. For example, they can pose profound challenges to cybersecurity in terms of unauthorized access to, or use of, data and public sector information. Public sector managers need to be just as aware of these unintended consequences as they are of those they expect when e-government is introduced.

Now, do not misunderstand me. E-government is a very good thing and has many clear and documented benefits. For example, there is a lot of evidence that digitizing back-office processes can lead to significant cost savings for government through more efficient and rational processes, joining up administrations to share and save resources, better design and targeted services, and more intelligent and evidence-based policy development with greater impact. As illustrated in a 2011 article in the *European Journal of ePractice*, e-government also has a lot to offer in tackling the financial and economic crisis. In the front-office, e-government services undoubtedly provide users with better, more convenient, time-saving services, available 24-7. Digitization encourages transparency, openness, and participation, and provides tools for users to get involved in designing and consuming services more appropriate to their individual needs.

For example, a 2010 survey from TechAmerica, an information technology (IT) trade association, shows how federal agencies and departments in the United States have increased efforts to publish data sets and utilize social media tools as part of the Obama Administration's push for transparency, yet continue to struggle with cybersecurity, IT infrastructure, and workforce issues. The shift toward a more open government has created threats as well as opportunities. According to the survey, some chief information officers (CIOs) see "millions of malicious attempts per day to access their networks"—from recreational hackers to sophisticated cyber-criminals.

This chapter illustrates some of the issues of moving public sector information online, showing that these have both direct and indirect ramifications across the large canvas of e-government areas often not considered. For example, many governments are making the mistake of trying to set security systems too high for the functionalities deployed, resulting in a waste of resources that could have been used to shore up more vulnerable systems. There have been many failed attempts to introduce sophisticated Public Key Infrastructure (PKI) and digital signature systems when simple passwords or PIN codes would suffice. The lesson is to take security and data protection extremely seriously and treat it as the most pressing technical challenge, but at the same time approach these issues incrementally and proportionally given that there is always a trade-off between increased security and usage. The approach to take is to build in security and data protection from the very start of any e-government initiative.

Web on the March

Since 2004 the evolution of the World Wide Web has moved from Web 1.0 (consisting of Internet websites and webpages, e-mail, instant messaging, short message service (SMS), simple online discussion, etc.) to Web 2.0 that also allows users to provide and manipulate content and get directly involved. Web 2.0 sites typically have an "architecture of participation" that encourages users to add value to the application as they use it, for example, through social media dialogue around user-generated content in a virtual community. There is also much discussion about the Web 3.0 evolution toward wide-scale ubiquitous seamless networks (sometimes called grid computing), networked and distributed computing, open ID, open semantic web, large-scale distributed databases, and artificial intelligence.

Some are also looking forward to Web 4.0 as the global semantic web (i.e., methods and technologies that allow machines to understand the meaning, or "semantics," of information on the web), including the use of statistical, machine-constructed semantic tags and algorithms. According to Tim Berners-Lee, the "father" of the Internet, we are indeed on the verge of the age of the semantic web that exploits the Internet of data rather than the Internet of documents we now have. This will enable intelligent uses of the Internet like asking questions rather than simply searching for key words, as well as more automatic data exchanges between databases, data mining, and similar uses.

E-government is affected by the march of the web with increasing focus on the Government 2.0 paradigm. This concentrates much more on the demand side, on user empowerment and engagement, as well as on benefits and impacts that address specific societal challenges, rather than simply providing administrative services online.

This is to be achieved by supporting the real transformation of governance arrangements away from silo and government centricity toward becoming more user centric and user driven. As noted by Millard in 2010, users and other legitimate stakeholders are being invited more openly into a participative and empowering relationship with government in relation to service design and delivery, the workings and arrangements of the public sector and public governance more widely, as well as public policy and decision making.

To this effect, tremendous e-government progress has been made over the last 10 to 15 years during which time the use of information communication technology (ICT) in the public sector has moved from being largely a concern of separate ministries in digitizing their records and processes, to one where ICT is used to join up ministries, reengineer processes, and offer many new services to citizens and businesses. E-government has become a top priority for governments around the world and a major focus of investment. This can be measured in the steady growth of the supply-side availability of e-government services across all countries since 2000. For example, according to ongoing benchmarking reports led by Capgemini, a consultancy, full online availability of a basket of the most common 20 e-government services in Europe increased from 20% in 2001 to 82% in 2010, while online sophistication increased from 45% in 2001 to 90% in 2010. Globally, the 2010 UN benchmarking survey "finds that citizens are benefiting from more advanced e-service delivery, better access to information, more efficient government management and improved interactions with governments, primarily as a result of increasing use by the public sector of information and communications technology" (p. 59).

These developments point inexorably in the same direction. As the web marches on and data of all types and qualities become increasingly ubiquitous, the issues are not only about whether we can keep them secure but also about confronting profound issues about who owns the data, where they are, how accurate they are, and who is accountable for them.

The Known Unknowns of Cybersecurity

There is no doubt that the biggest operational challenge to e-government is cybersecurity, including threats to identity, privacy, and data systems.

Adequate privacy and data protection, and the trust these support, are crucial for reaping the benefits of e-government. If they are in place and work well, they can provide stable, predictable, and confidence-building frameworks. In fact, these are key for any activity using information and communications technology (ICT) across society, whether in the public, private, or civil sectors, so should not be seen in isolation. But if they are not, it can have negative effects on usage. According to the European Commission (2009, p. 1), "Only 12% of EU Web users feel safe making transactions on the Internet, while 39% of EU Internet users have major doubts about safety, and 42% do not dare carry out financial transactions online." Ongoing news reports about lost credit card data and private information in both the private and public sectors are not likely to improve this image. For example, according to a November 2007 BBC News report, two password protected computer disks holding the personal details of all families in the United Kingdom with a child under 16, 25 million people in total, went missing. The package had not been recorded or registered and has never been found since being physically transported between two departments. This has been one incident among many severely questioning the way government handles sensitive data. There are also increasing numbers of malicious hacker attacks, financially motivated breaches, and even policy motivated efforts to shut off information, such as during the attacks on Estonia, the Iranian demonstrations in 2010, and the 2011 uprisings in the Middle East. We know a lot about the main cybersecurity threats, yet a lot less about how to meet them. As the foremost duty of government is to protect its citizens, the public sector must build highly effective and integrated systems to protect against crime, espionage, terrorism, and war in cyberspace.

Government's response to cybersecurity issues has, however, generally lagged the private sector, despite it arguably being more important, and, according to a 2008 Organization for Economic Cooperation and Development (OECD) report, there is limited availability of data on public sector efforts. Even in highly advanced e-government countries like Norway, only a minority of public administrations have been offering secure ways of communicating with their websites, despite many surveys showing that fears of data insecurity are perceived by users as the biggest deterrent to their use of e-government. However, it is also worth noting that the cybersecurity response is highly variable, for example central governments are much more likely to have adequate measures in place than local, obviously reflecting the size of populations involved and the resources available. But many e-government services are provided at the local or regional levels and the amount of information provided by these entities is rapidly increasing. One of the challenges of cybersecurity in e-government is that the public sector is characterized by a large amount of operational independence and "siloization" among its various parts, something not seen in the private sector to the same extent.

Security in government's cyberspace is thus of paramount concern, and it is clear that current systems, both organizational and technical, are not always meeting the challenge. Future solutions will also likely require solutions very different from those of today's systems that are predicated on relatively stable, well-defined, consistent configurations, contexts, and participants in security arrangements. A new paradigm is probably needed characterized by "conformable" security, in which the degree and nature of security associated with any particular type of action will change over time, with changing circumstances and with changing available information. In this endeavor, it is likely that the public sector will have to deal with challenges in five areas: privacy, trust, data security, loss of data control, and human behavior.

Privacy

Cybersecurity initiatives need to consider privacy implications that in many cases can significantly compromise their likely efficacy. For example, privacy and data protection will need conformable security systems, adapted to the changing access needs and identities of people and organizations. These systems will also need to operate across national borders, which will require not just political agreements but also data structures and standards that are compatible. Data security will also be improved by giving users much greater control over their own data and their own (often) multiple identities, for example, through trusted third parties. For services that can operate across borders, well-functioning identity and authentication systems will be vital. Information assurance is also needed as a holistic approach incorporating risk management, given that no system can provide complete security. Long-term data preservation and access are also important given the fast-changing technical formats and the huge increases in data generation expected.

Privacy needs to be upheld, for example, through regulation and international agreements like the European Data Protection Framework, including appropriate data ombudsmen, custodians, or trusted third parties. Care should be taken to avoid "mission creep," when data are used for purposes not originally intended, or the "race to the bottom" in interagency or cross-border data sharing by a reversion to the standards of the weakest member. User needs and trust must be built on an understanding of real human behavior when using data, as well as on technical requirements.

Trust

The technical aspect of cybersecurity may turn out to be the easy part. Clearly, understanding and catering for, what some call irrational or schizophrenic, human behavior can be a real challenge to cybersecurity.

Trust is a critical issue and is built through information minimalization (i.e., using as little data as possible to perform a task), and informing users or obtaining user consent when accessing and processing their data by enabling users to trace, own, or control their own data. Trust is also built by properly managing, explaining, and minimizing the risks of data loss or leakage. Trust is notoriously difficult to build but can be very quickly and devastatingly destroyed by one single breach. This underlines the need to consider trust as multidimensional. Clearly, for maximum benefit, users need to trust their government or service provider, but it is also becoming increasingly important for governments to trust users, for example, by allowing them to deploy public sector data and engaging them in policy development and decision making. E-government will also require personalizable and context-relevant ICT, customer (or citizen) relationship management systems, and decision-support and forecasting systems based on intelligent knowledge management and archiving. Personal e-governance modules/spaces are likely to become important that are context-sensitive, intelligent, and personalizable, also for tracking and tracing service progress.

Although much of the debate about cybersecurity, certainly in the mainstream media and in everyday discourse, is far from rational, informed, or accurate, it is also very difficult to be dispassionate. Just as in the physical world also in cyberspace, one person's terrorist is another person's freedom fighter—literally, in the case of WikiLeaks and Julian Assange. On the one hand is the view held by many governments that the more citizen data available the better citizens can be helped and protected. Compare this with the opposite view held by many citizens of fear of the surveillance state with nowhere to hide. If governments hold too much data, this intrudes into citizens' private lives. Moreover, governments have a poor track record of keeping data safe, and there are many examples of data misuse by government, either knowingly or unknowingly. However, at the same time, the same citizens who worry about "big brother" government, willingly provide private companies, which they know are only concerned with making money out of them, with much more personal data than they ever give governments. Many also scatter even more personal and often intimate details about themselves on social networking sites. Perhaps citizens perceive governments as so big, monolithic, and pervasive that any data misuse will have huge consequences, while the private sector or social networking sites are so differentiated and variegated in comparison that data misuse cannot be of much importance. Professionals know this is very far from being the case.

Data Security

Who owns data can be a deeply philosphical question, but it is of real practical importance when it comes to cybersecurity because it determines who can (or should) secure it. For example, do individuals or organizations own the data they give to governments or which governments collect, or does government own data once in its possession? Perhaps of greater importance is the right to use data regardless of ownership, especially if they have economic or other value. Recent studies in the United Kingdom, such as one by Newbery, Bently, and Pollock, and by the European Commission have shown that "public sector information" (PSI) has clear and significant economic value that can be sold to commercial or other organizations to provide revenue streams for government. This has been the norm in most advanced countries for many years, but a concerted "free-our-data" campaign in the United Kingdom over the last few years has led to most government agencies releasing PSI in machine-readable and easily accessible formats for free use by anyone. The main argument being that even greater economic value for society as a whole is thereby created when entrepreneurs of all types can develop new offline products (such as business services around economic data), as well as new online smart services (or "apps") that may in their own right be given away freely. Freeing up data in this way is now part of a burgeoining "open government" movement, such as the UK's Transparency and Accountability Initiative 2010, although still only significant in a few countries.

Many argue that data security will be improved by giving users much greater control over their own data and their own (often) multiple identities, as they then take a direct interest in ensuring its safety and accuracy. For example, in 2003, a Data Protection Act was passed in Estonia covering information relating to an identified natural person's physical, mental, physiological, economic, cultural, and social characteristics, relations, and associations. On request, the natural person has a legal right to access all personal data relating to him or her, the purposes of these data, their categories and sources, and third persons or categories to whom transmission of the data is permitted. According to the country's Personal Data Protection Act, the person has the further right to request the termination of processing of their personal data, to correct in the case of errors, and to block or erase their data, through the Data Protection Inspectorate or courts. Issues surrounding the security of the person's home computer when examining their data on the official website are not addressed in this legislation, as this is largely beyond the government's control, but are felt to be of less concern as any data leakage would be piecemeal rather than wholesale. However, very few countries have data ownership and rights provisions as well developed as Estonia, and this is likely to skew the way governments implement cybersecurity and the attitude citizens have about the issue.

Loss of Data Control

There are burgeoning and very beneficial examples of outsourcing where cybersecurity does not seem to have been compromised, but the very fact that data are widely shared, no longer under direct government control, and moved around increases the risks. These arise from technical incompatibilities and because of the often very different organizational and workplace cultures and intentions involved, where it becomes increasingly difficult to maintain common control and to monitor standards.

Introducing e-government implies the need to completely redesign both organizational structures (essentially, smashing the silos) as well as data architectures to enable the sharing of services and resources across and between public administrations. This is increasingly taking place in shared service centers and also covers ICT applications, e-government building blocks, information and data, as well as common business processes. This can also facilitate outsourcing to other actors, including outside the public sector, if costs can be cut. However, a major criticism is that costs may not be saved in the longer term, it may reduce quality, and certainly leads to loss of control by governments that are, in the final analysis, democratically accountable unlike private contractors.

It is clear, however, that significant disruptions do take place. According to Davenport (2005) we are on the edge of a major move toward the ICT-based commoditization of large numbers of business processes, and this will also profoundly affect the public sector, making outsourcing as well as greater user involvement much more likely. All types of business processes, not just in relation to designing and delivering services, but also from developing software, through hiring personnel to at least some aspects of policy modeling and development through automatic modeling, scenario, and simulations, are being analyzed, standardized, and routinized, and this knowledge is being codified and facilitated by ICT. This could lead to process commoditization and outsourcing on a massive scale. The widespread use of ICT undoubtedly means that the public sector must grapple to avoid the simultaneous loss of knowledge and control over basic processes and over the competencies, decisions, and policies needed to support these and which lie at the basis of all public services. There is a need to better understand which aspects of the public sector's activities can and should be codified, commoditized (e.g., through ICT) and outsourced or "networked" with other actors including both private and civil sectors, and as increasingly seems likely, with users. The jury is still out on all these issues, but in the context of the financial crisis their importance is dramatically increasing again as governments attempt to cut costs.

The Mother of All Known Unknowns—Human Behavior

Building in technical resilience with "graceful degradation" when under cyber attack, and ensuring rapid reconstitution of mission-critical functions, are key on the technical side. However, the main known unknown of cybersecurity, because we rarely stop to think about it and it is so unpredictable, turns out to be more important than the purely technical issue of how to make it work—human behavior. Most accept that security can never be perfect, but the reasons need greater scrutiny, especially when it also becomes clear that there is an inverse relationship between the use of systems (which we obviously want to encourage) and the security of those systems. It is like the old adage, that if you want to be completely safe and take no risks stay in bed all day—though this says nothing about earthquakes, so even that is not risk free. But that is no way to run a society, develop an economy, let alone live a life. Human behavior, whether rational or not, lies at the core of cybersecurity—how people think about their identity, data about their identity, who owns it, has access to it, and how it is used. We do know that a better understanding of the relative risks of cyber insecurity compared to the benefits of system use is the core challenge, but we do not yet know much about achieving good balances. This is particularly the case in the government sector, compared to the private sector, where it is not possible or desirable to employ market solutions to find the balance. It needs to instead be explored through trial and error, evidence collection, as well as the conscious application of ethical and democratic principles.

Government Loses Control—Who Is Now in Charge and Why It Matters

With the adoption of Web 2.0 tools and approaches, many governments are moving into the "Governance 2.0" paradigm that enables "coproduced" services in which users actively cooperate with service providers, and "self-created" services in which it is mainly users who determine the service. This can also lead to "crowd-sourcing government" where content and inputs are sourced from a wide range of users and others actors who have particular knowledge and interests not possessed by the government. The cybersecurity concern for the public sector and for citizens and businesses is how these data are dispersed, shared, and used, as well as by whom. Perhaps of even greater importance, is it possible to find out who is using the data? Losing control is one thing, but not knowing who now has control compounds the problem. For example, specific parts of Australia still remain blurred on Google Earth. Google says that it removed the high-resolution photos due to a problem with one of the image providers, but *IT Security*, an online publication, point to fears that the maps could be used as a terrorist tool. Some of the blocked areas include (or have included at some point) The Garden Island Naval Depot, the Lucas Heights Reactor, Parliament House, and the Australian Defense Force headquarters in Canberra.

Less of a security issue but still of concern to the public sector is not only are the data secure but also can they be preserved and made available for authorized use in the long term, given constantly changing data formats and standards. Here again, the need for a trade-off between security and use is evident. For example, data preserved on floppy disks 15 years ago today require specialist intervention resorting to museum artifacts to access them. Cloud computing may help as it potentially enables data and other resources to be dispersed potentially in multiple servers somewhere on the Internet. But even if this solves the "where" challenge, long-term preservation still requires standards and formats to be accessible in the long term.

When data preservation is outsourced to a specialist private company, or when e-government services, for example, can be automatically delivered from the "public cloud," there are profound issues of control and ownership, including possible loss of accountability and democratic oversight. Another example in the Netherlands shows not only loss of government control, but also of usurpation of everything a government does because others can access or even create their own data relevant to an erstwhile public function. This involves the combination of Web 2.0 tools and consumer electronics, like high-resolution recording equipment, sensors, and cameras that are increasingly available in the high street to everybody and not just professionals. The complaints by people who live near Schiphol Airport in Amsterdam about aircraft noise levels were ignored or dismissed by the public authorities, leading to the residents developing their own measurement system based on sensor technology linked to a computer and the Internet. The system has been installed in the gardens of the protesters and records the level of aircraft noise. This is captured electronically, collected, mashed up with other data and applications, and published on their own website, http://www.geluidsnet.nl/en/geluidsnet/. This illustrates an increasing trend whereby professional hardware and software are becoming commodities available to everyone to design and implement their own "user-driven" services, in this case showing how public agencies can have their competence and reliability both undermined and usurped. After some battles, the public authorities accepted that the residents' system was more accurate and reliable, and this has now become the de facto service. Perhaps some backhanded benefits for government here could include the fact that by losing control they might also lose responsibility, both political and financial, although that remains a challenge to be negotiated.

Another aspect of loss of control by government is the fairly disappointing use of e-government portals and growth of alternative user-driven tools. For example, the direct.gov.uk portal in the United Kingdom acts as a gateway to all public services and has often been praised as world class. However, citizen use has been admittedly low, according to William Perrin (2008) at the Transformational Government Unit in the UK Cabinet Office, and, as evidenced by several sources, including the European Commission, OECD, and McKinsey (2009), a consultancy, this is a common problem for e-government portals around the world. Instead, whether governments like it or not, access to public sector data is becoming dispersed, both by the rise of third-party providers, but also by governments. In fact, some countries are now moving away from the portal concept to multichannel service delivery methods that offer the citizens direct access to local services, simplifying the services and reducing the time taken to carry through a service request by eliminating the number of steps needed to complete a transaction. Such moves illustrate the "no-wrong-door" approach providing direct service access wherever the citizen might be on the Internet. In a recent unpublished survey undertaken by the author, experts and practitioners cited a number of reasons why the dominance of portals is coming to an end: "Why go to a portal first when I am already somewhere else on the web? I want to go direct to the service I need." "Everything (services, applications, platforms, infrastructure) is—or will be—in the cloud anyway as a 'service,' so just use Google or other search engines to find what you need." "Do we hang on to grandiose portals because they are a show-case—just like an imposing town hall—but what do they really do for all that money?"

Loss of government control of data is also likely to lead, in the e-government services context as for other commercial and personal services, to organizations, enterprises, and individuals increasingly making their data (content and functionalities) available in the cloud rather than via a portal or even a website. This means that service users will be able to create their own content and services on their own plat-forms typically through avatars or automatic electronic agents. Going through the "front door" of a website will probably be seen by an increasing number of users as an extra unnecessary step. There is also rapid growth of new ICT channels, like mobile and digital TV, all of which is leading to the proliferation of a multitude of channels and platforms, where portals and websites constitute one, probably small, part of the offering.

These developments are likely to mean that cybersecurity could become even more relevant, because even if the web is declining in importance, increased ICT usage across diverse channels makes it more important overall as well as more challenging for e-government. Alongside high-profile attacks on government websites (with the White House, the Pentagon, the cyber attack on Estonia, all being prominent examples), this could, in turn, scare off many users. This would further decrease trust in using e-government and might tempt users to demand a return to more traditional face-to-face services that in their view are more secure. The fact that this view is often entirely wrong, because paper records are more easily perishable, lost, or destroyed, and information much less accessible when needed, might be difficult to establish.

What e-government is good at doing is making data available as ser-vices to users in ways never before imagined, and there are many good examples of this such as the FixMyStreet website, http://www.fixmys-treet.com/, in the United Kingdom. However, it is not always govern-ment doing it, as in this example where a third sector organization collected data from all authorities about their responsibility for main-taining and repairing streets and local neighborhoods—everything from broken paving stones to graffiti and rubbish. These data are then used to automatically direct complaints, simply accompanied by a post code, to the responsible authority, making this e-government service one of the most used in the United Kingdom.

Another 2011 example, also from the United Kingdom, is the website availability of crime statistics on local maps, intended as a service to citizens. According to the *Guardian*, a British paper, immediate problems arose that had not been anticipated. First, there were fears that house prices in high crime areas would fall with some home owners threatening to sue the relevant agency for their loss. Second many of the data were wrong or badly calculated or mislocalized, often giving completely inaccurate impressions. Scale is very important, not just of data presentation on the map but even more of collection and allocation. Issues arose around how the data were collected, who did the data collection, and how they were recorded and where. The apparent objectivity of data showed again to be subject to the machinations of less than perfect human behavior that became magnified by ICT. The advantage of seeing these problems in the public sector does, however, raise awareness of similar problems that almost certainly exist in private commercial services that hide, or attempt to hide, them. It also makes us realize that such problems have always existed, and one advantage of digitization is that it makes them transparent even if it might magnify them.

Who Gets In and What Gets Out When Government Opens the Door?

As well as coordination and integration within the public sector, there is an increasing trend toward cooperation with other actors, from both private and civil sectors, as well as with users. All this is generally very beneficial to all involved. Although the private sector has for many years acted as an important partner to government, the civil sector is now also starting to become a significant and often new source of resources and expertise for undertaking public sector tasks and delivering services. So, in addition to public–private partnerships (PPPs) the trend is also toward public–civil partnerships (PCPs). For example, the voluntary sector and social entrepreneurs, especially when they function as intermediaries between the government provider and the constituent user, can contribute grassroots resources, knowledge, innovation, and even useful competition.

Government is thus becoming collaborative, open, and porous, in ways and to an extent not seen in other sectors, and this could lead to beneficial disruption of the way in which the public sector operates and the responsibilities it has. First, in order to deliver better services and better governance, technology is helping to turn the public sector inside-out, by exposing the way it works and pushing its activities out into society. For example, e-government enables civil servants and politicians to roam free of the confines of the town hall and engage directly with citizens on the streets or in their homes and with businesses on their own premises, while always being in touch with the intelligence and knowledge they need in the back-office. Second, the technology is helping to turn the public sector outside-in by inviting commercial, civil, and constituent actors inside to participate in designing and delivering services as well as providing them with tools to join in the making of public policy and decisions.

All this generally brings many benefits, but there are also dangers or at least challenges that should make us stop and think. When government is just one player among many in the public sphere, which now also legitimately consists of private and civil sector actors, new forms of accountability need to be found. A pair of researchers, Bovens and Loos (2002), addressed this issue when they described the shift from legality to transparency. A new form of accountability is needed when governments have to share data, power, and responsibility, for example because of the processes of horizontalization, deterritorialization, and scalability. Horizontalization allows the partial shifting of the production of generally binding rules away from the traditional legislative power to other regulatory parties that may have no democratic legitimacy, such as independent administrative bodies (cf. quangos), umbrella organizations, and interactive policy partners. The process of digitization can make it possible for all authorities, including those in the private and civil sectors, to move faster than legislators in the public sector and in parliament.

Deterritorialization refers to the fact that the many challenges and issues faced by government across borders (e.g., trade, pollution, migration, crime, etc.) can present the national legislature with accomplished facts over which it has no immediate control. Globalization and rapid change and turbulence cause the formal legislature to lag behind and require new flexible forms of regulation. The 2008 financial crisis and crash were enabled if not caused by the "big-bang" in the mid 1980s when the financial services sector went digital enabling billions of dollars to be moved around the globe in a millisecond. For both horizontalization and deterritorialization, cybersecurity needs not only to cope with public sector or national data dispersion and systems but also with global threats increasingly in real time. This implies not just technological complexity but also political, organizational, cultural, and behavioral complexity on a massive scale.

The limits of government action are increasingly visible. Complex policy challenges ranging between international and personal levels—in such diverse areas as climate change, aging populations, and obesity—cannot be "solved" by government action alone. Tackling them effectively will require the concerted efforts of all actors in society including individual citizens. Governments everywhere are under pressure to do more with a lot less. Most are working hard to deliver effective policies and services at least at cost to the public purse; many are trying to leverage resources outside the public sector. Last but not least, governments are seeking to ensure and maintain high levels of public trust, without which government actions will, at best, be ineffective and, at worst, counterproductive. At the same time, more educated, well-informed, and less deferential citizens are judging their governments in terms of their democratic, policy, and service delivery performance.

The role of the public sector may be to retain competence and control over these high-level issues in the public interest and with the public good and public value in mind. The danger of not doing so could be that the public sector, as we understand it today, could disappear or shrink to a rump of only doing things that the market is not interested in, while everything is commoditized, outsourced, and privatized, or passed to the whim and partiality of charitable organizations. Such developments are already apparent in the United States. This could be one of the biggest challenges to public service and to the public service ethic as we know it today. In such a scenario, protecting the public sector from cyber threats will be even harder as data will be dispersed. This can also mean that private sector entities, in practice, would need to protect public sector data. Would they have the bottom line as their prime concern or the public good? However, despite the problems raised by loss of government control of data, some would argue that dispersed ownership, control, and use of public sector data can be beneficial as it mitigates the concentration of power and increases responsibility, creativity, and innovation. This very dispersion may also improve cybersecurity because, although the risk of having a security breach clearly increases, any damage is likely to be much less and more manageable than a low-risk but highly catastrophic breakdown in security of a highly centralized system that controls most if not all data. Once again, it is clear that the core cybersecurity challenge is not technical (however, important and intractable this is) but is the need to balance cybersecurity with system use in the context of often unpredictable organizational and individual behaviors and needs.

Back to Basics: Trust, Transparency, and Accountability

Trust, transparency, and accountability are arguably the three biggest challenges confronting successful e-government, and all are inextricably interlinked. Without trust in the public sector, online government will fail. It is a truism that trust is difficult to grow and easy to degrade, so it is imperative to find ways to reverse this trend. Trust and mistrust go hand-in-hand and need to be balanced. Trust reduces transaction costs, but a healthy mistrust encourages constructive criticism and debate. The trick is to know the difference. Governments can assist in this by maximizing transparency and openness so citizens can see how decisions are made, who takes them, and why. Suitable opportunities to challenge the decision-making process are also needed within clear rules.

As noted by the Hansard Society (2008), a UK nonprofit, although ICT, can be very important for increasing participation, it is crucial to have clear, transparent, rules-based accountability for all forms of participation in order to reconnect disaffected voters with politicians. Apart from ICT being used to give access to public information (which is a very important aspect of e-participation), ICT can support moves toward much more extensive transparency as part of the concept of open government. For example, enabling users to trace every interaction within the public administration right down to the name of the civil servant who is dealing with their query or case in real time.

In another example, as part of a move on from e-procurement, the UK government has recently set up a website showing the budgets and expenditure of all government agencies, and this is now being rolled out across local governments, following the lead set by Recovery.gov in 2009, the U.S. government's official website that provides easy access to data related to recovery act spending and allows for the reporting of potential fraud, waste, and abuse. Developments like this could be part of a move toward a situation, not just of transparency of information and of services, but also transparency of the purpose, actions, processes, and outcomes of government. This would mean that all could potentially have access to (near perfect) knowledge about what is going on, and the impact this has or is likely to have. As noted by a pair of researchers, Blakemore and Lloyd (2007), this would make it possible to relate decisions and actions very precisely to the whole set of diverse (sometimes contradictory, sometimes complementary) needs of all actors. The publication of heretofore confidential information by the WikiLeaks website is a powerful example that this trend is happening whether governments like it or not.

System and data transparency could enable users and civil servants to trace and track requests and cases through the public sector in order to follow progress, know which part of the system is currently responsible, and to better foresee and circumvent bottlenecks or roadblocks. The placing of responsibility (and intellectual property rights [IPR] where relevant) could be critical, especially in relation to users who, by way of their status or situation, may not be able to exercise their own responsibility, such as children, the elderly, the handicapped, and so forth. This will also allow users to become involved, to be better informed, and to be better able to exercise some control for their own benefit.

As noted by the European Transparency Initiative (2005), transparency is often the basis for trust. Transparency in the public sector actually implies really being able to "both see and get what we pay for" and to make this visible to all. It should also imply the end of invisible, divisive, Kafkaesque bureaucracies not knowing what they are doing except for serving their own ends. Transparency can also save time and money through reducing errors, pooling resources and knowledge, reducing duplication, and promoting cooperation. Transparency also reduces corruption. It is important to emphasize that although there is a continuing need to increase users' trust of government across all public sector tasks, governments also need to increase their trust in users so that they, with support and within clear guidelines, will be able to participate responsibly. Such trust is potentially manifest in many ways. For example when governments make available local crime data including in machine-readable format for re-mashing, they trust society to use these wisely to inform rather than a scaremonger. Similarly, when governments open up the decision- and policy-making processes to citizens, two-way trust is required. Clearly there is a learning curve for both governments and citizens in how to handle and interpret freed-up data sensibly and responsibly, and how to avoid the dangers of misuse in the many forms this can take.

Although it is clear that the widespread release of public sector data can have immense benefits, there are almost certainly legitimate interests that should be protected from total transparency and openness. For example, there are undoubtedly legitimate privacy needs and interests of citizens and businesses when their data are used by government. Just as important, however, are the interests of civil servants and politicians, especially during the decision- and policy-making process, for example from intrusive exposure and monitoring that could result from all their actions and decisions being made totally transparent. This could bring about stress and too much focus on measurement and performance at a personal level, and lead back to an overly bureaucratic stance, working strictly to rule-books rather than being flexible and prepared to take measured risk with policy ideas. It could also provoke an unwillingness to make decisions, or to take responsibility for them. According to a 2007 article in the *Guardian*, one top-ranking civil servant in the UK government is quoted as saying "I would never now write down advice to ministers," and accuses the 2007 Freedom of Information Act of "impeding the effective work of government, not least because officials face 'frivolous' or 'time-consuming' fishing expeditions from journalists, campaigners and citizens."

Accountability flows from responsibilities as well as from openness and transparency. It is also related to ethical considerations that are, both in theory and practice, highly important in the public realm. There are different types of accountability. First, political accountability should be exercised by politicians and democratically elected representatives. Second, administrative accountability rests on civil servants individually as well as on the public sector as an institution. This also includes the likelihood of changing accountability when private sector and civil organization partners are involved in undertaking public sector tasks, such as policy making or delivering services. Third, there is user accountability in not misusing or abusing public sector services or facilities, as well as in participating in legitimate and responsible ways. All these relate to responsibilities. Fourth is the general ethical and moral accountability of all actors, including citizens, businesses, communities, and the public sector. If things go wrong, the boundary of powers, accountability, and responsibility between government and user becomes important, so there also needs to be an open and fair appeals procedure. Formal agreements may need to be entered into, such as a Service Level Agreement (SLA) or citizen charter, both for individuals or groups of users, as exemplified by Burgerlink, the e-government citizens charter in the Netherlands (Burgerlink, 2006). Accountability needs to be clear and traceable, so that if things go wrong it is clear who is responsible and how the situation can be resolved. Simplicity helps all of these issues by increasing understanding and awareness of the democratic process. However, as this chapter has shown, e-government often leads to increasing complexity and massive blurring between roles and tasks when so many actors are involved and so many voices are clamoring to be heard.

How to Swim in an Ocean of Insecure Data

The purpose of this chapter is not to provide answers for tackling cybersecurity threats to e-government, but five main challenges do emerge clearly from the issues reviewed in this chapter:

1. The public sector is characterized by a large amount of operational independence and "siloization" among its various parts, which makes tackling cybersecurity extremely challenging and probably more challenging than in the private sector.
2. Important public data are now being created, held, and applied by actors and individuals outside of government, so that the

definition of public sector security must be expanded and rethought.

3. Human behavior, whether rational or not, lies at the core of cybersecurity—how people think about their identity, data about it, who owns it, who has access to it, and how it is used.

4. There is an inverse relationship between the use of systems (which we obviously want to encourage) and the security of those systems, but we do not yet know much about achieving good balances.

5. Users of e-government may be in need of just as much cyber-security protection from government as government is from third parties, particularly where governance regimes are incompetent or corrupt, but the issue is more general and related to the proper role of the public sector vis-à-vis other actors.

The consequences of these challenges are that coordination and control become increasingly difficult and that the range of cyber-security threats that need to be addressed have multiplied in scope and scale for all actors in the public realm. Some responses to the first four challenges are obvious. Clearly, government-wide, end-to-end strategies for meeting cybersecurity challenges must be developed and applied, working closely with the private sector that will provide some of the solutions, but also need to be agile and aware of the ever-changing landscape of threats. International cooperation and frameworks need to be negotiated and put in place, given that there are no political borders to such threats. Perhaps most important of all, cultural changes within organiza-tions need to be driven through in relation to awareness of cyber-security issues, responsibility for tackling them, and the working practices that underpin these.

Other responses flow from these general tenets, as noted by Booz Allen Hamilton (2009), a consultancy, and *Fed Tech* magazine, to include the need to improve the overall governance and coordination of cybersecurity, simplification of processes and rules, and the need to foster appropriate talent and skills in the public sector. The 2010 survey undertaken by TechAmerica noted that "a high percentage of security breaches occur because internal users are careless or fail to follow procedures" (p. 8). Local governments are probably even more threatened than central administrations due to their relative lack of resources and expertise, but even here much can be done. According to a nontechnical guide to cybersecurity published by the Multi-State Information Sharing and Analysis Center in collaboration with the U.S. Department of Homeland Security, this includes recognizing the problem; designating responsibility; protecting essential hardware, software, and information; controlling access; improving training and awareness; and ensuring safe disposal.

Responses to the fifth challenge are less straightforward and may need a slowly evolving mindset change to tackle. However, as pointed out by this author in a 2010 article in the *European Journal of ePractice*; much evidence now points to the benefits of establishing neutral trusted third parties to stand between governments and data providers on the one hand and citizens on the other, and to ensure that the interests and rights of all stakeholders are fairly upheld. Such third parties could be commercial, civil, or even arms-length government agencies but need to be legally and operationally independent and seen to be so. They might advantageously perform some of the following tasks:

- Act as a "champion" and "watchdog" for users in relation to using data and engaging in policy and decision making, thus act as a sort of "ombudsman" for users vis-à-vis the government.
- Agree and publicize a citizen charter of rights and responsibilities for users in using public data and in public engagement, building on what is there already in law or regulation, and open these to debate and amendment by users.
- Identify and implement frameworks for real motivation, incentives, and rewards for user engagement in service design and policy participation.
- Continuously monitor the potential risks and inform users about these, as well as offer possible solutions and assistance.
- Provide both proactive and passive moderation on Web 2.0 media, as well as help frame debates in a neutral and balanced way, if requested and appropriate.

- Monitor and uphold users' privacy and data protection rights vis-à-vis governments and other interests. This would include preventing the misuse of personal data whether provided consciously by users or collected automatically during service use.
- Ensure that all "public" services, whoever provides them, identify the provenance of all data and other sources used, while complying with other open source requirements concerning relevant ownership and liability. This should also include monitoring and referral functions to ensure that any service developed for public use lives up to agreed standards of accuracy, quality, and the "public good."
- Despite the immense potential benefits of releasing all types of public data, there is a danger of data overload and data misuse. Data, like statistics, can be seriously corrupted to mean anything anybody wishes. A trusted third party should monitor and provide neutral and transparent guidance as well as intervention on such issues.

It is important to put in place safeguards like these to ensure that governments or any actors do not inappropriately manipulate other actors. This will also be facilitated by ensuring that public data and processes are open and transparent, as this balances power across all actors and mitigates misuse and corruption.

References

Author's interview with William Perrin, Transformational Government Unit, UK Cabinet Office, London, 5 June 2008.

BBC News. November 20, 2007: http://news.bbc.co.uk/2/hi/7103566.stm.

Blakemore, M., and Lloyd, P. (2007). "Trust and transparency: Pre-requisites for effective eGovernment," *Citizen-Centric eGovernment Think Paper*, 2007: 10.

Booz Allen Hamilton. (2009). "Cyber IN-Security: Strengthening the Federal Cybersecurity Workforce," Partnership for Public Service, July 2009: http://www.ourpublicservice.org.

Bovens, M., and Loos, E. (2002). "The digital constitutional state: Democracy and law in the information society," *Information Policy*, Vol. 7, No. 4, 2002, pp. 16, 185–197.

Burgerlink (2006). (Workbook e-Citizen Charter," Version 2.2 (December 2006); http://www.burgerlink.ml/Documenten/burgerlink-1.0/live/binaries/burgerlink/pdf/citizen-charter/workbook-e-citizen-charter-english.pdf.

Capgemini, IDC, Rand Europe, Sogeti, and DTI. (2010). "Digitizing Public Services in Europe: Putting ambition into action—Ninth Benchmark Measurement," for the European Commission, Directorate General for Information Society and Media, December 2010.

Davenport, T.H. (2005). "The coming commoditisation of processes," *Harvard Business Review,* June 2005, pp. 101–108.

Digital Agenda website: http://ec.europa.eu/information_society/newsroom/cf/pillar.cfm?pillar_id=45.

European Commission (2009). "Consumer Rights" Commission wants consumers to surf the web without borders." IP/009/702, 5 May 2009: http://europa.eu/rapid/pressReleasesAction.do?reference=IP/09/702.

European Commission workshop. June 16, 2009. "i2010 eGovernment Action Plan Progress Study (SMART 2008/0042)" Brussels, hosted by FG INFSO, European Commission.

European Journal of ePractice. (2010). "Government 2.0—Hype, Hope, or Reality?" Number 9, March 2010: www.epracticejournal.eu.

European Journal of ePractice. (2011). "e-Government for the economic crisis," Number 11, March 2011: www.epracticejournal.eu.

European Transparency Initiative, IDABC European eGovernment News Roundup. November 2, 2005, No. 116.

Givans, N. (2009). "Cybersecurity and the government CIO," June 11, 2009. http://fedtechmagazine.com/article.asp?item_id=655.

Guardian newspaper. June 15, 2007.

guardian.co.uk. Online crime maps crash under weight of 18 million hits an hour by A. Travis and H. Mulholland: http://www.guardian.co.uk/uk/2011/feb/01/online-crime-maps-power-hands-people.

Hansard Society. (2008). "Digital Dialogues 3": http://www.hansardsociety.org.uk.

IT Security: http://www.itsecurity.com.features/51-things-not-on-google-maps- 071508/.

ISTAG (Information Society Technologies Advisory Group). (2002). "Trust, dependability, security and privacy for IST in FP6." The European Commission: http://www.cordis.lu/ist/istag.htm.

McKinsey. (2009). E-government 2.0, number 4, summer 2009 edition of McKinsey on Government, retrieved December 8, 2009, from: http://www.mckinseyquarterly.com/Public_Sector/E-government_20_2408.

Millard, J., and Horlings, E. (2008). "Research report on value for citizens: A vision of public governance in 2020," for the European Commission eGovernment Unit, DG INFSO: http://ec.europa.eu/information_society/activities/egovernment/studies/docs/research_report_on_value_for_citizens.pdf.

Millard, J. (2009). "eParticipation recommendations—Focusing on the European level." Deliverable 5.1d&e: http://islab/uom/gr/eP/index/php?option=com_docman&task=cat_view&gid=36&&Ite.

Millard, J. (2010). "Government 1.5—Is the bottle half full or half empty?" *European Journal of ePractice,* Number 9, March 2010: www.epracticejournal.eu.

Multi-State Information Sharing and Analysis Center. (undated). "Local government cyber security: Getting started—A non-technical guide." Published in collaboration with U.S. Department of Homeland Security, National Cyber Security Division: http://www.msisac.org.

Newbery, D., Bently, L., and Pollock, R. (2008). "Models of public sector information provision via trading funds." Cambridge University, February 26, 2008.

OECD. (2008). "Measuring security and trust in the online environment: A view using official data." Working Party on Indicators for the Information Society, Directorate for Science, Technology and Industry, Committee for Information, Computer and Communications Policy, DSTI/ICCP/IIS(2007)4/FINAL, 21 January 2008, Paris.

OECD. (2009). Rethinking e-Government Services: User-Centred Approaches." Paris, October 2009.

Personal Data Protection Act (RT I 2003, 26, 158). Estonia: http://www.dataprotection.eu/pmwiki/pmwiki.php?n=Main.EE#robject.

TechAmerica. (2010). "Tranparency and transformation through technology." Twentieth Annual Survey of Federal Chief Information Officers, March 2010.

Transparency and Accountability Initiative. (2010). "Open data study." May 2010; UK Cabinet Office (2009, June 10); The PSI Directive put in place in 2003 (IP/02/814): http://ec.europa.eu/information_society/newsroom/cf/itemdetail.cfm?item_id=4891

Ubaldi, B. (2011). "The impact of the economic and financial crisis on e-government in OECD member countries." *European Journal of ePractice*, Volume 11, e-Government for the Economic Crisis: http://www.epractice.eu.

United Nations. (2010). "e-Government Survey 2010: Leveraging e-government at a time of financial crisis." Department of Economic and Social Affairs, New York: http://www2.unpan.org/egovkb.

2

UNDERSTANDING CYBER THREATS

DEBORAH L. WHEELER

Contents

Introduction

You can't see it, taste it, smell it, or even feel it, unless you are sitting at a computer keyboard and staring at a screen. Even then, the vast labyrinth beyond your Internet Protocol (IP) address that makes up the ethereal world of cyberspace is a slippery, shape-shifting concept at best. Internet architecture is a misnomer; like taking the whole globe as a unit of urban planning. The Internet does not have an architect, it has architects galore. This would not matter much except that the systems that make up the network are integrated and dependent on the kindness of strangers. Unkind strangers, malicious code, breeches, kill switches, leaks and breakdowns—all of these factors and more can cause potential friction in the flow of bits and bytes and can lead to unauthorized trespassing, theft, denial of services attacks, and malfunctioning in any system dependent on the network, including a nation's critical infrastructures. It is from within this context that threat and opportunity in cyberspace are defined and implemented.

According to Myriam Dunn (2005, p. 5), a security researcher, as computers "become part of the Internet," every machine and the networks that link them become "susceptible to attack and intrusion." To illustrate how and the potential consequences, this chapter examines two cases in which the Internet facilitates cybersecurity threats and opportunities in the 21st century: Stuxnet and WikiLeaks. These cases provide emerging examples of why our security strategies will be altered by global networked communications and human relations they shape and maintain. Through these case studies we are able to more carefully explore what Ronald J. Deibert and Rafal Rohozinski (2010, p. 15) call "risks through cyberspace," in other words, "risks that arise from cyberspace and are facilitated or generated by its technologies, but do not directly target the infrastructures per se." Each case study concludes with a list of lessons learned, and a conclusion applies them to an interpretation of the Arab Spring of 2011 sweeping away old regimes and weakening others in the Middle East as a region to watch in the future of cybersecurity studies. The same tools that can promote U.S. interests can also bring down friendly regimes, destabilize oil prices, empower state repression, and place national critical infrastructures at risk. Navigating the pluses and minuses of this brave new security environment is surely among the greatest challenges for the 21st century.

Definitions

From cyber threats to cybersecurity to cyber opportunities and cyber vulnerabilities to cyberdefense and cyber power, not to mention cyber warfare in cyberspace, a new language is being created. A new realm and style of engagement is emerging. According to the U.S. President's 2010 Cyberspace Policy Review, cyberspace is defined as "the interdependent network of information technology infrastructures, and includes the Internet, telecommunications networks, computer systems and embedded processors and controllers in critical industries" (p. 1). The Internet has been with us as a public commodity and realm of engagement since the early 1990s. Why in the 21st century are some wishing we could shut it down? According to Patricia Titus, VP and Chief Information Security Officer (CISO) of Unisys, "in the past it was difficult for just anyone to play in this new game of cyber-espionage. Now with the low cost of computing resources available through the cloud, nearly anyone with some technical sense and a will to do harm can participate" (Masters, 2010, p. 30). Similarly, in the words of Richard A. Clarke (2010, p. xiii), the former U.S. presidential adviser on the matter, "If we could put this genie back in the bottle, we should—but we can't." According to an article in *SC Magazine*, a security publication, on "any given day," IBM's Global Operations Centers "monitors 140 countries and processes 5–10 billion security events" (Radcliff, 2010, p. 31). This impressive body of cybersecurity breaches gives a one-day snapshot of the global threats of the cyber era.

The overlapping layers of information technology (IT) capability, dependence, and vulnerability are huge, complex, and central to national security in the 21st century. Cyberspace, according to Deibert and Rohozinski (2010, p. 16), "connects more than half of all humanity and is an indispensable component of political, social, economic and military power worldwide." According to Nigel Inkster (2010, p. 1), Director of Transnational Threats and Political Risks at the International Institute for Strategic Studies (IISS) in London, "cyberwarfare is going to be a serious threat in the future; a threat that could have serious implications for all of us." From our transportation networks, financial markets, telecommunications networks, power grids, to corporate, government, and individual proprietary data, to the military battlefield and intelligence, cyberspace provides the ways and means to secure (or destabilize) the daily lives and futures of states and citizens.

According to the U.S. Department of Defense's (DoD) *Quadrennial Defense Review Report*, February 2010, "Although it is a man-made domain, cyberspace is now as relevant a domain for DoD activities as the naturally occurring domains of land, sea, air and space" (p. 37). Driven by the importance of threats, vulnerabilities, and opportunities in the cyber environment, an interdisciplinary community of scholars and policy makers, from Political Science to Computer Science and beyond, is trying to make sense of the meaning of cyberspace for the practice of politics, the business of war, and the securing of critical information infrastructures needed for daily life to function in wired societies. In spite of the growing awareness of the importance of cybersecurity, and, according to the IISS (2010, p. 2), "despite evidence of cyber attacks in recent political conflicts, there is little appreciation internationally for how to properly assess cyber-conflict." The quest to better understand cyber threats and how to effectively respond to secure the networks that enable life as we know it, animates policy debates in the United States especially. As explained by Mike McConnell (2010, p. B1), former director of the U.S. National Security Agency, this is because the more wired a country is, the more vulnerable it is to cyber attacks, and in his words, "the stakes are enormous."

The Global Context of Cyber Threats

Given the rapid global diffusion of Internet and social networking technologies, the degree to which societies around the world are increasingly linked is on the rise. With each new participant in the information age added to the network, the possibilities for threats and opportunities increase exponentially. Unfortunately, much of our cybersecurity analysis is myopic and U.S. based. We assume (incorrectly) that the United States is the most wired country in the world, so it is the most vulnerable. But throughout the globe, countries are going digital at breakneck speed. We would be wise to understand information environments beyond the West so that emerging cyber threats and opportunities do not take us by surprise. To provide a snapshot of how global cyberspace is, see Table 2.1.

One of the reasons that cybersecurity challenges and opportunities must be conceptualized in a global framework beyond a U.S.-centric approach is that only 13.5% of all Internet users reside in North America. That leaves about 87% of cyberspace outside of U.S. sovereignty. The highest concentration of Internet users worldwide reside in Asia, which constitute 42% of the total global community. Within Asia, about half of all regional users, or about

Table 2.1 World Internet Access

WORLD REGION	POPULATION 2010	INTERNET USERS DECEMBER 31, 2000	INTERNET USERS FEBRUARY 10, 2011	PERCENT (%) PENETRATION OF POPULATION	PERCENT (%) GROWTH 2000– 2010	USERS AS PERCENT (%) OF TABLE
Africa	1,013,779,050	4,514,400	110,931,700	10.9	2,357.3	5.6
Asia	3,834,792,852	114,304,000	825,094,396	21.5	621.8	42.0
Europe	813,319,511	105,096,093	475,069,448	58.4	352.0	24.2
Middle East	212,336,924	3,284,800	63,240,946	29.8	1825.3	3.2
North America	344,124,450	108,096,800	266,224,500	77.4	146.3	13.5
Latin America/ Caribbean	592,556,972	18,068,919	204,689,836	34.5	1,032.8	10.4
Oceana/ Australia	34,700,201	7,620,480	21,263,990	61.3	179.0	1.1
Totals	6,845,609,960	360,985,492	1,966,514,816	28.7	444.8	100

Source: Internet World Stats (www.internetworldstats.com).

420,000,000 people, live in China. This is 26% more Internet users than reside in the United States. Moreover, the United States is "increasingly willing to publicly acknowledge that China's network exploitation and intelligence collection activities are one of [the U.S.'s] most consuming counterintelligence challenges," according to a report by Bryan Krekel of Northrop Grumman, an American defense contractor. As of 2007, for example, Krekel noted that the United States estimates that "China has successfully ex-filtrated at least 10–20 terabytes of data from U.S. government networks" (p. 51). The United States is not the only target of Chinese cyber attacks. It is estimated that "60% of cyber attacks hitting Germany emanate from China," according to a piece in *The Weekly Standard* and quoted by Krekel. A recent report on Chinese cyber espionage cites known cases of Chinese cyber attacks occurring in South Korea, Australia, the Philippines, India, Pakistan, Portugal, the United Kingdom, Belgium, and New Zealand. India claims, again according to the Northrop Grumman report, that "China is behind almost daily attacks into networks belonging to the government and India's private sector" (Gartzke, 2007, quoted in Kevkel, 2009).

The U.S. Cyber Consequences Unit estimates that more than 70% of known cyber attacks originate from computers located outside of the United States, thus illustrating the ways in which cyber threats are global in nature. A 2010 article in *The New York Times* (Markoff, 2010) states that "a secret cyberwar arms race is under way as a number of countries build sophisticated software and hardware attack capabilities." According to Jeffrey Carr (2010, p. 1), "there are over 120 nations leveraging the Internet for political, military and economic espionage activities." The first known act of cyber war occurred in 2008 when the Russian government, in addition to rolling tanks into South Ossetia, launched a denial of services cyber attack on the Georgian government's communication and banking sectors, according to a report in CNET News, among others.

In addition to China and Russia, the Middle East and North Africa, where the Internet is spreading faster than on any place on the planet, is another important location for cybersecurity knowledge and understanding. Both of the case studies analyzed for this chapter have a geographic link with computer networks in the Middle East. Each of these cases teaches us something about the nature of cyber threats as they emerge in individual, national, and international contexts. From these case studies, the public and private sectors, governments, and the international community can all learn important lessons about future cybersecurity.

Cybersecurity Questions and Issues

Before turning to the case studies, this section provides a summary of the complex web of competing interests, explanations, and policy recommendations that animate the emerging field of cybersecurity studies. We can conceptually map this process in terms of those points on which there is agreement, and those places where agreement is absent within the emerging cybersecurity community.

There is relative agreement across disciplines and communities on the following:

1. We (states, citizens, and the global community) agree that our lives as we know it are network dependent—that cyber is key to life.

In practice, this translates into a growing recognition that dependence on critical information infrastructures to live life in the 21st century makes us increasingly vulnerable to cyber threats.

2. We agree how serious the potential threats are, given this dependency on networks and known cases of cyber vulnerability.

The two case studies below indicate different layers of cyber vulnerability and opportunity, from critical infrastructures to international relations.

3. We agree that we are currently not winning the war against cyber threats; attacks occur, with increasing frequency and consequences over time.

As the case studies and conclusion suggest, states are vulnerable to overthrow, nuclear energy programs are vulnerable to cyber attack, and states and their diplomatic relations can be damaged by leaks of information and coordinated Facebook revolutions.

4. We agree that something has to be done to make our digital lives and interests more secure.

Although the case studies analyzed below do not provide specific answers with regard to solving cybersecurity challenges, they highlight several real-world examples of what is at stake if collectively we do not act to better secure our digital future. Recognizing the nature and scope of the problem is the first step toward solving it in the future.

5. We agree that cyberspace represents a "real" relatively new domain of engagement (locally and globally) as important as air, sea, land, and space. "Cyberspace" is not science fiction. It is deserving of all the rules of engagement, defense, and attention that the other domains receive.

The case studies below show how "real" cyber engagement, risk, and opportunity can be in the 21st century. Any asset that depends upon networked communications, from diplomatic relations, to nuclear centrifuges, to entire government infrastructures can be threatened by cyber attacks.

Meanwhile, disagreement still exists in the following areas:

1. Who/what organization(s) and individual(s) should be responsible for cybersecurity (both offensive and defensive)?

Geography has especially complicated this picture of responsibility. Who safeguards the network? The private sector? An individual government? A community of states? Individual companies? International organizations? The case studies below show how global in scope cybersecurity issues are. Organizations, whether families, corporations, or states, will have to learn how to best defend themselves based on past attacks and vulnerabilities. In the cyber era, a single individual with an ax to grind can challenge the United States and all their allies in the Middle East (WikiLeaks). Disgruntled publics abused by bad governments can rebel, throwing off old regimes and wreaking havoc in the global economy (Middle East Facebook Revolutions). Cybersecurity strategies have to be flexible enough and wide enough in scope to account for these and millions of other eventualities as they emerge today and in the future. Determining who will best keep us (meaning the human race) safe and cyber secure is an ongoing debate.

2. What exactly will make us more secure in cyberspace (policy/government/technology communities/private sector all debating this issue—no consensus yet—solutions sometimes violate privacy or proprietary issues and thus are delayed)?

The law and culture both get involved to make this issue very sensitive within the global community. The search for solutions is still ongoing. Is Julian Assange a criminal (maybe yes because of sexual indiscretion) or a hero because he made public the sometimes seedy backroom discussion and gossip orienting how nations interact? This is the kind of question we can expect to encounter more frequently in the emerging cybersecurity field. How are Assange's actions any different from a Google executive who uses a Facebook site to overthrow a bad government in Egypt? There is a need for new ethics to govern cyber interaction, similar to the universal declaration of human rights. There needs to be an agreed-upon set of cyber rights and responsibilities. Estonia has made access to the Internet a basic human right. We have laws against human trafficking and child pornography that govern certain cyber-business transactions. Especially the issue of cyber-espionage needs legal consequences, as do cyber attacks on critical infrastructure.

3. What are the best policies for implementing cybersecurity?

Because the threats are so diverse at all levels, local, national, and international, it is difficult to know what strategy or set of strategies will make us safe.

4. What legal frameworks need to be in place to (a) hold attackers responsible for cyber operations and (b) to be able to respond even preemptively to a cyber attack or threat (real or perceived)?

The threats in or through cyberspace are emerging more quickly than the legislation to regulate cybersecurity. This makes the determination of such issues as when a cyber attack or leak is an act of war and how and against whom a state, company, or individual has a right to respond.

5. How should the advent of cybersecurity issues change our thinking (conceptual frameworks) about the world, from the way we do science to how we train future generations to how we conceive of where potential future attacks will emerge?

There are obvious needs to reconceptualize security in the cyber era. The network that links our lives, states, and businesses touches every aspect of life as we know it both directly and indirectly. Reliance on networked communications is increasing over time, as are the vulnerabilities that result. The case studies below provide examples of the multiple layers of threat and opportunity that exist in the cyber era. Some conclusions regarding the need to rework our security frameworks in light of these cases are offered at the close of this chapter.

Figure 2.1 provides a graphic organizer of the complex angles of players and interests that illustrate why there is so much potential for contention in all of the above points.

There are potential links and disconnects between these players. The technology at the foundation of the equation is constantly changing. Change is in part fed by research and development (R&D) in the private sector. Individuals also create new techniques and tools that animate our digital futures. Standing by, looking to shape the process so as to regulate and secure cyberspace, especially when overt

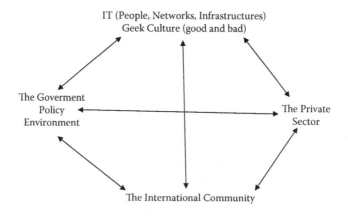

Figure 2.1   The cybersecurity environment.

breeches or challenges emerge, is the local and global government/ policy sector. The private sector has a stake and interest in regulation and security, too. Cybersecurity is thus a moving target, a live organism not a static environment. Perpetual motion makes cybersecurity more complex than the sum of its parts.

Two Cases of Threats to Cybersecurity

The following case studies illustrate the changing nature of the security environment in the cyber era. Stuxnet shows how malicious code can be used to deal serious setbacks to a country's nuclear infrastructure. Speculation is that this act of cyber sabotage was wielded by a state or a partnership of states, given the complexity and costliness of the project. WikiLeaks illustrates what can happen when an individual whistle-blower within an organization decides to share proprietary information with the world. The WikiLeaks website encourages transparency and gives individuals a relatively safe and secure online environment within which to pursue processes of cyber-espionage. Together these cases reveal that cybersecurity can pose state against state, individual against state or states, and states against individuals. Sorting through these complex relationships is the goal of the section that follows. The lessons learned apply to individuals and complex organizations worldwide. Anyone or anything with a life on the screen can gain insights into the strategic challenges of cybersecurity from these cases.

Stuxnet

In 2005, a skeptical security researcher, Myriam Dunn, observed that the link between national security and cyber vulnerabilities was sometimes difficult to substantiate because of threats to critical infrastructure, "the menacing scenarios of major disruptive occurrences in the cyber-domain triggered by malicious actors have remained just that—scenarios" (p. 10). Stuxnet changed that. For the first time in history, we have overt proof that cyber attack can be used to take critical infrastructure not only offline, but as well, to physically destroy systems (in this case nuclear centrifuges). According to one article in *The New York Times*, Stuxnet, as such, is "the most sophisticated cyber weapon ever deployed" (Broad et al., 2011, p. 1).

Stuxnet illustrates that, according to an article in the *Wall Street Journal*, "malicious software attacks...represent a growing corporate espionage and national security threat" (Fuhrmans, 2010, p. B3). Liam O. Murchu a cybersecurity researcher with Symantec, was quoted by *Business Week* as saying Stuxnet "shows what can happen when bad guys gain control of industrial systems" (Hesseldahl, 2010). In *Computerworld*, an industry publication, Joseph Weiss, partner at Applied Control Solutions, a consultancy, point out that "Stuxnet drives home the need for more federal oversight of cybersecurity in the utilities sector." In his words, "hacking a control system does not take rocket science, protecting one does." Advantage awarded to the hackers. Jon Miller, director of Accuvant Labs explains in *SC Magazine*, an industry publication, that "The people writing malicious code only have to write one good piece of malware. The people fighting against the malware have to protect against a multitude of different types of malware. So even if the numbers of defenders and protectors were equal, the defenders would be at a disadvantage" (Masters, 2010, p. 31).

Given the self-propagating nature of Stuxnet, control over the virus' spread was relinquished. As a result, Stuxnet was traced to multiple global intrusions, even though Iranian nuclear centrifuges bore the brunt of the attacks and are believed to be the intended target. In fact, 60% of all systems infected by Stuxnet were located in Iran, according to *SC Magazine*. Figure 2.2 shows which countries were most affected by Stuxnet.

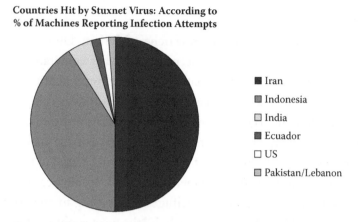

Figure 2.2   Countries affected by Stuxnet. (From Microsoft Malware Protection Center Threat Research and Response Blog http://blogs.technet.com/b/mmpc/archive/2010/07/16/the-stuxnet-sting.aspx.)

According to a 2010 article in *The New York Times* (Broad, p. 1), Tom Parker, an IT security specialist from Securion LLC, noted that because Stuxnet had spread widely across countries it could be seen as a failed operation. In fact, more than 40% of the computers hit by the virus were not the intended target. 45,000 industrial control systems, systems that are responsible for a nation's critical infrastructure like "electric power grids oil and gas pipelines, dams, or communication networks" were infected with the virus worldwide, according to *SC Magazine.* The structure of the virus, however, "was not designed to do damage wherever it landed," according to a *Newsweek* article (Dickey et al., 2010). Instead, the same piece noted that "it is structured to target a specific set of devices manufactured only in Finland and Iran that are used to determine the speed at which the centrifuges rotate." Further, Stuxnet "was designed to do nothing to computers that didn't connect with the control mechanisms it targeted." Thus, although the virus was detected on computers throughout the world, it seems to have only had a damaging impact on Iran's nuclear centrifuges. In this sense it was a smart weapon.

The difficulty in determining exactly where Stuxnet originated means that cyber threats like this one are hard to deter. What we do know is that Stuxnet was unlikely to have been the work of a single hacker, or even a team of hackers. The nature of the worm indicates that it is the work of a state or coalition of states. Analysts maintain this interpretation of the virus' origins for a number of reasons. First, according to an article in *The New York Times*, "the malicious code...would have required an organization with substantial financial resources to develop, test and then release such a program" (Markoff, 2010, p. 5). More specifically, the virus uses four zero day security vulnerabilities to attack the targeted systems,* and purchasing each one of these vulnerabilities from the hacker underground, according to *Red Herring* (2010), "adds up to a decent fortune, placing the virus out of the budgets of most private hacking teams." Second, according to an article on *BusinessWeek.com* (Hesseldahl, 2010), Liam O. Murchu of cybersecurity firm Symantec, "estimates that Stuxnet was written by a team of a dozen programmers working for at least six months, at a cost of more than USD\$3 million." Microsoft, meanwhile, estimates that "building the [Stuxnet] virus likely took 10,000 man-days of labor by top-rank software engineers," according to a 2010 article in *The New York Times* (Hesseldahl, 2010). In January 2011, *The New York Times* (Dickey et al., 2010) published another article in which it argued, based upon intelligence sources, that the Dimona nuclear power plant in southern Israel served "as a critical testing ground in a joint American and Israeli effort to undermine Iran's efforts to make a bomb of its own." While Israel and the United States are not openly taking responsibility for the cyber war against Iran's nuclear program, evidence increasingly points in that direction.

For security reasons, industrial control systems are often run on computers not connected to the Internet. In this instance, too, the Stuxnet worm was unusual because it attacked control systems that were not hooked to the Internet. The Stuxnet virus bypassed this security arrangement by (1) being uploaded by a universal serial bus (USB), either intentionally or unknowingly; (2) telling the host computer to dial the Internet, thus establishing a connection between the host computer and the supposedly offline computer programs running the industrial control system; (3) after establishing Internet access, the virus provided details of the system to a server reportedly in Denmark or Malaysia; (4) that server responded with instructions to change part of the software in the control computer, which in Iran's case meant

---

* Zero days are "holes in a computer program's security that were unknown to the developer" and have yet to be detected (Sugrue, 2010, p. 7).

to reset the centrifuges to maximum speed; (5) as Norman Friedman (2010, p. 88), a security analyst, has noted (2010), "each of the thousands of centrifuges at Natanz has a software-driven controller. Each controller presumably runs the same software, and many if not all are linked so that software revised for one computer can be spread to the rest"; and, as a result, (6) thousands of Iranian centrifuges, the devices that spin at supersonic speeds to enrich uranium, were destroyed. The virus was designed to alter the electric frequencies that control the spin rate of the centrifuges, sending them wildly out of their normal pattern, until they crack or cannot spin properly any more. A second part of the virus covered the change in the frequency converter drives by sending "normal readings to cover its tracks," according to an article in *The Economist* (2010, p. 8713).

A 2011 *New York Times* article estimated that Iran lost one-fifth of its nuclear centrifuges through this attack. Greg Thielmann and Peter Crail, writing for the *Christian Science Monitor*, note that this attack was helped along by the inherently buggy, reversed engineered Iranian nuclear program, based on the Pakistani model, stolen from the Dutch in the 1970s. Thielmann and Crail (2010) say Iran's nuclear program is at best thus, "temperamental and fault-prone." According to the same source, "reverse engineering faulty, smuggled equipment, as Iran has tried to do, only makes this challenge worse." Nuclear enrichment via centrifuge technology "requires constructing complex machinery at precise specifications to allow the cylindrical devices to spin at supersonic speeds, day in and day out." Given the design weaknesses of the Iranian nuclear program, the system was more vulnerable to attack than say a nuclear power plant in the United States or Europe.

The Stuxnet attack was accompanied by targeted assassinations of Iran's top nuclear scientists. One of the hits was against Majid Shahriari, who was "killed in Tehran on November 29th by a bomb stuck to his car by assassins on motorbikes," according to *The Economist* (2010), which also noted that Mr. Shahriari was at the time of his murder in charge of eradicating Stuxnet from the Iranian nuclear program, according to Debka, an Israeli website that specializes in security news. The *Newsweek* article estimated that the Stuxnet cyber attack, along with targeted assassinations of Iran's top nuclear scientists, set the Iranian nuclear program back several years and decreased the likelihood of a more traditional military attack (e.g., cruise missiles, aerial bombardment), giving diplomacy a chance and saving innocent lives.

Lessons learned:

1. Do not allow the use of USB drives.
2. Do not have Windows systems set to automatically boot when a USB drive is inserted.
3. Frequently replace hardware and software to "raise the bar for any enemy attacking," as Norman Friedman (2010, p. 89) put it in his article.
4. Just because critical information infrastructures are not linked to the Internet does not mean that they are invulnerable to cyber attack.
5. Cyber attacks can come from any direction (east or west, states or individuals, friends or foes) and are harder to anticipate, predict, or deter than they are to implement—advantage to the bad guys/aggressor; disadvantage to the defender.
6. Stuxnet makes it difficult to determine who the bad guys and the good guys are, both because of the anonymity of the attack's origin, as well as due to various value judgments regarding the attack's goals (some might think it is a good thing to delay Iran's nuclear program; others might defend the country's right to develop technology as it sees fit, and see the attack as an act of war/illegal sabotage).
7. Stuxnet is just the beginning, but it provides a wake-up call, an early warning system, so to speak, for any organization dependent on cyber networks to function. Large sums of money need to be dedicated to beefing up cybersecurity defenses including early detection and tracking of intrusions or abnormalities. Frequently changing and upgrading systems, both hardware and software, will make us safer in the short run.
8. The advent of cyber warfare means another realm of potential vulnerability, and opportunity is added to the security calculus of any state or business. Security in the 21st century just got infinitely more complex, for all the reasons examined in this chapter. As noted in the November/December 2010

issue of *Process Engineering*, Stuxnet is "just the latest incident showing a marked growth in computer hacking, Internet fraud, data loss, and malicious software in the industrial and utilities sectors."

9. *Process Engineering* (Nov/Dec 2010), also noted that Stuxnet reveals how simple and destructive it is for an employee or an outside contractor to introduce malware into a cyber infrastructure, with grave implications for the systems that run on such infrastructures.

10. *Newsweek* called Stuxnet "the paradigm of covert cyberweapons to come" and "the first time we've actually seen a weapon created by a state (or states) to achieve a goal that you would otherwise have used multiple cruise missiles to achieve" Dickey et al., 2010).

11. The fact that the Stuxnet code is widely available now means reverse engineering and copycat crimes might make its creators and the rest of the world increasingly vulnerable to pernicious cyber attack. In other words, the "worm could turn," as *Newsweek* noted.

12. *Newsweek* also noted that Stuxnet shows how covert cyber actions can buy time and "gives diplomacy a chance."

13. According to the *US Federal News Service* (2010), Stuxnet indicates an escalation in cyber warfare because it represents the advent of "countries launching attacks against other nations."

14. Also according to the *US Federal News Service* (2010), Stuxnet suggests the need to expand or revise the Geneva Conventions, the rules that govern warfare, to take account of cyber warfare, where the target may be physical or may be instead "soft or cyber damage—like the corruption of data or services."

WikiLeaks, Freedom of Information, Espionage, and the Future of Diplomacy in the Cyber Era

WikiLeaks is a nongovernmental organization established in 2006 in order to increase government transparency, encourage the emergence of better journalism, more enlightened foreign policy, and more effective governance in the global community. As noted by, among others, the *Christian Science Monitor*, Australian-born Julian Assange is the editor and figurehead of WikiLeaks, which is currently best known for a series of classified document leaks, the sum total of which are said to have had a detrimental effect on U.S. foreign policy and foreign relations. Hillary Clinton, for example, said in an article in the *Sydney Morning Herald* that "it will take years to undo the damage caused by WikiLeaks revelations" (Warrick, 2011, p. A11). *Human Events* called WikiLeaks a "security tsunami," the largest public breech of classified documents in history and a wake-up call to any organization trying to secure proprietary information in the Internet age. WikiLeaks brought into the public domain, more than half a million classified government documents, many of which cast an embarrassing light on certain dark sides of U.S. foreign policy, the war efforts in Afghanistan and Iraq, and U.S. global diplomacy assessments.

The leaks resulted in top U.S. officials losing their jobs, including P.J. Crawley, State Department Spokesman, for his comment about the "stupidity" of private Bradley Manning's (the alleged leaker) treatment in prison; U.S. Ambassador to Ecuador Heather Hodges, for her WikiLeaked comment regarding corruption in the Ecuadorian police force; and U.S. Ambassador to Libya Gene Cretz for his leaked comments about Gadhafi's "voluptuous nurse." The release also put at risk relationships between the United States and key allies by calling into question the American ability to keep privileged information private. Leaked information regarding the wars in Iraq and Afghanistan is said to have potentially put U.S. service member's lives at risk. Some of the leaked documents embarrassed allies, especially heads of state in several Middle Eastern countries. For example, during a December 2010 trip I took to the United Arab Emirates as a member of a U.S. Naval Academy delegation, U.S. Embassy staff and Emirati foreign policy officials discussed the WikiLeaks debacle and agreed that Emirati leaders would be less frank in future dealings with the U.S. government, given the ways in which the leaks embarrassed the Emir by publicizing the head of state's frank assessment of the Iranian threat.

WikiLeaks, in the debate between the state's right to privacy in world affairs and the public's right to know, sides with the public. On the organization's website (a mirror site, because the organization has been cyber-ousted from the public domain by its host), WikiLeaks is said to operate based upon the following principles:

Publishing improves transparency, and this transparency creates a better society for all people. Better scrutiny leads to reduced corruption and stronger democracies in all society's institutions, including government, corporations and other organizations. A healthy, vibrant and inquisitive journalistic media plays a vital role in achieving these goals. We are part of that media. (http://www.wikileaks.ch/About.html)

WikiLeaks is a product of new information environments enabled by the Internet and the increased flow of information supported by the technologies globally. WikiLeaks believes, as Justice Black ruled in a 1971 Supreme Court case involving freedom of the press, stimulated by the Pentagon Papers leak, that "only a free and unrestrained press can effectively expose deception in government." As Hillary Clinton noted in her 2010 speech at the Newseum, in the aftermath of the China-Google scandal, "information networks are helping people discover new facts and making government more accountable" (Black, 1971). Similarly, President Barack Obama noted, during a 2009 visit to China, that "the more freely information flows, the stronger societies become" because "access to information allows citizens to hold their own governments accountable."

So if wider more transparent information flows make society better off and more democratic, according to Clinton, President Obama, and WikiLeaks, why is the United States launching a campaign to censor the site and to charge Assange with espionage? The answer, of course, has to do with the fact that WikiLeaks is leaking classified, protected state secrets. And the whistle-blowers who aid WikiLeaks in its effort to expose deception in government are going beyond their right to free speech, breeching the limits of freedom of information, and potentially, according to the *Christian Science Monitor*, violating the 1917 Espionage act for "damaging US security by publishing the documents" (Grier, 2010, p. 1). In another article from the same source, when Bradly Manning, a 23-year-old Army private working in the intelligence field, allegedly copied and delivered to WikiLeaks nearly one million classified documents, he violated the Uniform Code of Military Justice by "communicating, transmitting and delivering national defense information to an unauthorized source" Grier, 2010, p. 1). The documents he allegedly leaked include

1. Secret archive footage of an Apache helicopter attack on civilians and journalists in Iraq that occurred in a suburb of Baghdad in July 2007 (leaked April 2010)
2. Afghan War Diary archive of 92,000 "field situation reports" from soldiers on the ground fighting in Afghanistan, giving their assessment of the war effort (leaked July 2010)
3. Iraq War log, including nearly 392,000 reports that collectively mapped every death and casualty in the Iraq war (leaked October 2010)
4. State Department Diplomatic Cables, about 250,000 pieces of frank assessment of U.S. friends and foes worldwide (leaked November 2010)

Learning from WikiLeaks So how does a data breech of this magnitude happen and what lessons can we learn from it about how to defend our cyber borders and infrastructures? According to *Forbes* magazine, WikiLeaks, if nothing else, "should serve as a reminder for the information security community" that "a single whistleblower with a conscience can turn your entire organization inside out." The *Christian Science Monitor* (Grier, 2010, p. 1) meanwhile reports that according to Manning, he "had unprecedented access to classified networks 14 hours a day 7 days a week for 8+ months." He "would come in with music on a CD-RW…erase the music…while exfiltrating possibly the largest data spillage in American history." So what weaknesses allowed Manning to create this "data tsunami?" Manning explains in an article in the *Christian Science Monitor*, "Weak servers, weak logging, weak physical security, weak counterintelligence, and inattentive signal analysis."

WikiLeaks played a role, too. As the organization explains on its website,

> As a result of technical advances particularly the internet and cryptography—the risks of conveying important information can be lowered. We believe that it is not only the people of one country that keep their own government honest, but also the people of other countries who are watching that government through the media. In the years leading up to the founding of WikiLeaks, we observed the world's publishing media becoming less independent and far less willing to ask the

hard questions of government, corporations and other institutions. We believed this needed to change. (Current WikiLeaks mirror site: http://213.251.145.96/About.html)

Some argue that WikiLeaks reveals that less information should be classified. In the words of Christopher Graham, UK Information Commissioner, as quoted in *The Guardian* (Borger and Leigh, 2010), "If all of us just accept that this is the people's information and 99.9% should be out there in all its tedium, you wouldn't have WikiLeaks." Plainly stated, according to the same source, "the best form of defense is transparency." WikiLeaks focuses a bright, clarifying light on weaknesses in the globe's information assuredness. This is because, in our present system, a 23-year-old Army private can download hundreds of thousands of sensitive documents while pretending to listen to a Lady Gaga CD. As CNN's Wolf Blitzer (2010) asks, "Is our security system that lax?"

The more important question is, if it was that lax, has the United States and other complex organizations like states and multinational corporations around the globe done anything to make it less so? According to *The Guardian* (Borger and Leigh, 2010), some three million U.S. public servants have access to classified information. Is this needed? Is there a way to limit, within the system, the documents to which analysts lower in the food chain have access? Wouldn't it make sense to limit the kinds of recordable devices that can be hooked up to a classified information network?

In general, the WikiLeaks case study yields six main lessons:

1. Keep in mind that cyber threats can be both external (common conception) and internal (whistle-blowers, disgruntled employees, former employees with an ax to grind, or criminals who operate behind the cover of loyal employee/good citizen).
2. Do not allow external storage devices to be hooked to computers linked with classified servers.
3. Monitor networks for unusual flows of bits and bytes.
4. Only give employees enough access to classified data as needed to do their job. Compartmentalize the rest to prevent sweeping breaches like WikiLeaks.

5. Remember, in the information age, privacy and censorship are an increasingly scarce resource even for authoritarian states. According to Admiral Blair, former Director of U.S. National Intelligence, the 21st century will be remembered as the time of mutually assured humiliation (Blair, 2011).

6. Just because information is made classified does not mean that bad policies can be hidden behind a veil of secrecy forever and always. If people in positions of power knew the whole World Wide Web was watching their behavior, would that behavior change to conform to public scrutiny? If so, then perhaps decisions are tainted, if they need to be kept secret in order not to create diplomatic upsets, public outcries, and regional unrest. As Graham, UK Information Commissioner observed in *The Guardian*, government and corporate transparency is the best defense against future WikiLeaks damage.

It is to the latter issue of IT-inspired regional unrest that we now turn. Both Stuxnet and WikiLeaks have clear links with the Middle East, but neither case study focuses upon a process that originated in the region at the grass roots. During the writing of this chapter, information technology has enabled everyday citizens in the Middle East to create processes of significant political change through a series of revolutionary events, as examined below.

Conclusion: Lessons for Global, Regional, and State Security in the Cyber Age

Is there a link between Stuxnet, WikiLeaks, and regional unrest that is sweeping the Middle East, including thus far, a regime collapse in Tunisia and Egypt, continuing unrest, as of 2011, and signs of civil war in Libya and Yemen, a new more repressive police state in Bahrain, continued unrest and governmental uncertainty in Oman, Jordan, and Syria, riots and demonstrations in Kuwait, Saudi Arabia, Iran, and Algeria? What role has enhanced information technology diffusion and use played in such regional unrest? Is it correct to call these "Twitter and Facebook revolutions?" What do the changes sweeping the Middle East teach us about cybersecurity? These questions form the foundation for this conclusion.

In states where there is a critical mass of people with IT skills and access, matched with robust indicators of social failure, cyber threats from these areas will be more likely. As illustrated by social media-enabled regime change in Tunisia in January 2011, and Egypt in February 2011, unemployment, large pockets of poverty, inequitable access to education, demographic factors such as the youth bulge, a lack of meaningful pathways to political participation, patterns of state repression, human rights violations, and corruption all combined with IT capabilities among the public to create threats to national, regional, and international security. When citizens throughout the Middle East read WikiLeaked documents about their government's corruption, it added one more log to the fire of their desire for good governance and regime change. In addition, groups working for regime change in Egypt, for example, "the April 6 youth movement" which has 70,000 followers on Facebook, "uses social networking sites to orchestrate protests and report on their activities," thus revealing the link between IT access, activism, and unrest in the Middle East, according to *The Telegraph* online.

As General Petraeus's (2010) report on the CENTCOM AOR illustrates, U.S. national security strategy considers regional stability in the Middle East and North Africa as crucial to global security interests, especially as the region contains vast energy resources and has been a venue for attacks on western interests in the past. Global cybersecurity strategy needs to be sensitive to what author Jeffrey Carr (2010) calls "latent tensions" in the world. Developing criteria for "latent tension" and identifying regions, countries, and movements that may now or in the future contribute to regional and global instability is an important element in mapping potential hot spots for cyber insecurity.

When and How Did the Middle East Become so Tech Savvy?

From June to July 2009, I spent a month in Kuwait researching emerging Internet cultures and attitudes. My research, especially a survey of more than 300 Internet users conducted by my students at American University of Kuwait, illustrated that in "far-away places," in countries relatively "underdeveloped" politically, vibrant, socially networked, and politically active Internet communities continue to spread at phenomenal speeds. The majority, more than 80% of those interviewed for this project, stated that Internet use was having a significant impact on politics. Most of those interviewed had a Facebook page, with large, extended friend networks. Text messaging, blogging, and using new media technologies to experiment with new freedoms of expression and organization continue to grow. What these findings indicate is that cyberspace is globally shared, locally constructed in the imaginations of digital citizens around the world. We should not assume that the network of networks has boundaries but rather is a globally vibrant and spreading imagined community.

The Internet continues to spread more rapidly in the Middle East than on any other place on the planet. The U.S. government has made getting free and open access to new media technologies to citizens of the Middle East, especially those living in hostile, authoritarian regimes like Iran, a matter of U.S. National Security Strategy. While this is an interesting "non-Military" strategy designed to enable domestic pressures for regime change, with each new member of the global Internet user community added, the potential for cyber-vulnerabilities and attack grows. The study of Kuwaiti Internet cultures reveals that even in conservative Islamic societies, Internet use, for more than 20 hours a week, is becoming a regular feature of everyday life. While not every user added to the network is a threat we should be aware of, the rapid increase of Internet use in the Middle East, a current theater of Department of Defense (DoD) operation, and a location from which hostile uses of the Internet to coordinate and implement acts that challenge U.S. security interests, have originated in the past. From the coordination of terrorist attacks, to recruitment, to computer network breeches, to jihadi website proliferation, and ideological warfare—of all these hostile acts take place because of the rapid growth and increasing dependence of the region on computer networks and communication. Unfortunately, it is not only democrats who are empowered by the networks, but hackers, jihadis, and thieves as well.

The increasingly bold forms of new media enabled public opposition to regimes in the region, from Shia opposition to Suni rule in Bahrain, to Internet-enabled opposition to state brutality and unaccountability in Egypt, to more subtle forms of push for democracy in Kuwait and not so subtle socially networked forms of opposition to Ahmadinejad's Iran. Each of these processes, while small steps forward for democracy in the region, also eat away at stability and security in a region vital to U.S. security interests. We should be aware of the potential unintended consequences of using the Internet to support processes of social and political reengineering in a region hostile to colonialism, even in electronic form. Due to the possibilities for "clashes" of civilizations, so overtly pronounced in the tragic 9/11 attacks, in which the Internet was the handmaiden to the organizers, we should not underestimate the creativity, tech-savvy, and dedicated mindset of our potential enemies, as well as the potentially destabilizing effects of Internet use on regimes with which the United States is allied. Both friends and enemies are enabled by the spread of new computer and media technologies. As we have seen in the past, even if dictators pull the plug on the Internet, when it gets used to challenge governmental authority, this is not an effective act for stopping revolution. This is because the public has other ways of communicating its opposition, and as well, the offline impacts of online behaviors have deep and lasting impacts on society that cannot be erased by a temporary kill switch.

The Clinton-led State Department has openly declared the Internet as a tool for regime change and has stated its desire to get safe Internet access in the hands of all global citizens. Although it may be clearly in U.S. interests for such tools to destabilize regimes in Iran and China, just like Stuxnet hitting targets outside of Iran, Internet access once diffused to the far reaches of the globe can be used to destabilize the regimes of our friends, raising oil prices, creating security challenges throughout the region.

Our stereotypes of Arab and Muslim cultures of being relatively backwards, both in social ideals and technological prowess, may leave us vulnerable as we try to map and to predict future cyber attacks from unexpected locations. We need to peer beyond the veil and think outside of the box of our cultural blinders. What happens if Iran or someone else reengineers the Stuxnet virus to attack U.S. critical infrastructures? Where will the WikiLeaks debacle end? What other diplomatic crises will result, and how will U.S. foreign policy makers and diplomats alter opinions and policies to restore the U.S.'s image and influence in the global community? How can the United States promote good governance and increased human security in the region without fostering short-term chaos and increased economic hardship for the region's poor and disenfranchised youth? Cybersecurity opportunities and strategies have a role to play in making the Middle East and the world a more stable and equitable place for all. At the same time, increased cyber threats if not anticipated and prevented through proactive and effective security strategies have the potential to change the world as we know it. Stuxnet, WikiLeaks, and Information Technology for regime change as explored in this chapter all provide important lessons about what is at stake in the cyber era as well as best practices for making the future more secure and safe than in the past.

References

Blair, Admiral D. (2011). "Cybersecurity Address." U.S. Naval Academy Foreign Affairs Conference (April 15).

Blitzer, W. (2010). "Awaiting Leaks of More US Secrets." *The Situation Room Transcript* (November 29). http://edition.cnn.com/TRANSCRIPTS/1011/29/sitroom.01.html (accessed April 3, 2011).

Black. (1971). Black, J., Concurring Opinion, Supreme Court of the United States 403 U.S. 713 *New York Times Co. v. United States* Certiorari to the United States Court of Appeals for the Second Circuit No. 1873. Argued: June 26, 1971; decided: June 30, 1971.

Borger, J. and Leigh, D. (2010). "Siprnet: Where America Stores Its Secret Cables." *The Guardian* (November 28), p. 2. http://www.guardian.co.uk/world/2010/nov/28/siprnet-america-stores-secret-cables (accessed April 3, 2011).

Broad, W. J. et al. (2011). "Israeli Test on Worm Called Crucial in Iran Nuclear Delay." *New York Times* (January 15), p. 1A.

Broad, W. J. et al. (2010). "Worm in Iran Was Perfect for Sabotaging Nuclear Centrifuges." *New York Times* (November 19), p. 1A.

Carr, J. (2010). *Inside Cyber Warfare* (Sebastopol, CA: O'Reilly).

Clarke, R. (2010). *Cyberwar: The Next Threat to National Security and What to Do About It* (New York: Ecco).

Curtis, P. (2010). "Ministers Must 'wise up not clam up' after WikiLeaks Disclosures." *The Guardian* (December 31), p. 2.

Cyberspace Policy Review: Assuring a Trusted and Resilient Information and Communications Infrastructure. (2009). United States, Executive Office of the President. http://www.archive.org/details/cyberspacepolicyreview (accessed January 30, 2011).

Deibert, R. J., and Rohozinski, R. (2010). "Risking Security: Policies and Paradoxes of Cyberspace Security." *International Political Sociology.* 4:1 (March), 15–32.

Department of Defense. (2010). *Quadrennial Defense Review Report, February 2010.* Washington, DC: Department of Defense. http://www.defense. gov/qdr/images/QDR_as_of_12Feb10_1000.pdf (accessed March 30).

Dickey, et al. (2010). "The Shadow of War." *Newsweek* (December 20), 156:25 (cover story).

Dunn, M. (2005). "A Comparative Analysis of Cybersecurity Initiatives Worldwide." Background Paper, WSIS Thematic Meeting on Cybersecurity, Document: CYB/05, June 10, 2005.

Espinger, T. (2008). "Georgia Accuses Russia of Coordinated Cyber Attack," *CNET News*, August 11, 2008, http://news.cnet.com/8301-1009_3-10014150-83.html.

Friedman, N. (2010). "Virus Season." *Proceedings: United States Naval Institute* (November), 136:11, 88–89.

Fuhrmans, V. (2010). "Corporate News: Siemens Halts Computer Virus as Threat Spurs Effort against Attack." *Wall Street Journal* (August 13), p. B3.

Gartzke, U. (2007). "Outrage in Berlin over Chinese Cyber Attacks." *The Weekly Standard* (August 31). http://www.weeklystandard.com/weblogs/ TWSFP/2007/08/outrage_in_berlin_over_chinese.asp.

Greenburg, A. (2010). "WikiLeaks Reveals the Biggest Classified Data Breech in History." *Forbes* (November 22), 186:9, 38.

Grier, P. (2010). "WikiLeaks Chief Julian Assange: 'Terrorist' or Journalist?" *Christian Science Monitor* (December 20), p. 1.

Hesseldahl, A. (2010). "How Bad Guys Worm Their Way into Factories." *Business Week.com* (October 15).

Inkster, N. (2010). Cyber Warfare." CBC Radio "As It Happens." February 10, 2010, http://www.iiss.org/whats-new/iiss-in-the-press/february-2010/ cyber-warfare.

International Institute of Strategic Studies (IISS). (2010). "The Military Balance 2010 Press Statement." http://www.iiss.org/publications/military-balance /the-military-balance-2010/military-balance-2010-press-statement/ (accessed March 29, 2010).

Knickerbocker, B. (2010) "WikiLeaks 101: Five Questions about Who Did What and When." *Christian Science Monitor* (December 1), p. 1.

Krekel, B. (2009). *Capability of the People's Republic of China to Conduct Cyber Warfare and Computer Network Exploitation* (McLean, VA: Northrup Grumman Corporation).

Maginnis, R. (2010). "WikiLeaks Case Must Spur Major Changes in Secrecy Proceedings." *Human Events* (November 1), pp. 1, 9.

Markoff, J. (2010). "A Code for Chaos." *New York Times,* October 3, p. 5.

Markoff, J., and Sanger, D. E. (2010). "In a Computer Worm, a Possible Biblical Clue." *New York Times,* September 30, p. 1.

Masters, G. (2010). "Raids from Afar." *SC Magazine* (November) 21:11, 30–32.

McConnell, M. "How to Win the Cyber-war We're Losing." *Washington Post,* February 28, 2010, p. B1.

Microsoft Malware Protection Center, "The Stuxnet Sting." July 16, 2010. http:// blogs.technet.com/b/mmpc/archive/2010/07/16/the-stuxnet-sting.aspx.

Obama, B. (2009). Transcript: President Obama's Town Hall Meeting with Students in Shanghi (November 16). http://www.cbsnews.com/stories/2009/11/16/politics/main5670903.shtml (accessed March 27, 2011).

Petraeus, D. H. (2010). Statement of General David H. Petraeus, U.S. Army Commander, U.S. Central Command before the Senate Armed Services Committee on the Posture of the U.S. Central Command (March 16).

Process Engineering. (2010). "Analysis: A Whole New Can of Worms" (November/December).

Radcliff, D. (2010). "A Long Haul." *SC Magazine* (December), 21:12.

Red Herring. (2010). "New, Super Virus Worms through Iran Government Databases." (September 28). http://www.redherring.com/home/26435 (accessed March 14, 2011).

Ross, T., Moore, M., and Swinford, S. (2011). "Egypt Protests." *The Telegraph* (January). http://www.telegraph.co.uk/news/worldnews/africaandindianocean/egypt/8289686/Egypt-protests-Americas-secret-backing-for-rebel-leaders-behind-uprising.html (accessed April 16, 2011).

SC Magazine. (2010). "The Stats" (November), 12:11, 15.

Strobel, W. (2011). "WikiLeaks: 'Voluptuous' Nurse Cable Costs Diplomat His Job." *Huffington Post* (January 4). http://www.mcclatchydc.com/2011/01/04/106191/wikileaks-voluptuous-nurse-cable.html. (Accessed Sept. 8, 2011).

Sugrue, M. (2010). "Virus May Be Targeting Iran's Nuclear Program." *Arms Control Today* (November) 40:9, 7.

The Economist. (2010). "Yet to Turn" (December 18), 397:8713.

Thielmann, G., and Crail, P. (2010). "Chief Obstacle to Iran's Nuclear Effort: Its Own Bad Technology." *Christian Science Monitor* (December 8).

US Federal News Service (wire). (2010). "Cyberwars: Already Underway with No Geneva Conventions to Guide Them," (October 15) (Proquest Document URL: http://search.proquest.com/document/758206443?accountid=14748) (accessed February 1, 2011).

Vijayan, J. (2010). "New Malware Targets Utility Control Systems." *Computerworld* (August 9).

Warrick, J. (2011). "WikiLeaks Damage Will Last for Years, Says Clinton." *Sydney Morning Herald* (January 11), p. A1. http://www.smh.com.au/technology/technology-news/wikileaks-damage-will-last-for-years-says-clinton-20110110-19l8f.html (accessed March 27, 2011).

3

CYBERSECURITY IN EAST ASIA

Japan and the 2009 Attacks on South Korea and the United States

MOTOHIRO TSUCHIYA

Contents

Introduction

Cybersecurity is a new global security concern and East Asia is no exception. In July 2009, a large-scale distributed denial of service

(DDoS) attack targeted South Korean Internet services in addition to those in the United States. The identity of the attackers remains unconfirmed, but the incident made the region's governments realize the importance of defending their countries from cyber threats.

The more our social system becomes dependent on computers, the more vulnerable our society becomes to attack by cyber terrorists. The problem is that computers and networks remain "black boxes" to many of us in that we do not fully understand them. It is also becoming increasingly difficult to understand the threat. We may not even know when an attack is taking place. Attacks such as the demolition of a dam via remote control over a network are obvious, but if a computer database is covertly accessed with the objective of modifying its records, it is quite likely that the time and perpetrator of the attack may go unknown. This is the reason that cyber terrorism has become a difficult concept that evokes unease.

Because targets cannot always recognize an attack the involvement of law enforcement agencies may not be enough and intelligence agencies must therefore be involved in the defense against cyber attacks, especially regarding serious attacks concerning national security. This chapter analyzes public documents and draws on personal interviews with relevant organizations to shed light on the current organizational arrangements for cybersecurity in Japan. It begins with an overview of various forms of cyber threats and attacks before analyzing how Japanese government agencies responded to the July 2009 attacks against the United States and South Korea, in particular the cooperation and competition between intelligence and law enforcement agencies. The chapter concludes with an overview of the current situation in East Asia.

Cyber Threats

The world is increasingly dependent on information and communication networks, and likely to become ever more reliant on cyberspace as the information society emerges. Cybersecurity is also a global problem, and as more countries move to the information society stage, the challenges will increase. Unless we cut computer and network cables, there will be new types of threats and we need security to protect against them. There are various kinds of criminal activities in

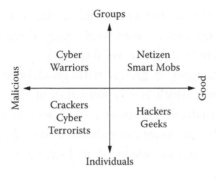

Figure 3.1 Concepts around cybersecurity.

cyberspace, and perpetrators vary, too. One way to view the concept of cyber terrorism is to break it down into multiple categories based on the subject being a group or an individual, and the objective being mental or physical.

Imagine a two-dimensional plane separated into four quadrants by two axes, one vertical and one horizontal (Figure 3.1). The horizontal axis signifies the intent of the user, ranging from "malicious" to "good." The vertical axis signifies the number of users in question, which ranges from "group" to "individual." The four categories created in this way show four different categories.

People in the first category are "hackers," individual users who possess good intentions. The term "hacker" originally meant an individual with considerable computer knowledge and did not signify malicious intent. In modern language, they may also be called "geeks" (Katz 2000). A geek is defined as "a peculiar or otherwise odd person, especially one who is perceived to be overly intellectual." Net culture, which is developed by geeks, is quite different from government culture. One of the leaders in the Internet community, Dave Clark of MIT (Massachusetts Institute of Technology) in the United States, once said, "We reject kings, presidents, and voting. We believe in rough consensus and running code."* Rough consensus means that they keep on discussing issues until almost all of the members agree, even if it takes several years. But nobody has a veto. And running codes imply that they try to be as practical as possible. They don't

---

* Clark didn't intend to advocate anarchism. But his words spread in cyberspace and were widely share among hackers without a context of his speech. Interview with David Clark on July 21, 2008.

accept abstract idealism and unworkable codes. It might be difficult for government agencies to work with geeks. These geeks, however, are increasingly controlling our social systems.

The second category is groups with good intentions. They are known as netizens, which is a combination of the words "net" and "citizen," or alternatively as "smart mobs," a term used by Howard Rheingold (2000), an American cultural writer (2002). These users utilize technology and knowledge shared over a network to achieve group objectives.

The problem consists of users with malicious intent. Groups that possess malicious objectives can be dubbed "cyber warriors." They may be sponsored by governments or nongovernment entities. Either way, they are users who abuse network technology in order to achieve organizational goals.

Last, there are individual users with malicious intentions. As pointed out by Steven Levy (1984), an American journalist and author, these users were once known as "crackers" rather than "hackers." However, users who conduct destructive activities with political motivations rather than mere personal enjoyment can be labeled "cyber terrorists." It should be assumed that, in general usage, the term "cyber terrorist" includes "cyber warriors" as well.

Activities conducted by users with malicious intent can further be divided into two categories depending on their specific objectives. Researchers John Arquilla and David Ronfeldt at the RAND Corporation, headquartered in Santa Monica, California, differentiate between the terms "netwar" and "cyber war" (Arquilla and Ronfeldt, 1993). Netwars consist of societal-level ideational conflicts and take place between both countries and societies. Their aim is to disrupt, damage, or modify what a target population "knows" by targeting the public or elite opinion, or both. Simply stated, the objective of netwar is to mess with people's heads.

In contrast, cyber war is the conduct of military operations according to information-related principles. Warfare is moving from physical territories to networks. For example, it is now common that command controls of military forces are dependent on information and communication networks, and a modern digitalized military force cannot fight without them.

In order to clarify the difference of meanings between netwar and cyber war, the former could be termed "head war," because netwar is the act of trying to modify or change something in your head, while the latter could be called "body war," as an objective of cyber war is physical damage.

Cyber Attacks

The scope of cyber attacks and cyber crimes is increasingly wide and spread from individual to international (White House, 2003, 2008, 2009). Broadly speaking, there are four main types of cyber attacks: (1) physical damage, such as demolition of a dam or clash of airplanes; (2) financial damage, such as unauthorized access to bank account or illegal stock exchange; (3) psychological damage, such as web falsification or service disruption; and (4) virtual damage, which are not recognized by victims, such as a covert operation.

As an illustration of trends, Figure 3.2 shows the increase of reported unauthorized access in Japan. As the National Police Agency collected information in a proactive manner in 2001, this number is unusually high. For example, private sector companies are otherwise often hesitant to share such information with the public in order to avoid a bad reputation. The trend is stable after 2001 but has turned sharply upward since 2005. Figure 3.3 shows the number of reported web falsification. It rose sharply in the fourth quarter of 2009.

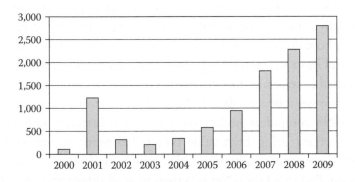

Figure 3.2   Reported unauthorized access. (From National Police Agency. http://www.kantel. go.jp/jp/singi/shin-ampobouei2010/dai7/siryou2.pdf.)

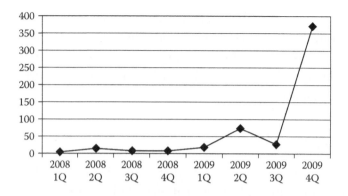

Figure 3.3 Number of web falsification (first quarter of 2008 to fourth quarter of 2009). (From JPCERT/CC. http://www.kantel.go.jp/jp/singi/shin-ampobouei2010/dai7/siryou2.pdf.)

Internationally, examples of large-scale cyber attacks are Estonia in 2007 and Lithuania and Georgia, both in 2008. Many important websites in the three countries were shut down as a result of attacks from Russia, though it does not necessarily mean that the Russian government was involved. Richard Clarke, the former U.S. presidential adviser, provides an example with physical repercussions in his latest book (Clarke and Knake, 2010). Allegedly, Israel disabled the Syrian air defense network in 2007 as the Syrian army could not find any Israeli jet fighters in its radar systems.

In a modern espionage mystery, in 2008, two Canadian researchers, Ronald Deibert of University of Toronto and Rafal Rohozinski of SecDev Group, a consultancy, found strange transmissions of Internet Protocol (IP) packets on the Internet (Information Warfare Monitor, 2009). Because it was unclear who was operating the network they eventually came to term it "GhostNet." A typical virus creates infection and duplicates itself, but the malware they found did not do so. Instead, GhostNet secretly entered target computers and was remotely controlled to send files to somewhere without the owner's knowledge. The two researchers analyzed the traffic of the malware and found that 1,295 computers in 103 countries were infected with 30% of the infections being high-value targets belonging to governments, financial corporations, human rights groups, and others. Traffic patterns implied that GhostNet was used to send information to China; however, further research and analysis could not be done legally as GhostNet traffic went beyond national borders and raised a problem of legal jurisdiction. As such, Deibert and Rohozinski had to give up their research. Instead, they wrote a report about the issues and made it public online in March 2009. Their warnings were widely echoed in cyberspace.

It is easy to say that cybersecurity is important, but it is hard to pinpoint its real importance. But in 2009, a massive scale of attacks broke out on the east and west sides of the Pacific Ocean, an event that came to illustrate clear and present danger to the region's governments.

The Cyber Attacks against South Korea and the United States in July 2009

In July 2009, right after the U.S. Independence Day holiday, someone started distributed denial of service (DDoS) attacks against more than 20 governmental and commercial Internet sites in the United States, including the White House, Department of State, Department of Justice, Department of Defense, and commercial enterprises such as Yahoo! and amazon.com (Nakashima et al., 2009; Sudworth, 2009; and Goodin, 2009).

Similarly, important South Korean websites, such as Ministry of Defense, National Congress, National Intelligence Service (NIS), and those in the financial services sector were also attacked, beginning on July 7 and lasting two days. Major attacks occurred in a wave fashion at 18:00 on July 7, at 18:00 on July 8, and at night on July 9 (KST: GMT+9). The attacker(s) propagated malware through online storage sites and embedded the predefined targets and schedules in the malware (Cho, 2010). According to a report in *Korea Times* (Han, 2009), in an emergency measure to recover disabled online networks, the Korean Communications Commission (KCC) ordered the nation's Internet operators KT (Korea Telecom), SK Broadband, and LG Dacom to deny Internet access to nearly 30,000 virus-infected computers until their operating systems were cleaned (Author's interview at KCC on January 28, 2011). According to the Korean Internet and Security Agency (KISA), many of the hard drives in certain PCs that were hijacked and remotely controlled, "Zombies," were destroyed after the attacks (Author's interview at KISA on January 27, 2011). All kinds of document files and programs were erased while the attacking source files were overwritten or encrypted. In addition, fixed disk MBR (Memory Buffer Register) was overwritten with specific meaningless values. All Internet browsing histories in the Zombie PCs were also removed in order to make it impossible to identify the original source of the malware (Claburn, 2009).

"This is an attack against our country's system and an act or provocation to our national security," said the Chief of the Korean Prime Minister's Office in a task force meeting. KCC officials kept working four nights without sleep to stop the attacks and fix problems. Later analysis indicated that the attacks against South Korea came from the same program as those used against the United States.

At first, Korean National Intelligence Service told some members of the National Congress about the possibility of North Korean involvement. But no clear evidence was presented, although the South Korean government also received information saying that the North Korean government had issued an order to develop computer programs to crack South Korean communications systems. Two weeks later, the government saw signs of simulation tests targeting KISA and a university in Pusan. All these pieces of information lead to continued suspicions about North Korean involvement.

After the attacks against the two countries, the South Korean government sent an inquiry to the Japanese government regarding eight computer servers in Japan. These servers appeared to be used as stepping stones for the attacks, according to my personal interview with the National Police Agency (2010). A stepping-stone is a way of hiding the real attacker. The eight servers were owned by the private sector and their owners had no idea that they were used in the attacks. Three of the eight had a fixed IP address, which allowed them to be identified, and specific stepping stone programs were found on them. The other five were used by commercial Internet service providers, and dynamic IP addresses were allocated to them. It is against secrecy of communications to identify them, and the five are still unknown.

The programs, which were found in the three servers, were the same, and a code to direct targets was found. Only the targets listed were attacked. But the program could not be fully revealed, and it was not possible to locate the route of which the servers had been infected. As such, no information revealing the real attacker or where he or she was located was available, and any North Korean involvement could not be proved.

But the fact that the United States, a Japanese ally, and South Korea, its neighbor, were simultaneously attacked concerned Japanese leaders. The second part of this chapter will detail how they responded to this event, focusing on the National Police Agency, the Ministry of Defense, and the National Information Security Center (NISC), starting with an organizational overview.

Organization of Japan's Intelligence Activities

Today's Japanese intelligence community, even though it was not clearly defined by law, includes National Police Agency, Ministry of Foreign Affairs, Public Security Intelligence Agency, and Ministry of Defense. But the scale and scope of intelligence activities in Japan used to be smaller and narrower (Fukuda, 2010; Hori, 1996; Kitaoka, 2009; Kotani, 2004; Omori, 2005; Sugita, 1987; and Tsukamoto, 1988). During the Cold War most of intelligence came from the United States under the Japan–U.S. Security Treaty. Japan did not have IMINT (Imagery Intelligence) capabilities and had limited HUMINT (Human Intelligence) and SIGINT (Signal Intelligence) capabilities. However, these situations started changing in the post–Cold War era. The emergence and development of cybersecurity and the rise of cyber threats was also a reason to push for intelligence reforms. Cybersecurity is not necessarily an issue to be dealt with by an intelligence agency, but as cyber attacks become larger in scale and affect national security, they also become more serious and it is necessary to involve intelligence agencies to prevent attacks (Nye, 2010; Saka, 2004; and Tsuchiya, 2007).

Growing concerns regarding cybersecurity, especially in light of the 2009 attacks, have added a new dimension to Japan's intelligence activities. Although the revival of intelligence agencies such as the Cabinet Intelligence Research Office (CIRO) after the Japanese defeat in World War II was relatively quick, the National Police Agency has been more powerful both in intelligence and law enforcement activities than any other security-related agency. That is, there has been no clear wall between law enforcement and intelligence activities in terms of organizational functions. However, new cyber threats are forcing changes to the system because they are too complicated and elusive to respond to under the existing organization.

The National Information Security Center (NISC), established in 2005, is a key player in this new environment (Yamada et al., 2010). It is an agency under the Cabinet Office of the Prime Minister. It used to focus on technical measures for cybersecurity, but after the July 2009 attacks it quickly acquired national security perspectives. If NISC were to be a cross point of intelligence and law enforcement, this cooperation system between law enforcement and intelligence agencies could be a first step to reorganize the Japanese intelligence system to prepare for future cyber and other types of threats.

The first government agency to respond to cyber threats is the police. If a cyber attack can be categorized as a crime, a police agency will attempt to catch and prosecute a perpetrator. However, if the attack goes beyond a simple crime and is perceived as a national security threat, a military force (Self Defense Force in the Japanese case) will respond. For example, falsification of websites is just a crime, but physical attacks on critical infrastructure, such as power grids or national transportation systems are different. Similarly, the third corresponding agency is intelligence. It tries to forecast and prevent attacks beforehand, primarily against targets such as nuclear facilities, transportation systems, or financial systems. In order to prevent those attacks, intelligence activities such as wiretapping are needed.

In the case of Japan, these three types of government agencies and organizations are overlapping and cannot be separated in a rigorous manner. For example, the Security Bureau of the National Police Agency is a powerful intelligence section inside a law enforcement agency. The Intelligence Headquarter of the Ministry of Defense is also an intelligence section for signal intelligence (SIGINT). The top director position of the Cabinet Intelligence Research Office (CIRO) has been always occupied by officers from the National Police Agency, and the position of deputy directors has always been occupied by officers from the Ministry of Foreign Affairs. Among many related agencies, the National Information Security Center (NISC) is playing a central role in these situational changes. The central problem, however, is how these overlapping Japanese government agencies responded to the large-scale cyber attacks in July 2009, the scale of which had impressed Japanese government leaders.

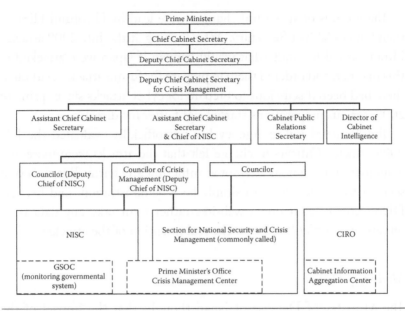

Figure 3.4 Crisis management structure for cybersecurity. (From a document obtained during author's interview on July 2, 2010 at National Police Agency.)

The Japanese Government Response to the 2009 Attacks

National Police Agency

The attacks in July 2009 heightened tensions in the National Police Agency. Attacks to the neighboring country made the Japanese government recognize cyber attacks as real and direct threats. The agency started making plans to prepare for future attacks, and the July 2009 attacks became a good example to which to refer. On March 19, 2010, the government set up a new structure to deal with cyber issues (Figure 3.4). Under this structure cyber attack is recognized as a crisis similar to natural disasters, such as earthquake or eruption. Thus, when an attack breaks out, crisis management mechanisms will start working.

In addition, the National Police Agency has a fixed 24-hour monitoring system of Internet traffic in 150 locations around Japan as well as contacts with 600 private sector critical infrastructure operators, which will report suspicious activity to the agency. The operators are advised to make security policy and to set up a nighttime response window.

These kinds of structural changes were lead by Hirofumi Hirano, then Chief Cabinet Secretary. After looking at the July 2009 attacks, Hirano asked his staff what would happen if Japan were attacked in this manner, and ordered them to prepare for future attacks. Although there had been discussions to prepare for cyber attacks since spring of 2008, serious preparations started right after his direction.

The National Police Agency has not officially evaluated the July 2009 attacks. Officers in charge felt that the attacks were more of a demonstration than an attempt at inflicting any harm. But the event seemed to last too long to simply be a demonstration, and because DDoS attacks shut down websites rather than take any data from servers, it is difficult to know the real intention of the attacker.

Ministry of Defense

The Ministry of Defense of Japan thought that the impact of the July 2009 attacks on them were minimal because their systems, including the Self Defense Force (SDF), were independent from the Internet, according to my personal interview with them (2010). In fact, until the release of "Information Security Strategy for Protecting the Nation" in May 2010, the Ministry was thinking of cybersecurity as a computer system level challenge. Now, however, the Ministry started thinking that it should be considered as a national security issue.

Unlike the United States, which deploys troops in several places overseas, the main goal of Japan's Ministry of Defense is to protect its command and control systems inside Japanese territories, as SDF is not expected to deploy overseas due to constitutional limits. The Ministry is preparing enough to threats from outside Japan, but there is still a problem of internal threats as William J. Lynn, Deputy Secretary of Defense in the United States, wrote in his 2010 article in *Foreign Affairs*. Although users of the systems are strictly limited, devices such as USB memory sticks are easy to use and very difficult to stop from being used for malicious activity. Confidential information can be carried out through such devices and virus or malware can be brought into systems (Lynn, 2010).

Unlike the National Police Agency, the Ministry has no monitoring system and can only detect attacks against itself and cannot

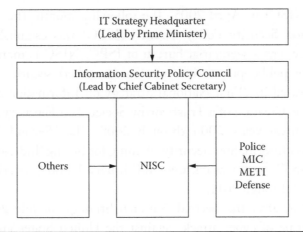

Figure 3.5 Organization for national information security in Japan. (From Cabinet Office)

therefore grasp the whole picture of attacks against the Japanese government. It needs to get information through the NISC. In case of emergency, the National Police Agency and the Ministry of Defense are mandated to cooperate to respond to the situation (Figure 3.5). In order to make it happen, the Ministry temporarily sends seven self-defense officials to NISC to work with them.

The Ministry also does not analyze attacks by itself. Cyber Clean Center (CCC) which is jointly operated by the Ministry of Internal Affairs and Communications and the Ministry of Economy, Trade and Industry will do such analysis. For the Defense Ministry, it does not matter much who is attacking. In terms of defense, the SDF must protect the nation from any enemies but identifying or catching them is out of scope for them.

The Ministry is interested in USCYBERCOM, the U.S. Department of Defense agency responsible for cybersecurity, which the Obama Administration set up in 2009. According to *Japan's Defense and its Budget* (2010), a Japanese Ministry of Defense publication, it is possible that it will set up a similar organization in 2011 under the SDF, tentatively entitled the "cyber space defense unit."

National Information Security Center (NISC)

In February 2000, the Information Security Section was created under the Cabinet Office; it became the National Information Security

Center (NISC) in April 2005. The following month, the National Information Security Policy Council (ISPC) was established, and NISC serves as a secretariat bureau of ISPC. NISC is mandated to coordinate public–private information (or cyber) security policies. ISPC released its "First National Strategy on Information Security: Toward the Creation of a Trustworthy Society" on February 2, 2006, covering fiscal years 2006 through 2008. The "Second National Strategy on Information Security: Aiming for Strong 'Individual' and 'Society' in IT Age" was released on February 3, 2009, covering fiscal years 2009 through 2011.

However, after the Second National Strategy, in July 2009, the massive scale of cyber attacks against the United States and South Korea broke out. In August 2009 the Liberal Democratic Party (LDP), which had been in a ruling position for a long time, lost the national election, and the Democratic Party of Japan (DPJ) came into a coalition government. This was a historic regime change and it affected the ISPC and the NISC in that previous LDP policies were being revised, starting with the release of "the Information Security Strategy to Protect the Nation" on May 11, 2010. This strategy covers FY 2010 to 2013 including the Second National Strategy and mandated that an annual plan to be created. The cyber attacks against the United States and South Korea played a critical role in the revision of Japanese cybersecurity measures, as the first page of the Strategy stated:

> After the Second National Strategy on Information Security was resolved, a large-scale cyber attack took place in the United States and South Korea in July 2009. Also, numerous incidents of large-scale private information leaks occurred one after another.
>
> The large-scale cyber attack in the United States and South Korea particularly alerted Japan—where many aspects of economic activities and social life are increasingly dependent upon Information and Communication Technology (ICT)—to the fact that a threat to information security could be a threat to national security and require effective crisis management.

The basic principle of the Strategy has three points: (1) strengthening of policies and upgrading of countermeasures, (2) establishment of information security policy that can be adjusted in new or changing environments, and (3) transformation from reactive information security measures to proactive ones. It is not fair to say that cyber attacks were neglected or considered less serious in the First National Strategy and the Second National Strategy; however, it is noteworthy that cyber attack concerns hitched to the fore in the May 2010 Strategy.

About a month after the release of the Strategy, Prime Minister Yukio Hatoyama resigned and Naoto Kan, new leader of DPJ, succeeded the administration. Under the new cabinet, the National Information Security Policy Council's meeting was held on July 22, 2010, and it authorized its annual plan called "Information Security 2010." The first item in it is "upgrading counter measures for large-scale cyber attack situations," and 19 policy items were listed in the plan.

Concluding the Japanese Response

The response to the July 2009 attacks differed among the three main Japanese government entities, the National Police Agency, the Ministry of Defense, and the National Information Security Center (NISC). But while the response varied, the outcome remained the same: along with government leaders, they all realized the importance of developing new strategies to meet the rising cyber threat.

As an example of this, Japan, for the first time, joined the "Cyber Storm" exercise in September 2010. Organized for the third time by the U.S. Department of Homeland Security, it is the world's largest simulation in the area and involves cooperation between the government and the private sector. In this effort, Japan was, represented by NISC, National Police Agency, Ministry of Economy, Trade and Industry, and the nonprofit JPCERT/CC (Japan Computer Emergency Response Team/Coordination Center), an independent organization dealing with computer security incidents. According to an article in *Asahi Shinbun*, more than 3,000 people in 13 countries participated in the simulation overall (Toh, 2010).

Recent East Asia Developments

East Asia is a region that continues to be a hotspot for cyber activities, including cyber attacks. The numbers of Internet users are growing rapidly in this part of the world mainly due to China, which, along with South Korea greatly influence regional developments. Due to historical disputes, Japan is sometimes a target of cyber attacks from China and South Korea, though this is not the sole reason of course. To provide a broad picture of cybersecurity in East Asia, this chapter concludes with a brief overview of the recent situation in these two countries.

China

Chinese presence in cyberspace is becoming greater and greater. The world's Internet population is estimated at around two billion and China constitutes about one-fourth of that, despite the fact that the Chinese penetration ratio is still low. If it reaches the same ratio as developed countries, its presence will be overwhelming.

China is notorious for attacking other countries online. In 2007, *The Times*, a British paper, reported that China is trying to achieve "electronic dominance" over each of its global rivals by 2050, particularly the United States, Britain, Russia, and South Korea (Reid, 2010). According to the same article, Chinese cyber terrorists were suspected of penetrating hundreds of U.S. State Department computers all over the world and also disrupting the U.S. Naval War College's network. Overall, the article noted that the Pentagon had logged more than 79,000 attempted intrusions in 2005. Further, according to MSNBC (2009), an American news channel, China's elite hacker community may have ties to the government, though there is little hard evidence per se (Baldor, 2009).

In January 2010, Google, the Internet search engine giant, began a dispute with China over censorship it claimed it could not follow but that was mandated by the government. Google also claimed their systems, in particular the free e-mail service Gmail, were being attacked by China. With the support of the U.S. government, Google tried to change the Chinese government's policy in vain and instead withdrew from the market. In the end, Google received a service license to reroute their search engine to its Hong Kong site.

These kinds of news regarding China are flooding media coverage yet the government is denying claims that the Chinese Communist Party or its People's Liberation Army is involved in any cyber attacks.

Instead, it says, China is being continuously attacked by foreign powers. *Norton Online Living Report* 2009 reported that 53% of Chinese Internet users say they had experienced cyber intrusion into their computers, the highest among surveyed countries (Symantec, 2009).

It is quite strange that there are a lot of cyber crimes and attacks in China because the government is maintaining strong control over the Internet. Both Internet connection service providers and content service providers must be registered and providers watch their customers in detail. Even when a Chinese citizen uses an Internet café, he or she must register an ID. The government is also regulating international traffic because all of international gateways are under control of the government. If the government is really serious, it can stop "illegal" or suspicious traffic. This point makes people outside China believe in the government's involvement in cyber attacks against foreign countries, though there is still no hard evidence of this. According to a 2009 report in *The Wall Street Journal* (Gorman, 2009), a spokesman for the Chinese Embassy in Washington, Wang Baodong, said that the Chinese government "resolutely oppose[s] any crime, including hacking, that destroys the Internet or computer network" and has laws barring the practice.

South Korea

South Korea experienced a serious economic downturn in the Asian economic/financial crisis in 1998, something that would come to determine its future as a digital nation. In order to recover, President Kim Tae-jung proposed "Cyber Korea 21" in 1999 and introduced ambitious technologies and policies to make the country adapt to the new political and economic modes of the digital age. Key technological developments stemming from the initiative include semiconductor chips, ADSL (Asymmetric Digital Subscriber Line) for Internet broadband access, and CDMA (Code Division Multiple Access) for mobile phones. Samsung and other South Korean digital vendors went global, leaving their Japanese competitors stuck to their domestic market.

There are many reasons why South Korea advanced in broadband adoption specifically. One of them is that it is costly to lay broadband access technologies in vast areas, but the population in South Korea is concentrated in cities. More than one-fifth of the total population is living in Seoul and most of them are living in apartment complexes. There was also a culture of people competing to gain faster speeds in order to get jobs, educate their children, buy cheap goods online, play games, among other things.

The success in broadband penetration made South Korea proud of its new cyber culture and today it is an important part of life. However, at the same time, new cyber threats emerged, in particular ID theft. A big boom of the online economy in South Korea was made possible by its resident registration number, which is assigned to every citizen in South Korea in order to burn out North Korean agents hidden in South Korean society. All Internet service sites requested users to register their own numbers. The number system also helped service providers to understand customers better; however, theft of ID numbers became a serious social problem. Financial fraud, impersonation, privacy invasion, and other crimes and attacks were seen. In addition, computer viruses and spam mails were getting worse. For example, according to *The New York Times*, South Korea's former President Roh Moo-hyun's ID number was used to gain access to 416 sites requiring personal identification, including 280 pornographic sites. According to Hotwired Japan, an online publication, 4,552 fraud cases were reported in the first half year of 2004 alone, the consequence of which saw the government introducing an improved online system to fix the problem in 2006 (Tsuchiya, 2004).

In 2008 President Lee Myung-bak reorganized the Ministry of Information and Communication, and its functions were transferred to Ministry of Public Administration and Security (MOPAS), Ministry of Culture, Sports and Tourism, and Ministry of Knowledge Economy (MKE). And Korea Communications Commission (KCC) is regulating the industry now. However, national security perspective of cybersecurity is administrated by the National Intelligence Service (NIS). Under NIS, National Cyber Security Center (NCSC) is the core of policy making. Outside the government, KISC (Korea Internet Safety Commission) is a CSIRT (Computer Security Incident Response Team) and KISA (Korean Internet and Security Agency) is playing a role to bridge between the government and the private sector.

Because their neighbor, North Korea, is a potential threat, it was easy to expect that they might start a cyber attack. But the severity of the July 2009 attacks was a big shock to South Korea and damaged the country's pride. One Korean journalist wrote, "South Korea was proud to be an Internet advanced nation and its economy is supported by exports of IT-related technologies. The biggest loss in this attack was that its image was hurt" (Cho, 2009).

We still do not know who attacked South Korea, but its government is now more aware of the importance of defending its cyber domain. For example, in February 2010, the South Korean government proposed to set up an organization for international cybersecurity under the United Nations and to locate it in Seoul. It was not agreed, but the government understands well why it must protect its cyber infrastructures.

Conclusion

In order to respond to changing situations in East Asia, widening scope of intelligence activities is an important policy agenda in Japan. Rising possibilities of cyber attacks in recent years added a new role to intelligence agencies. Perhaps because of good intelligence, there has been no successful large-scale cyber attack against Japan.

Either way, the attacks in July 2009 built a momentum to improve Japanese cybersecurity measures. The change of administrations is an important factor, but it is also noteworthy that the Second Information Security Basic Plan was overwritten while it was still active after the attacks.

NISC is not within the Japanese intelligence community, but it must help the community and political leaders to find better approaches. Its role is critical in cybersecurity preparedness. We need to define NISC's role more clearly in national security environments.

Widening the scope of intelligence in society might raise anxieties over privacy and other basic human rights. For example, we might need executive power to wiretap communications to prevent cyber terrorism, which Japanese law does not allow (but wiretapping for law enforcement purposes is allowed). ISPC and NISC are publishing a series of strategies, but we need concrete policy measures to fulfill them. Among other things, the Prime Minister and his cabinet's political will are needed to move forward ISPC, NISC, and other related agencies and private sectors toward better preparation to protect the nation.

References

Author's interview at KCC (Korean Communications Commission) on January 28, 2011.
Author's interview at KISA (Korea Internet and Security Agency) on January 27, 2011.
Author's interview at the Ministry of Defense of Japan on October 4, 2010.
Author's interview at the National Police Agency of Japan on July 2, 2010.
Arquilla, J., and D. Ronfeldt, "Cyberwar is Coming!" *Comparative Strategy*, Vol. 12, No. 2, Spring 1993, pp. 141–165.
Baldor, Lolita C., "Report: China's Cyberwarfare Capabilities Grow," MSNBC. com. http://www.msnbc.msn.com/id/33439397/ns/technology_and_science-security (accessed October 22, 2009).
Cho, C., "Korean Government Was Attacked in Blind Spots," July 15, 2009, http://it.nikkei.co.jp/internet/news/index.aspx?n=MMIT1300001507 2009 (accessed May 2, 2010).
Claburn, T., "Cyber Attack Code Starts Killing Infected PCs," *InformationWeek*, http://www.informationweek.com/news/government/security/showArticle.jhtml?articleID=218401559 (accessed July 10, 2009).
Clarke, R. A., and Robert K. Knake, *Cyber War: The Next Threat to National Security and What to Do about It*, New York: ECCO, 2010.
Fukuda, M., *Terrorism and Intelligence*, Tokyo: Keio University Press, 2010 (Japanese).
Goodin, D., "US Websites Buckle under Sustained DDoS Attacks," *The Register*, http://www.theregister.co.uk/2009/07/08/federal_websites_ddosed/ (accessed July 8, 2009).
Gorman, S., "Electricity Grid in U.S. Penetrated by Spies," *Wall Street Journal*, http://online.wsj.com/article/SB123914805204099085.html (accessed April 8, 2009).
Han, J., "Cyber Attack Hits Korea for Third Day," *Korea Times*, http://www.koreatimes.co.kr/www/news/biz/2009/07/123_48203.html (accessed July 9, 2009).
Hori, E., *Intelligence War Record of a Japanese Imperial Headquarter Staff*, Tokyo: Bungei Shunju, 1996 (Japanese).
"ID Theft Strikes South Korean Leaders," *New York Times*, http://www.nytimes.com/2006/06/28/world/asia/28iht-roh.2070985.html (accessed June 28, 2006).
Information Warfare Monitor, *Tracking GhostNet Investigating a Cyber Espionage Network*, March 29, 2009, http://www.infowar-monitor.net/research/.
Kitaoka, H., *Introduction to Intelligence*, 2nd Edition, Tokyo: Keio University Press, 2009 (Japanese).

Kotani, K., *Intelligence Diplomacy in the U.K.*, Tokyo: PHP, 2004 (Japanese).

Katz, J., *GEEKS: How Two Lost Boys Rode the Internet out of Idaho*, New York: Crown, 2000.

Kumon, S., *The Age of Netizen*, Tokyo: NTT, 1996 (Japanese).

Levy, S., *Hackers: Heroes of the Computer Revolution*, New York: Dell, 1984.

Lynn, W. J., III, "Defending a New Domain: The Pentagon's Cyberstrategy," *Foreign Affairs*, vol. 89, no. 5, September/October 2010, pp. 97–108.

Ministry of Defense, "Japan's Defense and its Budget," Ministry of Defense, 2010, p. 8.

Nakashima, E., B. Krebs, and B. Harden, "U.S., South Korea Targeted in Swarm of Internet Attacks," *Washington Post*, http://www.washington-post.com/wp-dyn/content/article/2009/07/08/AR2009070800066.html (accessed July 9, 2009).

National Information Security Council. "First National Strategy on Information Security: Toward the Creation of a Trustworthy Society," http://www.nisc.go.jp/active/kihon/pdf/bpc01_ts.pdf (accessed February 2, 2006).

National Information Security Council, Information Security Strategy for Protecting the Nation, May 2010, http://www.nisc.go.jp/eng/pdf/New_Strategy_English.pdf.

NISC, Information Security Strategy for Protecting the Nation, May 2010, http://www.nisc.go.jp/eng/pdf/New_Strategy_English.pdf. (Accessed May 2, 2010)

Nye, J. S., "Cyber Power," Harvard Kennedy School Belfer Center for Science and International Affairs, May 2010.

Omori, Y., *Japanese Intelligence Agencies*, Tokyo: Bungei Shunju, 2005 (Japanese).

Reid, T., "China's Cyber Army Is Preparing to March on America, says Pentagon," Times Online, September 8, 2007, http://technology.time-sonline.co.uk/tol/news/tech_and_web/the_web/article2409865.ece (accessed May 9, 2010).

Rheingold, H., *Smart Mobs: The Next Social Revolution*, New York: Basic Books, 2000.

Saka, A., "Counter Cyber Terrorism Measures in the United States," *Keisatsu-gaku Ronshu*, vol. 57, no. 5, 2004, pp. 1–45 (Japanese).

Sudworth, J., "New 'Cyber Attacks' Hit S Korea," *BBC News*, http://news.bbc.co.uk/2/hi/asia-pacific/8142282.stm (accessed July 9, 2009).

Sugita, I., *War Leadership without Intelligence*, Tokyo: Hara Shobo, 1987 (Japanese).

Symantec, Norton Onlne Living Report 2009: *Survey Data* (Japanese version, April 7, 2009, http://www.symantec.com/ja/jp/about/news/resources/press_kits/ (accessed October 30, 2011)

Toh, E., "13 Countries Cooperate to Combat against Cyber Attacks," *Asahi Shinbun*, October 4, 2010.

Tsuchiya, M., "Flying Personal Information (Tobikau Kojin Joho)," *HotWired* Japan, September 14, 2004.

Tsuchiya, M., *National Security by Intelligence*, Tokyo: Keio University Press, 2007 (Japanese).

Tsukamoto, M., *Record of a Intelligence Officer*, Tokyo: Chuko Bunko, 1988 (Japanese).

U.S. Department of Defense, Quadrennial Defense Review, http://www. defense.gov/qdr/ (accessed February 2010).

U.S. Government Accountability Office, *Critical Infrastructure Protection: Sector-Specific Plans' Coverage of Key Cyber Security Elements Varies,* http:// www.gao.gov/new.items/d08113.pdf (accessed October 2007).

U.S. Government Accountability Office (GAO), *Cyberspace: United States Faces Challenges in Addressing Global Cybersecurity and Governance*, GAO-10-606, Washington, DC, July 2010.

Yamada, Y., A. Yamagishi, and B. T. Katsumi, "A Comparative Study of the Information Security Policies of Japan and the United States," *Journal of National Security Law and Policy*, vol. 4, no. 1, 2010, pp. 217–232.

White House, *The National Strategy to Secure Cyberspace*, Washington, DC, February 2003.

White House, *National Security Presidential Directive 54/Homeland Security Presidential Directive 23*, Washington, DC, January 8, 2008.

White House, *Cyberspace Policy Review: Assuring a Trusted and Resilient Information and Communications Infrastructure,* http://www.white-house.gov/assets/documents/Cyberspace_Policy_Review_final.pdf (accessed May 2009).

4

TOWARD A GLOBAL APPROACH TO CYBERSECURITY

MARCO OBISO AND GARY FOWLIE

Contents

Introduction

Information and Communication Technologies (ICTs) transform modern lifestyles through global real-time access to an almost unlimited amount of information. At the same time, these innovative tools also create opportunities for exploitation and abuse.

Cyber threats have become one of the biggest global issues of our time. The proliferation of constant connections creates a global network of open conduits. While these bring untold benefits in terms of

77

access to information, they also lead to an alarming rise in the number and scale of cyber threats, cyber criminals, and cyber terrorists. For example, according to the International Multistakeholder Partnership Against Cyber Threats (IMPACT), more than 12 million ICT systems worldwide are affected at any given time by malware.

Cybersecurity is one of the most critical concerns of the information age. It forms the cornerstone of a connected world. It is a global issue that demands a truly global approach. Because of light-speed communications and ubiquitous networks, cyber criminals and cyber terrorists do not need to be anywhere near the scene of the crime. International cooperation and response is the only answer. And there is little time to waste.

The power of the virtual world increases every day. By the time you have read this chapter, that power will have grown even further. A young student in a developing country will have accessed the library of a prestigious university in the West; a senior citizen who has never traveled abroad will have virtually visited a nation on the other side of the world; a small-business owner will have attended an international conference without leaving her office. With each of these achievements, the virtual world brings about another real-world victory for education, dialogue, and better understanding between peoples.

Unfortunately, there is nothing virtual about the hazards that accompany modern communications technologies. The Internet may open our minds to new possibilities, but it also exposes us to the pitfalls and dangers of cyber threats.

Like many of the challenges facing our planet today, these dangers know no borders. Just as viruses and bacteria can spread from region to region, computer viruses spread from computer to computer, regardless of physical location.

The United Nations, through the International Telecommunication Union (ITU), its specialized agency for information and communication technologies, has a vital responsibility to ensure the safety of all those who venture online, especially as online services become an integral part of peoples' lives. Technology is improving direct and democratic access to health, financial and telecommunications services, among many others. None of us would stand idly by during attacks or theft at the hospital or bank or phone company; we must provide the same security to the increasing number of people who work with these institutions online. Leaders strive to ensure the safety of their citizens on their countries' highways and roads; the attention to safety on the information superhighway, where people young and old travel for hours each day, should be no different.

The ITU has dealt with security issues since its inception in 1865: from the invention of the telegraph, through the era of radio and television to the deployment of satellite and Internet-based technologies. The goal remains to forge partnerships and support projects whose goal is to create a safe and secure environment. Access to communications is useless if peace and safety cannot be guaranteed.

ITU recognizes that information and technology security are critical priorities for the international community. Cyber threats are global; therefore, the solutions must be global, too. It is vital that all countries arrive at a common understanding regarding cybersecurity, namely providing protection against unauthorized access, manipulation, and destruction of critical resources. However, any successful global strategy must first start by identifying existing national and regional initiatives already in place in order to find common ground that will increase the likelihood that an international strategy can effectively engage all the relevant players and establish clear priorities for action.

The need for a global framework to secure cyberspace is also being fueled by the growing realization that ICTs play a decisive role in the development process. More than five billion people will be connected in cyberspace by 2015. It is both desirable and necessary to provide them with a safe and secure cyber environment conducive to bringing about economic growth.

Given the global nature of the cyber threat, this is not a problem any one nation can solve alone. A global framework is needed, giving us international principles to match hackers' international range, and allowing rapid coordination between countries at the regional and global levels. In order to accomplish this goal, the ITU created The Global Cybersecurity Agenda, the elements of which will be outlined in this chapter.

Cyberspace—No Longer Just a Virtual World

The Internet has become an integral part of modern societies, propelling the end user to the forefront of communication. All sorts of information and opinion are available in various languages on almost any topic.

The difficulty with the ever-growing multitude of resources is effectively sorting through the vast amount of information available on the Internet. How much of that information is factual, or even genuine? The real concern is not just with the dissemination of inaccurate or misleading information, but above all with malicious content. Fraud, theft, and forgery exist online just as they do offline. If users are to benefit from the full advantages of the Internet, then confidence in its infrastructure is of utmost importance.

Cyber threats such as malicious software (malware) are becoming extremely sophisticated. This is especially true with the increased presence of organized criminal groups online. The Internet has ceased to be the domain of the technically competent. User-friendly software and interfaces have enabled all types of users, including children and novices, to interact online. Consequently, cyberspace contains a gold mine of valuable information and potential victims. The complicated infrastructure of the Internet also makes it difficult to track down criminals.

But criminals are not the only threat on the Internet. The vulnerabilities of ICTs also extend to cyber warfare, espionage, and terrorism, all of which can pose serious threats to critical information infrastructure.

Even though national measures are being taken, cyber threats remain an international problem. Loopholes in legal frameworks are being exploited by perpetrators, and harmonization between existing laws is far from satisfactory. For example, different laws regarding spam or phishing, or even those related to the identity of online users, allow cyber criminals to originate criminal acts from localities where they cannot be detected or prosecuted. Coupled with the absence of international organizational structures and national level outfits that can coordinate internationally (such as computer incident response teams, CIRTs), there is a genuine problem in responding to cyber threats.

This is without considering the constant evolution and sophistication of such threats as well as the vulnerabilities in software, and more recently hardware, applications. With the phenomenal growth in mobile ICTs and new trends such as cloud computing and virtualization, it is increasingly likely that cyber threats will spread to new levels. For example, in 2007, the ITU noted that the rise of spam had become a broader cybersecurity threat, acting as a platform for other scams such as phishing and hacking.

A Unique Global Forum, a Unique History

In 2000, global leaders gathered at the United Nations in New York and pledged themselves and their countries to achieving eight Millennium Development Goals (MDGs), ranging from halving extreme poverty to halting the spread of HIV/AIDS and providing universal primary education, all by the target date of 2015. The MDG goals have galvanized unprecedented efforts to meet the needs of the world's poorest. For example, Millennium Development Goal number 8 calls for a global partnership that challenges world leaders to cooperate with the private sector to make available the benefits of information and communications technology to those with the least access to them.

Given the interdependencies that are created by ICTs, a commitment by all UN member states is needed to ensure that MDG Goal 8 is achieved and that the Global Cybersecurity Agenda is adopted as an appropriate framework for cooperation. The development potential of eHealth, eEducation, eCommerce, and eGovernment programs and services will only be successful if the ICT infrastructures that they rely upon for delivery are secure.

Founded on the principle of international cooperation between governments and the private sector, the ITU represents the unique global forum for action to promote cybersecurity and to tackle cybercrime. In order to ensure that the benefits of the information society are extended to all of the world's citizens, ITU was asked to organize, on behalf of the United Nations, a two-part World Summit on the Information Society (WSIS) in Geneva (2003) and Tunis (2005). It was during the WSIS process that leaders and governments entrusted the ITU to take the lead in coordinating international efforts in the field of cybersecurity.

From broadband Internet to the latest-generation wireless technologies, from aeronautical and maritime navigation to radio astronomy and satellite-based meteorology, from convergence in fixed-mobile phone, Internet access, data, voice, and TV broadcasting to next-generation networks, ITU is committed to connecting the world.

However, building confidence in a global communication system that has been built by multistakeholder input will require a global multistakeholder solution.

Toward the Global Cybersecurity Agenda

The objective is clear: we need to ensure a global information society in which trust and security in the use of ICTs is the norm for the benefit of mankind. For this reason, on May 17, 2007, the ITU Secretary General launched the Global Cybersecurity Agenda (GCA) to provide a framework within which an international response to the growing challenges to cybersecurity can be coordinated and addressed. The GCA is an international cooperation framework and strives to engage all stakeholders, including governments, the private sector, civil society, and international organizations, in a concerted effort to build confidence and security in the information society. The GCA is built upon five pillars with seven strategic goals.

The five pillars are

1. Legal measures
2. Technical and procedural measures
3. Organizational structures
4. Capacity building
5. International cooperation

The legal, technical, and procedural measures and the organizational structures need to be undertaken at the national and regional levels but also harmonized at the international level as follows:

- National laws need to be put in place where they do not yet exist, and existing laws as well as regional and international agreements need to be based upon a shared understanding of what constitutes cybercrimes and cyber attacks, and how to confront them.
- Technical solutions need to be identified and developed, taking into account the principles of globally accepted standards, aimed at providing hardware and software security baselines that can be adopted by vendors, manufacturers, and end users.

- Appropriate organizational structures, such as coordination and response centers with national responsibility (e.g., Computer Incident Response Teams), need to be established in order to promptly respond to cyber attacks and coordinate with their counterparts at the international level.

The last two pillars cross-cut all areas and aim at elaborating strategies to ensure that the required capacity is available to allow IT security professionals to properly react in case of cyber attacks as well as to build relations and partnerships at the international level.

In order to carry out this work, ITU is collaborating with both UN member states and private sector partners to identify current challenges, consider existing and emerging threats, and propose global strategies to meet the following seven strategic goals:

1. Elaboration of strategies for the development of a model cybercrime legislation that is globally applicable and interoperable with existing national and regional legislative measures

2. Elaboration of global strategies for the creation of appropriate national and regional organizational structures and policies on cybercrime

3. Development of a strategy for the establishment of globally accepted minimum security criteria and accreditation schemes for hardware and software applications and systems

4. Development of strategies for the creation of a global framework for watch, warning, and incident response to ensure cross-border coordination between new and existing initiatives

5. Development of global strategies for the creation and endorsement of a generic and universal digital identity system and the necessary organizational structures to ensure the recognition of digital credentials across geographical boundaries

6. Development of a global strategy to facilitate human and institutional capacity building to enhance knowledge and know-how across sectors

7. Proposals on a framework for a global multistakeholder strategy for international cooperation, dialogue, and coordination in all the above-mentioned areas

In order to achieve these seven goals, the GCA has been structured in pillars to facilitate implementation and ensure an integrated and harmonized approach.

The Pillars of the Global Cybersecurity Agenda (GCA)

This section provides details on the pillars composing the GCA and the work currently undertaken by ITU in coordination and collaboration with its partners.

Legal Measures

Cyber criminals are an ever-present menace on the Internet while organized crime is on the rise. This is due to the fact that loopholes in national and regional legislation remain, making it difficult to effectively track them down. The main problem is the lack of international harmonization regarding cybercrime legislation. Investigation and prosecution are difficult if the categorization of crimes differs from country to country. The Internet is an international communication tool, and consequently, any solution to secure it must be sought at the global level.

Cybercrime Legislation Resources   The ITU assists member states in understanding the legal aspects of cybersecurity in order to move toward harmonizing legal frameworks. Through these cybercrime legislation resources, ITU addresses the first of the seven strategic goals of the GCA, which calls for the elaboration of strategies for the development of cybercrime legislation that is globally applicable and interoperable with existing national and regional legislative measures. This activity also addresses the ITU approach for organizing national cybersecurity efforts, highlighting that establishing the appropriate legal infrastructures is an integral component of a national cybersecurity strategy.

The adoption by all countries of appropriate legislation against the misuse of ICTs for criminal or other purposes, including activities intended to affect the integrity of national critical information infrastructures, is central to achieving global cybersecurity. Because threats can originate anywhere around the globe, the challenges are inherently international in scope and require international cooperation, investigative assistance, and common substantive and procedural provisions. Thus, it is important that countries harmonize their legal frameworks to combat cybercrime and facilitate international cooperation. The ITU (2009) cybercrime legislation resources currently consist of "Understanding Cybercrime: A Guide for Developing Countries," a publication, and the "ITU (2010) Toolkit for Cybercrime Legislation," described below.

"Understanding Cybercrime: A Guide for Developing Countries" This publication aims to help developing countries better understand the national and international implications of growing cyber threats; assess the requirements of existing national, regional, and international instruments; and assist countries in establishing a sound legal foundation.

The guide also provides a broad selection of resources for a more in-depth study of the different topics, such as an overview of the phenomena of cybercrime, which includes descriptions of how crimes are committed and explanations of the most widespread cybercrime offenses such as hacking, identity theft, and denial-of-service attacks. It also covers the challenges as they relate to the investigation and prosecution of cybercrime and a summary of activities undertaken by international and regional organizations in the fight against cybercrime. It concludes with an analysis of different legal approaches with regard to substantive criminal law, procedural law, international cooperation, and the responsibility of Internet Service Providers, providing examples of international approaches as well as good-practice examples from national solutions.

"Toolkit for Cybercrime Legislation" (2010) The toolkit aims to provide countries with sample legislative language and reference material that can assist in the establishment of harmonized cybercrime laws and procedural rules. Developed by a multidisciplinary international group of experts, the toolkit is a practical instrument that countries can use for the elaboration of a cybersecurity legal framework and related laws.

The sample language provided in the toolkit, while not intended as a model law, was developed after a comprehensive analysis of the most relevant regional and international legal frameworks currently in place. The toolkit language is consistent with these laws and is intended to serve as a guide for countries desiring to develop, draft, or modify their own cybercrime laws. The toolkit intends to advance the global harmonization of cybercrime laws by serving as a central resource to help legislators, attorneys, government officials, policy experts, and industry representatives around the globe move their countries toward a consistent legal framework that protects against the misuse of ICTs.

Technical and Procedural Measures

ICTs are a vital tool in information societies. However, they continue to be exploited by malevolent users, and this phenomenon is becoming intrinsically linked to organized crime on the Internet. Vulnerabilities in software applications are purposely sought out in order to create malware that enable unauthorized access and modification, thus compromising integrity, authenticity, and confidentiality of ICT networks and systems. With the increasing sophistication of malware, these threats cannot be overestimated as they could have dire consequences if critical information infrastructures are affected.

International Telecommunications Union (ITU) Standardization Work   ITU's Standardization Sector (ITU-T) brings together the private sector and governments to work and promote the harmonization of security policy and standards on an international scale, which are essential in ensuring cybersecurity.

Not only will harmonization of standards increase the level of security, it will also reduce the costs of building secure systems.

There are now literally hundreds of ITU standards (ITU-T Recommendations) on security, or which have cybersecurity implications. In particular,

- The X.500 series of Recommendations on directory services and authentication, including the well-known Recommendation ITU-T X.509. X.509 is a cornerstone for designing applications related to public key infrastructure (PKI) and is widely used in a wide range of applications from securing the connection between a browser and a server on the web to providing digital signatures that enable e-commerce transactions to be conducted with the same confidence as in a traditional system. Without wide acceptance of the standard, the rise of e-business would have been impossible.

- The X.800 series on Security Architecture includes Recommendation ITU-T X.805, which gives telecom network operators and enterprises the ability to provide an end-to-end architecture description from a security perspective. Key players from telecom network operators, manufacturers, and governments have defined the specifications that will alter the way that companies look at their networks. The Recommendation will allow operators to pinpoint all vulnerable points in a network and mitigate them.

- The Recommendation ITU-T X.1205 "Overview of Cybersecurity" provides a definition of cybersecurity and taxonomy of security threats. It discusses the nature of the cybersecurity environment and risks, possible network protection strategies, secure communications techniques, and network survivability (even under attack).

Ongoing ITU work on security includes architecture and frameworks; cybersecurity; vulnerabilities, threats, and risk management; incident handling and traceback; countering spam; telebiometrics; information security management; identity management; security for next-generation networks (NGN), IPTV, home networks, ubiquitous sensor networks, mobiles; and secure application services. ITU Study Groups are also starting to look at security concerns in emerging areas such as smart grids and cloud computing.

One particularly urgent area of work is in combating identity theft, which was identified in an ITU survey as the biggest fear preventing users from placing more trust in online networks. In 2009, a first set of ITU-T Recommendations dealing with identity management was approved for application in NGN, for globalization of existing solutions, and ensuring interoperability, and for user control of digital identity.

Study Group 17 is the lead study group on telecommunications security and identity management at the ITU. It is responsible for studies related to security, including cybersecurity, countering spam by technical means, and identity management and handles security guidance and the coordination of security-related work across all ITU-T study groups. Study Group 17 updates the manual on "Security in Telecommunications and Information Technology" and also electronically publishes a Security Compendium on its website containing a catalogue of approved ITU-T Recommendations related to security and presenting an extract of security definitions from ITU-T and other sources.

In addition, ITU-T's Cybersecurity Information Exchange (CYBEX) initiative will be importing more than 20 best-of-breed standards for platforms developed over the past several years by government agencies and industry to enhance cybersecurity. These platforms capture and exchange information about the security "state" of systems and devices, about vulnerabilities, about incidents such as cyber attacks, and related knowledge "heuristics." The CYBEX approach pursued pulls these platforms together in a coherent way to provide for (1) "locking down" online systems to minimize vulnerabilities, (2) capturing incident information for analysis when network harmful incidents occur, and (3) facilitating evidence for enforcement action if necessary.

As a starting point of CYBEX, Recommendation ITU-T X.1500 provides an overview of the landscape of current and forthcoming Recommendations on "Cybersecurity information exchange techniques." First, practical means for such cybersecurity information exchange techniques are specified in Recommendation ITU-T X.1520 "Common vulnerabilities and exposure (CVE)," which provides a structured means to exchange information security vulnerabilities and exposures that aim to provide common names for publicly known problems in the commercial or open source software used in communications networks, end-user devices, or any of the other types of ICT capable of running software. In that regard, X.1520 allows vulnerability databases and other capabilities to be linked together, and to facilitate the comparison of security tools and services.

Recommendation ITU-T X.1521 "Common vulnerability scoring system (CVSS)" provides an open framework for communicating the characteristics and impacts of information and communication technologies (ICT) vulnerabilities in the same context and allows the users of this Recommendation to speak from a common language of scoring ICT vulnerabilities.

Recommendation X.1209 "Capabilities and their context scenarios for cybersecurity information sharing and exchange" describes the foundational scenarios at a high level and identifies the supporting capabilities for cybersecurity information sharing and exchange. These provided capabilities are important for supporting interoperability between applications for the sharing and exchange of cybersecurity information.

The CYBEX activities are surrounded by Recommendation ITU-T X.1206 that yields "A vendor-neutral framework for automatic notification of security related information and dissemination of updates," and by Recommendation ITU-T X.1207 that captures best practices and "Guidelines for telecommunication service providers for addressing the risk of spyware and potentially unwanted software."

For CYBEX, ITU worked closely with the Forum of Incident Response and Security Teams (FIRST)—a global organization for coordination and cooperation among Computer Emergency Response Teams. Collaboration between other standards bodies and other technical bodies is an essential characteristic of ITU's work.

ICT Security Standards Roadmap Promoting Collaboration between International Standards Bodies The ICT Security Standards Roadmap promotes the development of security standards by highlighting existing standards, current work, and future standards among key standards development organizations. The Roadmap was launched by ITU Study Group 17 and is a joint effort with the European Network and Information Security Agency (ENISA) and the Network and Information Security Steering Group (NISSG). The Roadmap describes the different standards organizations, their structures, and the work they are undertaking in security standards, including International Telecommunication Union (ITU), International Standards Organization (ISO), International Electrotechnical Commission (IEC), International Engineering Task Force (IETF), Oasis Service Oriented Architecture (SOA) (OASIS), Alliance for Telecommunication Industry Solutions (ATIS), European Telecommunication Standards Institute (ETSI), Institute of Electrical and Electronics Engineers (IEEE), 3rd Generation Partership Project

(3GPP), and 3rd Generation Partnership Project 2 (3GPP2). The publication provides a database summarizing approved standards and gives an overview of standards under development by ITU and ISO/IEC. It also includes future areas of work in security standards where gaps have been identified or proposals made for new standards work as well as a repository of security-related best practices contributed by members and stakeholders.

ITU Radiocommunications   Radio spectrum global frequency management is increasingly important for building confidence and security and creating an enabling environment in the use of ICTs. Wireless applications, such as 3G, are becoming an integral part of daily life, and the global use and management of frequencies require a high level of international cooperation.

ITU's Radiocommunication Sector's (ITU-R) mission is to ensure rational, equitable, efficient, and economical use of the radio-frequency spectrum by all radiocommunication services, including those using satellite orbits, and to carry out studies and adopt recommendations on radiocommunication matters. It plays a pivotal role in facilitating complex intergovernmental negotiations needed to develop legally binding agreements between sovereign states in an increasingly "unwired" world.

International radiocommunication provisions are embodied in the ITU Radio Regulations (treaty status, which means they are binding once agreed to) that incorporate the decisions of the World Radiocommunication Conferences (WRCs) and in world and regional plans adopted for different space and terrestrial services. ITU Radio Regulations agreements apply to frequencies ranging from 9 kHz to 400 GHz and include information on how radio frequency is shared around the globe.

ITU-R specializes in developing radio standards, including spectrum identification and harmonization applicable to national, regional, and international broadband network infrastructure including the capacity to countries and their citizens for new ICT-based services through satellite systems. ITU-R ensures interference-free operations of radiocommunication systems and facilitates any new developments and the continuation of satellite services in a safe way.

Safeguarding quality of service against degradation or denial of service is vital for the secure functioning of networks in data transmission and service provision, and many of the Radiocommunication Sector's (ITU-R) latest Recommendations on generic requirements and the protection of radiocommunications against interference are relevant for security.

ITU's work in radiocommunication standardization continues, matching the constant evolution in modern telecommunication networks. For example, ITU established clear security principles for IMT-2000 (3G) networks (Recommendation ITU-R M.1078 and Recommendations M.1223, M.1457, M.1645 are also relevant) and also recommended that the security provided by mobile broadband IMT-2000 (3G) networks should be comparable to contemporary fixed networks.

International Multilateral Partnership Against Cyber Threats (IMPACT) Global Response Center The Global Response Center (GRC), part of the ITU's collaboration with the International Multilateral Partnership Against Cyber Threats (IMPACT), plays a pivotal role in realizing the GCA objective of putting technical measures in place to combat new and evolving cyber threats. The two highlights of the GRC are NEWS (Network Early Warning System) and ESCAPE (Electronically Secure Collaboration Application Platform for Experts).

The GRC is designed to be the foremost cyber threat resource center in the world. Working with leading partners, including academia and governments, the center will provide the global community with NEWS, a real-time aggregated early warning system. It will help countries identify cyber threats early on and provide guidance on what measures to take to mitigate them, including implementation of watch, warning, and incident response capabilities, establishment of computer incident response teams, and distribution of alerts, technical assistance, and security-related training.

The GRC will also provide ITU member states with access to specialized tools and systems, including the recently developed ESCAPE platform. ESCAPE is an electronic tool that enables cyber experts across different countries to pool resources and collaborate with each other remotely, yet within a secure and trusted environment. Access to ESCAPE is given to representatives selected by the member states, as well as to experts designated by ITU IMPACT partners. By pooling resources and expertise from many different countries on short notice, ESCAPE will enable individual nations and the global community to respond immediately to cyber threats, especially during crisis situations.

As of 2011, some 136 countries have joined ITU IMPACT, and access to the GRC is being given, including the necessary capacity building.

Organizational Structures

Watch and warning systems and incident response are essential when it comes to responding to cyber attacks, as is the free flow of information, collaboration, and cooperation within and between national organizational structures.

Collaboration at all levels of government and with the private sector, academia, and regional and international organizations is necessary to raise awareness of potential attacks and take steps toward remediation. Effective incident management also requires consideration of funding, human resources, training, technological capability, government and private sector relationships, and legal requirements. Efforts are being made to bring together organizational structures at the national and regional levels in order to facilitate communication, information exchange, and the recognition of digital credentials across different jurisdictions.

However, more needs to be done at the global level, and international cooperation between these different structures is indispensable.

In this regard, ITU is working with member states to identify the specific cybersecurity needs that they have and, based on this work, with the relevant national, regional, and international organizations to implement these activities.

Yet, there is still a low level of computer emergency preparedness within many countries, particularly developing countries. But the launch of an attack from networks of the less-prepared nations can affect global ICT networks because of a high level of interconnectivity. As such, several ITU initiatives are recommending that member states establish national cybersecurity response centers, such as computer incident response teams (CIRTs). For example, Resolution 58 of the World Telecommunication Standards Assembly in 2008 and Resolution 69 of the World Telecommunication Development Conference in 2009 emphasize that well-functioning CIRTs in developing countries will improve the level of readiness in responding to cyber attacks and contribute to achieving security in national ICT infrastructures, as well as achieve better coordination at the regional and international levels. In addition, they resolve to support the creation of CIRTs by identifying best practices to establish CIRTs, assess where they are needed, and support their implementation.

IMPACT Security Assurance Division In partnership with leading ICT experts, IMPACT aggregates and develops global best practice guidelines, creating an international benchmark that is especially relevant for governments. This division conducts, upon request, independent ICT security audits on government agencies or critical infrastructure companies, thereby ensuring that these organizations subscribe to the highest security standards.

The IMPACT Security Assurance Division functions as an independent, internationally recognized, voluntary certification body for cybersecurity.

Capacity Building

Capacity building is essential in order to develop a sustainable and proactive culture of cybersecurity. One of the key challenges of cybersecurity is effectively educating the end user. This is a matter that concerns all stakeholders from governments and industry to education both at school and at home.

Given the essential role that ICTs play in providing services in sectors as varied as health, education, finance, and commerce, awareness of the opportunities offered by a secure cyber environment and of the threats inherent to cyberspace are vital. Programs aimed at creating a level playing field in raising basic awareness and building capacity at all levels are important, and these also need to be undertaken within the international arena.

A National Cybersecurity Strategy Guide   The ITU has established a practical guide to assist member states wishing to design their national approach to cybersecurity and critical information infrastructure protection (CIIP).

Cybersecurity and CIIP are the shared responsibilities of government, business, other organizations, and individual users who develop, own, provide, manage, service, and use information systems and networks ("participants"). Managing inherent security risks requires the active cooperation of all participants, addressing the security concerns relevant to their roles. The collective goal is to prevent, prepare for, respond to, and recover from any incidents rapidly, while minimizing damage.

In any interconnected system, roles and responsibilities often overlap. Only when all participants share a common understanding of the security objectives, how to achieve them, and of their individual roles in the effort, can this collective goal of a safe and secure communications be achieved.

Governments are in a position to lead national efforts to enhance cybersecurity and improve CIIP. Many countries have already implemented national governmental efforts to protect critical (information) infrastructure. A common vision with well-delineated roles and responsibilities is essential in order to create a strategy for managing risks inherent in ICT use.

Once a nation has gained valuable domestic experience of addressing cybersecurity and CIIP issues, it can make more valuable contributions to global cooperative security efforts.

In this regard, the ITU National Cybersecurity Guide aims to assist ITU member states in developing their national strategy by examining their existing capacities for addressing challenges to cybersecurity and CIIP, identifying their requirements and outlining a national response plan. It is directed at leaders in the policy and management levels of government, providing them with guidance on how to assess their existing national policies, procedures, norms, institutions, and relationships in light of national needs to enhance cybersecurity and address critical information infrastructure protection. It also guides them on how to develop cybersecurity strategies after matching ends (objectives), means (resources and capabilities), and ways (how to use the means to achieve the ends), in line with the overall objectives and goals of the GCA.

ITU, through its Telecommunication Development Sector, provides member states with the assistance needed to undertake these efforts, as well as providing support for countries that are in the process of developing and reassessing their national cybersecurity strategies.

A Botnet Mitigation Toolkit   ITU is working with experts on developing a practical Botnet Mitigation Toolkit to assist developing countries in particular to deal with the growing problem of botnets.

A botnet is a collection of software agents, or robots, that run autonomously and automatically. The term is most commonly associated with malicious software, but it can also refer to a network of computers using distributed computing software. While botnets are often named after their malicious software name, there are typically multiple botnets in operation using the same malicious software families.

The Botnet Mitigation Toolkit is a multistakeholder, multipronged approach to track botnets and mitigate their impact, with a particular emphasis on the problems specific to emerging Internet economies. It will provide information and guidelines to member states on how to protect against and deal with botnets, and will also advise states on how to cooperate with local and regional stakeholders, including business and private industry, law enforcement agencies, Internet service providers (ISPs), and civil society organizations.

International Cooperation

Even though the Internet and ICTs have enabled unparalleled interconnection, they also limit the ability of countries to close their borders to incoming cyber threats and contain those coming from within. Attempts to solve these challenges at national or regional levels are important, but they can be undermined.

Cybersecurity is as global and far-reaching as the Internet. Therefore, solutions need to be harmonized across borders. International cooperation is necessary, not only at the government level, but also with industry, nongovernmental, and international organizations. For this reason, the GCA seeks to harness the power of multistakeholder collaboration in order to arrive at global strategies to enhance cybersecurity.

International Multilateral Partnership Against Cyber Threats (IMPACT)
The International Multilateral Partnership Against Cyber Threats
(IMPACT) is an international public–private initiative dedicated to
enhancing the global community's capacity to prevent, defend, and
respond to cyber threats. In May 2008, the ITU was invited to become
a member of the IMPACT Advisory Board. In November 2008,
IMPACT's headquarters in Cyberjaya, Malaysia, formally became the
GCA's operational, physical, and state-of-the-art home.

IMPACT Center for Policy and International Cooperation   Under the leadership of the ITU, and together with UN agency partners, Interpol,
Council of Europe, and Organization for Economic Cooperation
and Development (OECD), among others, the Center for Policy
and International Cooperation contributes to the formulation of new
policies and the harmonization of national laws around a variety of
issues relating to cyber threats, including cybercrimes.

The Center for Policy and International Cooperation also provides
advisory services to interested member states on policy and regulatory
matters for cybersecurity. With the support of the ITU, the center
fosters international cooperation through specific programs such as
coordinated cyber-drill exercises between countries.

IMPACT Training and Skills Development Center   In collaboration with
leading ICT companies and institutions, IMPACT conducts high-
level briefings for the benefit of representatives of ITU member states.
Many of IMPACT's key partners have made available their respective
chief technical officers, chief research officers, and other experts in a
unique high-level IMPACT program to keep governments abreast of
present and future cyber threats.

The ITU contributes its experience to the center in capacity-building
and developing frameworks for policy response to this program. Such
high-level, cross-industry briefings give countries invaluable exposure
and private sector insight about the latest trends, potential threats, and
emerging technologies.

IMPACT Research Division   The focus of the Research Division is to
direct academic attention, including from universities and research
institutes, to areas of concern that may not currently be adequately

addressed. This includes research into new areas as well as specialized niche areas, including research into vulnerabilities of nonmainstream systems, such as the legacy Supervisory Control and Data Aquisition (SCADA) systems still used by some countries.

With a small user base, niche technologies may not be commercially viable for industry-oriented solutions, making governments or organizations using such technologies vulnerable to threats.

IMPACT is committed to making facilities available and encouraging joint research efforts to address specific areas of concern. In collaboration with the ITU, IMPACT is making its research network available for the benefit of the global community. Besides the academic network, IMPACT global headquarters provides ITU member states with access to specialized ICT laboratories, specialized equipment, resource center, and other facilities.

A Cybersecurity Gateway   The Cybersecurity Gateway is an information resource on national, regional, and international cybersecurity-related initiatives worldwide.

In today's interconnected world, threats can originate anywhere, and thus our collective cybersecurity depends on the security practices of every connected country, entity, business, and citizen. Through the Cybersecurity Gateway, ITU aims to enable information access, dissemination, and online collaboration among stakeholders working in cybersecurity- and cybercrime-related areas. It serves as a platform to make stakeholders more aware of the various actors and groups working on the different areas of cybersecurity at the national, regional, and international levels.

The ITU invites all interested parties to explore the vast resources and links available through the Cybersecurity Gateway (http://www.itu.int/cybersecurity) and join in partnership with the ITU and others to build confidence and security in the use of ICTs.

Child Online Protection   Under the GCA umbrella, the ITU launched the Child Online Protection (COP) as an international collaborative network for action to promote the online protection of children and young people by providing guidance on safe online behavior in conjunction with other UN agencies and partners. The key objectives of the initiative are to

- Identify key risks and vulnerabilities to children and young people in cyberspace.
- Create awareness of risks and issues through multiple channels.
- Develop practical tools to help governments, organizations, and educators minimize risk.
- Share knowledge and experience while facilitating international strategic partnerships to define and implement concrete initiatives.

The COP initiative draws together an effective package of policies and practices, education and training, infrastructure and technology, and awareness and communication. It operates on a multistakeholder basis with the belief that every organization—whether online or mobile, educator or legislator, technical expert or industry body—has something to contribute.

Cybersecurity—The United Nations Acting as One   The ITU, as requested by the international community through the UN World Summit on the Information Society, has taken as a core principle of its mandate the need to build confidence and security in the use of ICTs. Information and communication technology may have changed since the advent of the telegraph, but the mission of ITU to "Connect the World" in a safe and secure manner has not.

ICTs have become an essential part of human development, 145 years after the ITU was established to deal with the challenges and opportunities of what was the very beginning of the information age. Today, management and provision of water supplies and power networks depend upon ICT networks. Food distribution chains, transportation. and navigation systems are built around them. Industrial processes and supply chains operate because of them while they help education, healthcare, government, and emergency services become more efficient.

The essence of the challenge of cybersecurity is that the global ICT networks that have grown around these vital aspects of our daily lives were never designed to be especially secure. The cyber environment of today is significantly different from that which existed when the ITU first became a specialized agency of the United Nations 60 years ago. It is an environment that challenges many of our traditional approaches to security and requires unique solutions. However, one thing is certain, cybersecurity is a global issue that can only be solved with global solutions.

As the leading UN agency for ICTs, the ITU plays a pivotal role in facilitating this global cooperation, and together with governments, the private sector, civil society, and international organizations, can expedite the process of achieving global cybersecurity, through

- Facilitating the harmonization of legal frameworks at national, regional, and international levels
- Providing a platform to discuss and agree on the technical measures to be implemented to mitigate the risks posed by misuse of ICTs
- Helping member states in establishing those organizational structures needed to responding proactively to cyberthreats, triggering coordination and cooperation with all stakeholders at national and international levels
- Promoting the importance of building capacity and international cooperation as key elements for countries to follow-up in order to obtain the necessary expertise to start elaborating and implementing national strategies as well as establishing mechanisms of cooperation at regional and international levels

In May 2011, the first step in this direction was taken as the ITU and the United Nations Office on Drugs and Crime signed a memorandum of understanding (MoU) to collaborate globally in assisting Member States to mitigate the risks posed by cybercrime with the objective of ensuring secure use of ICTs. It is the first time that two organizations within the UN system have formally agreed to cooperate at the global level in regards to cybersecurity.

The MoU enables the two bodies to work together on technical assistance to be provided to Member States on cybercrime and cybersecurity, making available the necessary expertise and resources to facilitate the establishment of legal measures and legislative frameworks at a national level, within the principle of international cooperation, and to the benefit of all countries in the world.

Establishing global cybersecurity may be a complex, multifaceted, and challenging task, but if we act as one, the benefits gained from our information society may provide humanity with the best chance it has ever had for sustainable peace, security, and development.

Acronyms

ATIS: Automatic Terminal Information Service
CIRT: Computer incident response team
CIIP: Critical information infrastructure protection
COP: Child Online Protection
CYBEX: Cybersecurity Information Exchange
DDoS: Distributed denial of service
ENISA: European Network and Information Agency
ETSI: European Telecommunications Standards Institute
GCA: Global Cybersecurity Agenda
ICTs: Information and communication technologies
IEC: International Electrotechnical Commission
IEEE: Institute of Electrical and Electronics Engineers
IETF: Internet Engineering Task Force
IMPACT: International Multilateral Partnership Against Cyber Threats
IMT-2000: International Mobile Telecommunications–2000
IP: Internet Protocol
ISO: International Organization for Standards
ITU: International Telecommunication Union
NGN: Next-generation network
NISSG: Network and Information Security Steering Group
OAIS: Open Archival Information System
OECD: Organization for Economic Cooperation and Development
PKI: Public key infrastructure
QoS: Quality of service
UN: United Nations
WSIS: World Summit on the Information Society
WTSA: World Telecommunication Standardization Assembly

International Telecommunications Union (ITU) Resolutions, Decisions, Programs, and Recommendations on Cybersecurity

Resolution 71 of the ITU Plenipotentiary Conference (Antalya, 2006)

This Resolution outlines the Strategic Plan for the Union for 2008–2011, including its mission and nature, strategic orientations and goals and detailed objectives for the Sectors. Under Goal 4, ITU should specifically engage in "developing tools, based on contributions from the membership, to promote end-user confidence, and to safeguard the efficiency, security, integrity and interoperability of networks," with information and communication network efficiency and security defined as including, inter alia, spam, cybercrime, viruses, worms, and denial-of-service attacks. Under Objective 3, ITU's General Secretariat has been tasked to facilitate the internal coordination of activities among the three Sectors where work programs are overlapping or are related, so as to assist the membership in ensuring that it benefits from the full complement of expertise available within the Union.

Resolution 130 of the ITU Plenipotentiary Conference (Revised, Guadalajara, 2010)

"Strengthening the role of ITU in building confidence and security in the use of information and communication technologies"

Resolution 174 of the ITU Plenipotentiary Conference (Guadalajara, 2010)

"ITU's role with regard to international public policy issues relating to the risk of illicit use of information and communication technologies"

Resolution 181 the ITU Plenipotentiary Conference (Guadalajara, 2010)

"Definitions and terminology relating to building confidence and security in the use of information and communication technologies"

Resolution 45 of the ITU World Telecommunication Development Conference (Revised, Hyderabad, 2010)

"Mechanisms for enhancing cooperation on Cybersecurity including countering and combating spam"

Resolution 69 of the ITU World Telecommunication Development Conference (Revised, Hyderabad, 2010)

"Creation of national computer incident response teams, particularly for developing countries, and cooperation between them"

Doha Action Plan Programme 2 of the ITU World Telecommunication Development Conference (Hydarabad, 2010)

"Cybersecurity, ICT applications and IP-based network-related issues"

Resolution 2 of the ITU World Telecommunication Development Conference (Revised, Hydarabad, 2010)

Annex 2 of Resolution 2—Question 22/1 "Securing information and communication networks: best practices for developing a culture of cybersecurity"

Resolution 50 of the ITU World Telecommunication Standardization Assembly (Johannesburg, 2008)

"Cybersecurity"

Resolution 52 of the ITU World Telecommunication Standardization Assembly (Johannesburg, 2008)

"Countering and combating spam"

Resolution 58 of the ITU World Telecommunication Standardization Assembly (Johannesburg, 2008)

"Encourage the creation of national Computer Incident Response Teams, particularly for developing countries"

ITU-T E.408

"Telecommunication networks security requirements"

ITU-T E.409

"Incident organization and security incident handling: Guidelines for telecommunication organizations"

ITU-T H.235.x Series Recommendations

H.323 security: Framework for security in H series (H.323 and other H.245-based) multimedia systems (a series of 10 Recommendations)

ITU-T J.170

"IPCablecom security specification"

ITU-T X.509

"Public-key and attribute certificate frameworks (global standard on identity management)"

ITU-T X.800 Series Recommendations

Global standards on key security aspects including authentication, access control, nonrepudiation, confidentiality, integrity, audits, and security architecture for systems providing end-to-end communications

ITU-T X.805

"Security architecture for systems providing end-to-end communications"

ITU-T X.811

"Information technology—Open Systems Interconnection—Security frameworks for open systems: Authentication framework"

ITU-T X.812

"Information technology—Open Systems Interconnection—Security frameworks for open systems: Access control framework"

ITU-T X.1031

"Security architecture aspects of end users and networks in telecommunications"

ITU-T X.1034

"Framework for extensible authentication protocol (EAP)-based authentication and key management"

ITU-T X.1035

"Password-authenticated key exchange (PAK) protocol"

ITU-T X.1036

"Framework for creation, storage, distribution and enforcement of policies for network security"

ITU-T X.1051

"Information technology—Security techniques—Information security management guidelines for telecommunications organizations based on ISO/IEC 27002"

ITU-T X.1055

"Risk management and risk profile guidelines for telecommunications organizations"

ITU-T X.1056

"Security incident management guidelines for telecommunications organizations"

ITU-T X.1081

"The telebiometric multimodal model—A framework for the specification of security and safety aspects of telebiometrics"

ITU-T X.1082

"Telebiometrics related to human physiology"

ITU-T X.1083

"Information technology—Biometrics—BioAPI interworking protocol"

ITU-T X.1084

"Telebiometrics system mechanism—Part 1: General biometric authentication protocol and system model profiles for telecommunications systems"

ITU-T X.1086

"Telebiometric protection procedure—Part 1: A guideline to technical and managerial countermeasures for biometric data security"

ITU-T X.1088

"Telebiometrics digital key framework (TDK)—A framework for biometric digital key generation and protection"

ITU-T X.1089

"Telebiometrics authentication infrastructure (TAI) "

ITU-T X.1111

"Framework for security technologies for home network"

ITU-T X.1112

"Device certificate profile for the home network"

ITU-T X.1113

"Guideline on user authentication mechanism for home network services"

ITU-T X.1114

"Authorization framework for home network"

ITU-T X.1121

"Framework of security technologies for mobile end-to-end data communications"

ITU-T X.1122

"Guideline for implementing secure mobile systems based on PKI"

ITU-T X.1123

"Differentiated security service for secure mobile end-to-end data communication"

ITU-T X.1124

"Authentication architecture for mobile end-to-end data communication"

ITU-T X.1125

"Correlative Reacting System in mobile data communication"

ITU-T X.1141

"Security Assertion Markup Language (SAML 2.0)"

ITU-T X.1142

"Web services security—eXtensible Access Control Markup Language (XACML 2.0)"

ITU-T X.1143

"Security architecture for message security in mobile web services"

ITU-T X.1151

"Guideline on secure password-based authentication protocol with key exchange"

ITU-T X.1152

"Secure end-to-end data communication techniques using trusted third party services"

ITU-T X.1161

"Framework for secure peer-to-peer communications"

ITU-T X.1162

"Security architecture and operations for peer-to-peer network"

ITU-T X.1171

"Threats and requirements for protection of personally identifiable information in applications using tag-based
identification"

ITU-T X.1191

"Functional requirements and architecture for IPTV security
aspects"

ITU-T X.1205

"Overview of cybersecurity"

ITU-T X.1206

"A vendor-neutral framework for automatic notification of
security related information and dissemination of updates"

ITU-T X.1207

"Guidelines for telecommunication service providers for
addressing the risk of spyware and potentially unwanted
software"

ITU-T X.1231

"Technical strategies for countering spam"

ITU-T X.1240

"Technologies involved in countering email spam"

ITU-T X.1241

"Technical framework for countering email spam"

ITU-T X.1242

"Short message service (SMS) spam filtering system based on
user-specified rules"

ITU-T X.1244

ITU-T "Overall aspects of countering spam in IP-based multimedia applications"

ITU-T X.1303

"Common alerting protocol (CAP 1.1)"

ITU-T X.1500

"Cybersecurity information exchange techniques"

ITU-T X.1520

"Common vulnerabilities and exposure (CVE)"

ITU-T X.1521

"Common vulnerability scoring sytem (CV1S)"

Resolution 45 of the ITU World Telecommunication
Development Conference (Doha, 2006)

"Mechanisms for enhancing cooperation on cybersecurity, including combating spam"

Recommendation ITU-R M.1078

"Security principles for IMT-2000"

Recommendation ITU-R M.1223

"Evaluation of security mechanisms for IMT-2000"

Recommendation ITU-R M.1457

"Security mechanisms incorporated in IMT-2000"

Recommendation ITU-R M.1645

"Framework and overall objectives of the future development of IMT-2000 and systems beyond IMT-2000"

Recommendation ITU-R S.1250

"Network management architecture for digital satellite systems forming part of SDH transport networks in the fixed satellite service"

Recommendation ITU-R S.1711

"Performance enhancements of transmission control protocol over satellite networks"

References

ITU. July 11, 2007. Evolving threats in cybersecurity. http://www.itu.int/osg/spu/newslog/Evolving+Threats+In+Cybersecurity.aspx.

ITU. February 2010. Toolkit for Cybercrime Legislation. http://www.itu.int/ITU-D/cyb/cybersecurity/docs/itu-toolkit-cybercrime-legislation.pdf

ITU. April 2009. Understanding Cybercrime: A Guide for Developing Countries. http://www.itu.int/ITU-D/cyb/cybersecurity/docs/itu-understanding-cybercrime-guide.pdf.

ITU. January 2008. Botnet Mitigation Toolkit: Background Information. http://www.itu.int/ITU-D/cyb/cybersecurity/docs/itu-botnet-mitigation-toolkit-background.pdf.

ITU. September 2010. National Cybersecurity Strategy Guide. http://www.itu.int/ITU-D/cyb/cybersecurity/docs/itu-national-cybersecurity-guide.pdf.

ITU. ITU called to play a key role in WSIS implementation of Action Line C5. http://www.itu.int/osg/csd/cybersecurity/WSIS/index.phtml.

United Nations. September 18, 2000. United Nations Millennium Declaration. http://www.un.org/millennium/declaration/ares552e.pdf.

United Nations Development Programme. Millennium Development Goal 8: A global partnership for development. http://www.undp.org/mdg/goal8.shtml.

5

THE CYBERSECURITY POLICY CHALLENGE

The Tyranny of Geography

ELAINE C. KAMARCK

Contents

Introduction

It is not uncommon to begin a paper on the role of the government by imagining how surprised Presidents George Washington and Thomas Jefferson would be at the concerns of the day. But for cybersecurity one only has to go back to the first Clinton Administration to realize that it is a unique problem unlike anything government has ever faced. A search of major newspapers on LexisNexis, an information provider, finds *one* article that mentions cybersecurity prior to 1996, and that is a story of how credit card companies tried to go online and suffered near instantaneous security breaches. Part of the problem stems from the speed with which the Internet moved from a tool used by a handful of researchers to trade information into something that is at the center of everything that modern people do. When I went to serve in the Clinton Administration in 1993, there was no World Wide Web. The Internet became available in the White House in 1996, but by the time I left government in 1997 I had never browsed the web. Today, hardly a day passes without me using it.

Because the Internet began benignly and grew rapidly, the government has played catch up and seems destined to continue to do so for quite some time. The American governmental father of cybersecurity, Richard A. Clarke, has a clear message in his best-selling book on the topic: America invented the Internet; it is the most wired country in the world, and hence, it is the most vulnerable—in spite of its sophistication. Clarke's insight has a historical distinctiveness that should not be overlooked. Technological advantages in warfare have always been associated with greater security for those who possessed them. But in the case of the Internet, technological advantage has simultaneously created vulnerability. In a brief amount of time the entire communications infrastructure of the nation has changed in ways that have made us more vulnerable to attack in spite of our economic and military advantages. Responding to these new threats poses policy challenges that are new to modern government.

But beyond being simply new, another reason that cybersecurity puts the government in uncharted territory has to do with geography, or in this instance, the absence thereof. From inception, government has relied on geography. Kings ruled kingdoms—areas of land with borders—sometimes imprecise, often disputed—but always defining the geography within which the state could act. In modern government geography exercises a tyranny over organization. The tyranny of geography defines the distinction between domestic and foreign, between nation and state, between state and town. Geography defines jurisdiction, "the power or right to exercise authority" per the *Merriam-Webster* dictionary. In modern government jurisdiction is implicit in everything from war between nation states to controversies between national and local authorities, as exemplified by tensions between the Federal Bureau of Investigation (FBI) and local police departments in the United States.

Cyberspace, however, transcends geography and herein lays the fundamental governmental problem. No one can put yellow police tape around the cybercrime scene, and no one can define the battle-field. The absence of geography makes the traditional governmental tasks of protection and retribution especially difficult. It is also unclear who is in charge of protecting cyberspace. In the United States, the Department of Defense (DoD) created the first Cyber Command in 2010 while the FBI has traditionally taken jurisdiction in crimes that cross state lines as nearly all cybercrimes do. But when a cybercrime or cyber attack occurs, we have trouble finding out where the criminals are. We have established protocols, arrangements with other countries that allow us to extradite murderers, child molesters, and all sorts of other undesirables so that they can be brought to justice. But often we have no idea or cannot be sure where the cyber criminal is. If another country attacks us we know where the missiles come from and we can decide how to retaliate. But it is very difficult to know where hack-ers are. Sometimes we can pinpoint the country in which they sit but cannot determine whether the attack is an intentional attack by a government or an attack by a group of criminals who happen to be in a given country at a given time and who perhaps have also attacked sites in that same country.

This is why cybersecurity is a challenge unlike anything govern-ments have encountered before. When we are able to establish juris-diction, we are able to establish rules, laws, and accountability for adherence to the law—the three bedrock principles of modern demo-cratic governance. In the absence of jurisdiction everyone is account-able and therefore no one is accountable. Other problems emerge from this underlying challenge to cybersecurity policy. Using the U.S. fed-eral government as a primary example but also showing that these issues are common challenges to other information age countries as well, this chapter highlights diffusion of responsibility between gov-ernment organizations and discusses three areas of complexity that flow from it: civil liberty and privacy issues, the challenge of public–private partnerships, and the people problem.

The Rise of Electronic Government

The Internet was created by the Defense Advanced Research Projects Agency (DARPA), an American government entity tasked with developing innovative technology for the military, and evolved from there to a system used by the entire world. But less well known is that demand for computing was not only created by the United States but also by large, domestic, data-driven agencies like the Social Security Administration. Testimony to this fact was that when the year turned from 1999 to 2000, the infamous "Y2K" problem that was supposed to wreak havoc with computers around the world turned out to be largely an American problem, not a global one. The reason was that the U.S. government had practically single-handedly created the information age, and it alone, therefore, was the owner of "legacy" systems that were vulnerable to the Y2K problem.

By the time President Clinton and Vice President Al Gore came to office in 1993 the information age was already transforming the private sector. Gore, whose landmark legislation brought the Internet out of DARPA and into global use, was given the task of "reinventing government." To do so, he was determined to use new information technologies to bring to the public sector the same large-scale productivity breakthroughs that had occurred in the private sector; hence, the term electronic government, or simply e-government, was born.

With lightning speed the Internet became critical to operations within government and to communications between citizens and government. As Gore led the Clinton Administration's efforts to put the government online, it became evident that the Internet could promise huge savings to government and improved convenience to citizens. Initially most government agencies put information and forms online. But by the end of the Clinton/Gore Administration people wanted more than information—they wanted to be able to conduct transactions as well. For most of the world's information age economies, the movement from "information" to "transactions" on the Internet was swift. As long as a country had a large number of citizens online and had a banked economy (i.e., not a cash economy), the move from office transactions to Internet transactions was relatively easy. New private sector entrants such as Ezgov.com and established corporations such as Microsoft and IBM also discovered a large new market opportunity in helping governments move from paper to web.

Research from the Pew Internet and American Life Project, which has been polling Americans about their use of the Internet since 2001, illustrates the increased use of e-government. Its 2010 poll found that

[M]any more Americans are now completing simple transactions with government than was the case in 2001. At that time, just 2% of online government users had paid a government fine online—now, 15% of all Internet users have done so. Similarly, 4% of online government users had applied for a recreational license online in 2001, a figure that has now grown to 11% of all Internet users. Renewing driver's licenses and auto registrations has also become much more common—from 12% of online government users in 2001 to one-third of all Internet users today.

The most common form of online government transaction has become tax filing, which has been growing steadily over the course of the past decade. In 2010, the Internal Revenue Service (IRS) reported that 99 million people used e-file in the United States, thus keeping up with a trend of steadily increasing use of the Internet for purposes of paying tax. In Sweden, about half the population declares their taxes online.

While America might have led the way, e-government is a global trend fueled by two powerful factors—public demand and cost. By 2007 the percentage of people who had used the Internet in their transactions with public authorities averaged 32% for citizens in the OECD countries. As younger tech-savvy citizens got to the age where they had to file tax returns and register motor vehicles they expected to be able to do this online, because they were doing most of their other transactions online—from buying clothes to meeting members of the opposite sex. On the government side of the equation, public sector leaders discovered that online transactions were much cheaper than offline transactions. Ezgov.com, an online solutions provider, estimated that postal or telephone transactions cost from 5 to 10 times more than an online transaction and that face-to-face transactions cost from 50 to 100 times more.

But as the rate of online transactions has grown so has the risk. It is one thing to hack into someone's Amazon.com account; quite another to hack into their tax or health records. And so, as e-government has expanded to keep pace with private sector dependence on the Internet so have the vulnerabilities of average citizens to cybercrime and the need for modern governments to provide some sort of coherent defense for its citizens. But in order to achieve good cybersecurity, the public sector must tackle several problems, all stemming from the tyranny of geography.

Problem #1: Diffusion of Responsibility
between Government Organizations

The first recorded instance of computer espionage took place in 1986 and illustrated the problem with jurisdictional thinking when it comes to cybersecurity. The story is told in a 1989 book by Clifford Stoll called, *The Cuckoo's Egg: Tracking a Spy Through the Maze of Computer Espionage*. The author, a graduate student managing computers at the Lawrence Berkeley National Laboratories, is asked to resolve a $0.75 discrepancy in the lab's accounting system. As he tries to untangle this fairly minor issue, he discovers that someone is systematically hacking into or attempting to hack into U.S. military sites. As the saga unfolds and Stoll attempts to alert the authorities he is handed from one part of the government to another. The FBI initially cannot be interested in the problem because the amount of money involved is too small. The national security agencies are intrigued but do not know quite what to do. As Stoll is handed off from one federal agency to another, he encounters various parts of the government's national security apparatus—a culture shock for a self-described countercultural type. The story finally ends with the FBI coming back into the picture to arrest the hackers in Germany, an early illustration also of the fact that this is a global issue.

In the intervening years the governmental response to cyber threats has changed from the lackadaisical and somewhat quizzical attitude encountered by Stoll to one of intense interest, not to mention intense funding. But the cacophony of governmental entities in the game persists because in cyberspace the government is playing both offense and defense.

In the United States, the offense is and has been handled, not surprisingly, by the DoD and the National Security Agency (NSA), both of which have been involved in this area for a long time. For example, according to Clarke's new book, *Cyber War: The Next Threat to National Security and What to Do about It*, the first class of officers trained in cyber war graduated from the National Defense University in 1995. In 1996, cryptome.org, a military news website, reported that the Pentagon published a report of the Defense Science Board Task Force on Information Warfare Defense, which was one of the earliest to identify the possibilities and vulnerabilities of the United

States to information warfare. Also in 1996, the Central Intelligence Agency (CIA) was already dealing with the cyber world through its advanced technology panel. But within the U.S. federal government no agency has been as preeminent as the NSA, which, as the nation's premier organization for electronic spying, has had the technological and legal authority to explore infiltration of the Internet for intelligence purposes. Its long involvement and significant expertise has given it enormous capacity which is why General Keith Alexander assumed a dual position as Director of NSA and Commander of the U.S. Cyber Command, formed in 2010. The other reason that NSA is the preeminent government player in this area has to do with money. Although the portion of the cyber budget at DoD is difficult to determine because so much of it is for "black" or cybersecurity activities that are highly classified, most sources put it at somewhere around $2.3 billion—a number that dwarfs spending on the nonmilitary side of the budget.

The defensive side of cybersecurity has been located in the Department of Homeland Security (DHS) ever since it was created in the wake of the 9/11 attacks, a result of combining 22 existing agencies into one. The perception that the defensive, or domestic, side of the government's cybersecurity operation was weak has been reinforced by an overall impression that DHS was weak. In its early years, DHS was known in government as a dumping ground for mediocre civil servants. On the political side, DHS was known as the place where the Bush Administration placed people it owed political favors without regard to their preparation for the job. Colonel Robert Stephen, who was brought into the White House to work for then homeland security advisor Tom Ridge (whom he followed to DHS when the new department was created), recalls the early days of DHS: "The NSA was off doing its own thing, DoD was doing its own thing. Their two ships never crossed paths. There was a lot of contention between FBI and DHS over this.... We brokered a truce in the 2004 time frame [because] everyone was setting up their own cyberspace. DHS was the newer and weaker kid on the block" (Interview with Author, 2010).

The status of DHS in this area began to change in 2007 as a result of presidential attention. Again, according to Stephen (2010):

To be honest... none of it mattered until 2007 (late spring or early summer) when the Office of the Director of National Intelligence requested briefing time with President Bush and rolled in with a very scary cyber briefing. Bush got very interested in this after that and did a quick study. Within a few months after that at a briefing with the National Security Telecommunications Advisory Committee—Bush came in for 45 minutes and talked in depth about the cyber problem and pinged 30 CEOs in the room. ...When the President gets involved... first lots of money appears. ...From that moment on it became an interagency frenzy.

By 2008, President Bush's attention to cybersecurity was being felt throughout the government. Michael Chertoff, Secretary of DHS, made it one of his top priorities for 2008, admitting to reporters in a *USA Today* article that "It's the one area in which I feel we've been behind where I would like to be" (Wolf, 2008, p. 6A). Bush's budget proposed a 10% increase in cybersecurity funding. The increased attention coincided with an increase in reported security breaches to DHS and reports that Estonia's largest bank had been shut down for 3 weeks in 2007, a victim of cyber attacks.

President Obama came into office promising that he would put cybersecurity on center stage. One of the first things he did was to task Melissa Hathaway of the Office of the Director of National Intelligence to conduct a comprehensive 60-day review to assess U.S. cybersecurity. The plan, formally known as the "Cyberspace Policy Review," was released on May 29, 2009. The very first recommendation was to appoint an official responsible for coordinating the nation's cybersecurity policies and to create an National Security Council (NSC) directorate devoted to the interagency coordination of those issues. On January 6, 2010, the White House announced that Georgia Tech professor Howard Schmidt, a former Microsoft official with decades of experience in the field, would assume the role of cyber czar. His tenure has illustrated the divisions within government, reflected in the difficulties DHS has had in recruiting and retaining leadership and in the ongoing disputes within the government between the domestic and national security sides. For instance, Seymour Hersh, a veteran journalist, reported in a 2010 article in *The New Yorker* that the Director of the National Cybersecurity Center Rod Beckstrom had resigned, stating that DHS's cybersecurity efforts are "controlled" by the National Security Agency. Beckstrom is not the first DHS official to resign in frustration and thereby prompt attempts at solving the underlying problem of who's in charge of what. In 2005, Amit Yoran, the very first director of cybersecurity, left amidst speculation that he was frustrated at the lack of importance put on cybersecurity at the DHS. Michael Chertoff, the then Secretary of DHS, responded that summer by announcing the creation of the position of Assistant Secretary for Cybersecurity and Telecommunications. After Beckstrom's departure the Secretary of Defense Robert Gates and the Secretary of Homeland Security, Janet Napolitano signed a Memorandum of Agreement, published in October 2010, that would place DoD analysts at the National Cybersecurity and Communications Integration Center (NCCIC) and would place DHS personnel at NSA. This was widely praised as an important step in recognizing the difficulties inherent in trying to separate cybersecurity issues by organization. Nonetheless, some believe that this will not be enough and that the only solution will be to place cybersecurity in its own separate organization. A 2010 report by the Center for Strategic and International Studies (CSIS), a Washington think-tank that conducted President Obama's 60-day review of cybersecurity policy, stated: "Although the administration created a cybersecurity coordinator and a new office, we still believe that the nation will ultimately need something like the Office of the U.S. Trade Representative to lead and coordinate federal policy for what has become a central element of national security and economic life" (p. 6).

For the time being, however, the U.S. federal government seems to have opted for a decentralized approach to cybersecurity where the DoD controls offense and defends the dot-mil domain space and where DHS is responsible for the dot-gov domain space and attempts to coordinate security with the private sector. In practice this means leaving large portions of cyberspace to their own devices when it comes to security. This is similar to the current European approach where there is a strict division of labor between the civil and military approaches to cybersecurity, again leaving large parts outside of government domain. Specifically, European Union (EU) policy is developed only in regard to civilian defense of cyberspace, and the organization's member states are responsible for military operations.

Coordination of Western military response at the international level, another topic of diffusion of responsibilities, is primarily addressed through NATO's Cooperate Cyber Defense, located in Tallinn, Estonia, which was created in response to the 2007 cyber attacks on that country.

Those who feel that the current level of government involvement is not sufficient face major obstacles in attempting greater coordination and centralization—concerns about privacy and civil rights, difficulties in getting cooperation from the private sector and the problem of attracting talented information technology (IT) personnel to government service.

Civil Liberty and Privacy Issues

Civil liberty and privacy issues have been at the center of the government's attempts at cybersecurity since the very beginning and complicate efforts to achieve greater cooperation and centralization. In the United States, the involvement of NSA continues to rouse suspicions among privacy advocates. NSA is tasked with electronic spying on a global level but is prohibited from spying on U.S. citizens. In a world where jurisdiction could be defined by geography this was not a problem—in today's world it is. This dilemma came up early in the history of U.S. government involvement in cybersecurity. In the Carter Administration, the Department of Commerce was made responsible for the protection of unclassified computer information. But a 1984 executive order by President Reagan shifted responsibility for computer security to the DoD and the NSA. The outcry from the private sector, civil libertarians, and privacy advocates was swift. They did not want domestic computer systems coming under the Defense establishment. As a consequence, in 1987 Congress passed the Computer Security Act, which placed responsibility for the federal government's computer security in the hands of the National Institute of Standards (NIST) at the Department of Commerce while giving the DoD and NSA authority over classified computers.

By the mid 1990s, as security issues moved from securing the federal government's computers to securing a network that was dominating all aspects of society, the preferred position of those concerned with privacy was to advocate a "hands-off" policy. Government intervention, it was argued, would only ruin the Internet which was a truly self-regulating system. This laissez-faire attitude toward the Internet was so widely accepted that when Ira Magaziner, author of the ill-fated Clinton health care plan, was given a second governmental assignment—running a panel to look at governance of the Internet—he concluded that government should refrain from regulating the Internet. The irony was duly noted. The same person who had sought to get the government into the business of health care took a big step away from that position when confronted with the Internet.

Unfortunately, terrorism, like cyber terrorism, defies the jurisdictional lines upon on which modern government was formed where spying on fellow Americans was under the jurisdiction of the FBI and the court system; the national security agencies were supposed to stay away from Americans and from the homeland. None of this mapped very well to the terrorist and the electronic worlds, both of which arrived in the United States at about the same time. Thus, in response to the events of 9/11, President Bush created the Patriot Act that authorized NSA surveillance of American telephone and Internet communications without prior Foreign Intelligence Surveillance Act (FISA) approval. As the involvement of the big telecommunications companies in this arena came to light, the Electronic Frontier Foundation and the American Civil Liberties Union took the big companies to court. The cases were eventually dismissed in part because FISA was revised to make it somewhat easier to conduct electronic surveillance while building in safeguards for American citizens. Spying on fellow Americans now involves a complex set of legal procedures and a heavy dose of probable cause that a crime was in the works.

Although the anger and court cases over electronic surveillance are no longer front-page news, they left a powerful legacy of concern over privacy, most of which has its origin in the heavy involvement of NSA in cyberspace. The problem is tricky because while NSA has perhaps the best technical ability in the government, it is primarily a spy agency. And so in 2009, Amit Yoran, the first director of the National Cyber Security Division during the Bush Administration, testified before Congress as follows: "In news reports and discussions among privacy and civil liberties groups the role of the NSA in monitoring or defending domestic private networks is debated. Should such intelligence programs exist, DHS should be very careful to distance itself from participation, support or engagement in these activities."

By the time the Obama Administration issued its 60-day review in early 2010, privacy issues were not much closer to being resolved than they had been nearly 30 years before in the Reagan Administration. Out of the 10 near-term action items proposed in the review, two dealt specifically with privacy. The first advocated that a privacy and civil liberties official be assigned to the NSC cybersecurity directorate. The second called for building a program that addressed privacy, civil liberties, and privacy-enhancing technologies.

In contrast to the hands-off approach of the United States, the European Union takes an active role in regulating data protection with most policies in this area concerning privacy as in the protection of personal data. With a community of 600 million people across 27 member states, a number of initiatives cover data protection and privacy, including, perhaps most notably, the Data Protection Directive 95/46/EC, which offers strong protection of individual data. A formal review to update privacy legislation was started in 2009 in an effort to maintain protection while improving data-sharing. Like its American counterparts, European telecommunications companies have found themselves in the middle of the issue as they would need to breach personal data to properly address risk.

The fact of the matter is that this issue has no easy answers. To further complicate matters, in addition to the public at large and policy makers, privacy issues are also important to the private sector, which is often at the center of the debate.

The Public–Private Conundrum

Among the primary obstacles to cybersecurity has been and remains the fact that the bulk of IT systems vulnerable to attack are in the private sector. It was clear from the beginning that security enhancements to private systems would be expensive, cut into the bottom line, and compromise effectiveness. And no one was quite sure that this was even necessary. Typical of a debate that has not really been solved was a headline from *Kiplinger Business Forecasts*, on January 15, 2002, that read, "Keeping Systems Safe From Cyber Bugs Can Cut Productivity." When U.S. Republican Senator Robert Bennett of Utah proposed that the Securities Exchange Commission (SEC) adopt rules requiring public companies to disclose their readiness to meet cyber threats, the business community mobilized to argue that cybersecurity should be treated as a risk factor *where appropriate* but that it should not be an entirely new disclosure category, an argument that won out.

President Obama's 60-day review admitted that "the private sector often seeks a business case to justify the resource expenditures needed for integrating information and communications system security into corporate risk management and for engaging partnerships to mitigate collective risk." The report also acknowledges private sector concerns beyond the bottom line. In addition to being reluctant to make major investments in cybersecurity, businesses are cautious about sharing information about security breaches with the government for fears that such information can be subject to the Freedom of Information Act, lead to public disclosure, and ruin trust in a company or reveal trade secrets to its rivals. Further, businesses loathe disclosure of proprietary information and too much interaction with the government can lead to unanticipated regulatory actions. In other words, there are few incentives for the private sector to engage in the sorts of partnerships that are put forward as a solution to these problems. In spite of legislation such as the Trade Secrets Act and the Critical Infrastructure Information Act, both designed to deal with the problems posed by the Freedom of Information Act disclosures, private sector skepticism remains. All too often businesses prefer to defend themselves without the government.

Even in the case of large infrastructure companies, who are most vulnerable to attacks, the government has to tread lightly. In the United States, for instance, NSA is developing a program called "Perfect Citizen," a digital surveillance program to detect cyber attacks on private companies such as the electricity grid, dams, and nuclear power plants. But as the following quote from the *Wall Street Journal* (Gorman, 2010) indicates, the program is not mandatory: "While the government can't force companies to work with it, it can provide incentives to urge them to cooperate, particularly if the government already buys services from that company, officials said" (p. 3).

The tentativeness with which government is moving into the area of critical infrastructure is not limited to the United States. In

Great Britain, the Government Communications Headquarters, the UK's version of NSA, is seeking to broaden its mandate to watch for signs of attack on private systems. According to the *Computer Business Review*, an industry publication, the Prime Minister met with heads of major companies to discuss the plan but the government was careful to deny that the plan has any privacy implications.

Official pronouncements about the importance of public–private partnerships in the area of cybersecurity are ubiquitous. But the problem remains. As long as the private sector feels it can defend itself against attack or that it can quickly recover, the risks of greater government involvement will seem high. Government has been loathe to mandate security improvements that might be deemed too expensive, and it has been reluctant to force its involvement on private sector entities such as utilities and power plants where the consequences of cyber attacks can be catastrophic.

People Issues

It is generally difficult for the public sector to attract and keep talent in the area of cybersecurity because top IT professionals are always in demand by the private sector, whether the economy is good or bad. To deal with the issue in the United States, DHS Secretary Janet Napolitano recently received exemptions from civil service hiring and wage scales in order to hire 1,000 cybersecurity experts. But in spite of the exemptions and in spite of studies by respected institutions such as the National Academy of Public Administration urging new compensation structures for IT professionals, the government has trouble filling these IT posts. "We're all fighting for the same resources. We don't have thousands of unemployed security professionals," said Patricia Titus, chief information security officer (CISO) for information technology firm Unisys and former CISO at the Transportation Security Administration in a 2010 article in *SFGate.com* (Cabrera, 2010, p. 2). "Good IT professionals are still employed and trying to entice them from private sector into the government is going to be difficult."

The people problem was front and center in President Obama's 60-day review, which argued for new policies to attract cybersecurity expertise and improve retention. For example, while the review noted a small measure of improvement in recruitment, it acknowledged the time needed for security clearances remains inadequate. To deal with retention, the review promoted the idea that employees should be able to build their professional portfolios beyond a single agency, suggesting "Shared training and rotational assignments across agencies and potentially with the private sector would not only be efficient, but would promote beneficial cross-fertilization and the building of professional networks" (Cyberspace Policy Review, p. 15).

The people problem in the federal government exists at both the civil service and political levels. At the civil service level it is a subset from the bigger problem that the federal government suffers from an antiquated personnel system that is bad at attracting and retaining highly skilled workers. At the political level talented IT leaders have so many more lucrative opportunities outside of government that there is little incentive for them to stay on and fight the bureaucratic battles. The leadership problem is directly connected to the problems outlined above; the lack of clarity about the government's role in cyberspace means that, as we've seen, talented leaders in this field can easily feel that they are spinning their wheels and that they could make more of a contribution outside the government.

Conclusion

There is no doubt that public sector organizations throughout the modern world are more aware and more capable of dealing with threats to cyber infrastructure today than ever before. More money is being spent and more vulnerabilities are being identified. But in the nearly three decades since the U.S. federal government has been concerned with protecting first its own computers and then the Internet, the challenges of dealing with cybersecurity have not changed much.

At the heart of the cybersecurity policy challenge is the traditional government geographical division into foreign and domestic issues, which is now obsolete. A cyber attack can be both and the organizations needed to defend cyber infrastructure will probably involve both as well. Cybersecurity is one of the biggest challenges governments have ever faced—in part because there's never been a challenge like it.

Government has been organized around physical geography for centuries but the cyber threat is borderless and challenges the domestic and the national security sides of the government to achieve a seamless architecture of cooperation. Up until now both the public and private sectors have simply dealt with challenges as they have come up. While some of them have been embarrassing, they have been fixed, usually in an acceptable amount of time. In other words, so far the system of cybersecurity has largely been able to cope with the threat.

But that is because so far the threat has not been "existential"—to borrow a phrase from national security policy. There is still debate about the potential impact of cyber attacks on physical security but until it is settled we will continue to live with a somewhat cautious government involvement that is influenced by the original culture of the Internet—"open, untrammeled, … the Wild West…a self-organizing community led by private action where governments should play only a limited role," as described by the CSIS report. Until the assumptions inherent in the original culture of cyberspace prove to be obsolete, we will be left with a cybersecurity architecture that is suboptimal.

References

Author's interview with Colonel Robert Stephen, October 19, 2010.

Cabrera, A. M., "Demand Keeps Growing for Cyber Security Workers," April 2, 2010, in SFGate.com, p. 2.

"CCHQ to Monitor Private Networks for Cyber Attacks," by CBR Staff Writer, *Computer Business Review*, March 29, 2011.

Clarke, R., and Knake, R., *Cyber War: The Next Threat to National Security and What to do About It*, (Harper Collins), p. 34.

"Cybersecurity Two Years Later: A Report of the CSIS Commission on Cybersecurity for the 44th President," Commission Cochaird, Reps. James R. Langevin and Michael T. McCaul, Scott Charney and Lt. General Harry Raduege. http://csis.org/files/publication/110128_Lewis_CybersecurityTwoYearsLater_Web.pdf.

"Cyberspace Policy Review," The White House. http://www.whitehouse.gov/assets/documents/Cyberspace_Policy_Review_final.pdf.

Gorman, S., "U.S. Plans Cyber Shield for Utilities, Companies," *The Wall Street Journal*, July 8, 2010.

Hersh, S., "The Online Threat: Should We Be Worried about a Cyber War?" *The New Yorker*, November 1, 2010. http://www.newyorker.com/reporting/2010/11/01/101101fa_fact_hersh#ixzz15AvfyXiq.

McKenna, C. "Bill to Create Assistant Secretary for Cybersecurity at DHS Delivered to Full House," April 22, 2005. Digitalcommunities.com/articles/Bill-to-Create-Assisant-Secretary-for.html.

Moscaritolo, Angela, "Policy Makers Debate White House's Role in Cybersecurity," *SC Magazine*, April 28, 2009, http://www.scmagazineus.com/policymakers-debate-white-houses-role-in-cybersecurity/article/131513/.

Nakashima, Ellen, "U.S. Cyber-Security Strategy Yet to Solidify," *The Washington Post*, September 17, 2010.

OECD, The Future of the Internet Economy, A Statistical Profile, 2008.

Office of the Under Secretary of Defense for Acquisition and Technology, "Report of the Defense Science Board Task Force on Information Warfare–Defense (IW-D)," http://cryptome.org/iwd.htm.

Smith, A. "How Americans Use Government Websites." Pew Internet and American Life Project at: http://www.pewinternet.org/Reports/2010/Government-Online/Part-One/How-Americans-use-government-websites.aspx.

Stoll, C., *The Cuckoo's Egg: Tracking a Spy Through the Maze of Computer Espionage*. New York: Simon & Schuster Pocket Books, 1989.

Testimony of Amit Yoran before the House Homeland Security Committee, "Reviewing the Federal Cybersecurity Mission," March 10, 2009.

Wolf, Richard, "Bush Pushes Cybersecurity; President Wants to Raise Funding to $7.3 Billion," *USA Today*, March 14, 2008.

6

U.S. FEDERAL CYBERSECURITY POLICY

DANIEL CASTRO

Contents

Introduction

On December 22, 2009, U.S. President Barack Obama announced that Howard Schmidt would become the first-ever White House Cybersecurity Coordinator. The appointment of Schmidt to this position represents the culmination of decades of work by information security professionals, researchers, and government officials who have argued that protecting American computer systems is of such importance that it should be addressed at the highest levels of government. The selection of Schmidt, an individual with experience from both the public and private sectors, as the first "cyber czar" reflects the multifaceted nature of the federal government's role in cybersecurity, a part that has been changing and evolving for decades.

Federal efforts to address cybersecurity are a study in contradictions. Policy makers demand secure systems that are able to withstand assault by well-funded foreign adversaries and are impenetrable to attack, while at the same time insisting on digital tools capable of penetrating enemy networks and allowing the United States to engage in cyber warfare. For years Congress has recognized the importance of information technology to the economy while acknowledging the severe impact that a failure of these systems could have on America. Yet, many fear that without a strong catalyst, such as a "digital 9/11" with visible consequences, policy makers will continue to delay substantive reform. Efforts to improve cybersecurity have stretched on for decades across multiple presidential administrations even though many of the basic challenges have remained the same.

It is likely that many of these contradictions will remain unresolved in the years ahead. Yet policy makers continue to make progress, albeit slowly, and learn from the past. The focus of this chapter is to provide an overview of current cybersecurity efforts at the federal level including major threats facing federal agencies, the evolution of the current policy framework, and an understanding of how cybersecurity resources, both human and financial, get deployed across the federal government's civil agencies. It will also discuss the different approaches between the United States and Europe and highlight emerging policy challenges facing the federal government.

Federal Cybersecurity Threats

The U.S. government has had an interest in maintaining security for information systems and telecommunication networks dating back as far as the use of radiotelegraphs in the early 20th century, and the modern era of cybersecurity emerged out of the network and computer revolution in the 1970s. This era witnessed the introduction of networking innovations, like the Internet Protocol (IP) and the widespread use of ARPANET, which eventually grew into the Internet. Convergence between telephony networks and the Internet, along with an increasingly greater role for information technology in daily life, mean that cybersecurity is more important than ever.

Computers in the United States are regular targets for malicious activity and government systems are no exception. According to a 2009 survey by CDW, a consultancy, of federal information technology (IT) professionals, over half of all federal agencies experience a cybersecurity incident each week. The type and source of threats faced by the federal government vary as it must defend itself against many of the same threats faced by the private sector: malware, spam, identity theft, denial of service attacks, botnets, packet sniffing, system scans and probes, and unauthorized intruders. Federal employees are also subject to the same threats at home as business users including viruses, worms, spyware, and phishing. Federal workers using web-based tools, including social networking applications like Facebook and Twitter, or using Internet applications, like instant messaging clients or peer-to-peer file sharing, expose agencies to new risks and present new challenges. In addition, the increasing number of federal workers who take advantage of options to work remotely from potentially insecure home computers and public hotspots mean that the security of federal data and information systems must be balanced against other government initiatives such as workforce flexibility and productivity. This challenge will only increase as the government catches up to corporate America in this area: according to a 2010 (Telework, 2010) survey by FedScoop, an online media company, currently less than a quarter of federal government employees regularly telework compared to over 60% in the private sector.

The federal government faces many unique threats as well. Although cyberspace is a relatively new frontier for espionage and war, many countries are preparing to engage in this domain. Well-funded adversaries who wish to penetrate U.S. government networks and access or disrupt critical information systems pose a serious threat to both virtual and physical attacks. The national security of the United States depends on the nation remaining secure from cyber threats and information warfare.

Actors

Federal computer systems and networks are targeted by a variety of state and nonstate actors including foreign nations, terrorists, criminals, and other malicious actors. Foreign governments are developing the IT skills necessary to carry out espionage, gain an economic advantage, and fight wars online. Terrorist groups can use IT to launch attacks against critical infrastructure, such as the electric grid and the air traffic control system, or launch cyber attacks that destabilize financial systems, including banks and the stock market. Similarly, criminals increasingly use IT to coordinate, commit, and cover-up crimes including fraud, money laundering, and identity theft. Criminals, including malicious insiders such as disgruntled employees, may also use cyber attacks for revenge or retribution. Insiders use their knowledge of systems and networks to launch attacks that an outsider might not be able to perform. Insiders work from within an organization to commit cyber crime, such as stealing data or committing fraud. Finally, hackers present a threat to federal cybersecurity. Hackers range in skill from elite programmers who discover new software vulnerabilities to "script kiddies" who simply download prewritten hacking tools from the Internet. Hackers are often motivated to break into systems for the challenge or thrill rather than any particular monetary reward. Others in the hacking community work to advance a specific ideology. The term "hacktivist" is used to describe politically motivated individuals who use hacking tools to attack systems for the purpose of sending a political message.

Domains

Federal cybersecurity efforts encompass multiple related domains including military, intelligence, homeland security, law enforcement, and commerce. Each of these efforts has been created primarily to respond to the different sources of threats described above. However, over time it has become clear that while the motivations of different threat actors may not be the same, the means that they use to accomplish a cyber attack are often identical. Because the tools, techniques, and technologies to address threats are often the same it makes sense to have a more coordinated federal response to improve cybersecurity.

Military

A key purpose of the federal government is to protect the homeland and its citizens from foreign threats. While previously limited to invasion or violence, the role of government has expanded in the 21st century to meet the new digital challenges that affect American freedom and prosperity, including potential attacks on IT systems. The threat of cyber attack does not generally generate the same level of concern among policy makers as nuclear, biological, or chemical attacks. But the consequences of a well-designed cyber attack could have a profound impact on vital national interests, especially as the separation between virtual and physical is increasingly blurred and no international standards exist for what constitutes aggression online. Attacks on U.S. systems and networks, such as the power grid or transportation networks, can have life-and-death consequences in the real world, and countries that conduct cyber warfare operations can trigger physical retaliation and engagements. Moreover, identifying the source of a cyber attack is critical for deterrence, yet remains a significant challenge because the source of digital attacks can often be masked.

The importance of cybersecurity was highlighted in 1997 during "Eligible Receiver," the first cyber warfare exercise in the United States. By simulating an attack by a rogue state, military and civilian leaders demonstrated that critical infrastructures in the United States, such as the electricity grid and transportation networks, were vulnerable to a cyber attack. The Pentagon's Joint Task Force on Computer Network Defense also found that the United States was unprepared to respond to a coordinated attack on critical infrastructure, according to a report from the Congressional Research Service

(Hildreth, 2001). Since then, the military has admitted that hackers have broken into and stolen data from classified information systems. In a high-profile example, it was revealed in 2009 that data on the Defense Department's $300 billion Joint Strike Fighter project had been stolen by online hackers who appeared to have originated in China. But not all attacks happen over networks. As retold (Lynn, 2010) in a 2010 article in *Foreign Affairs*, in 2008, a foreign intelligence agency managed to infect classified and unclassified military networks after a flash drive infected with malware was inserted into a government laptop in the Middle East.

The U.S. military is developing offensive and defensive cyber warfare competencies. These capabilities are designed to resist cyber attacks, provide cyber attack capabilities, and serve as a deterrent to attacks by other countries. On May 21, 2010, the Department of Defense (DoD) launched the U.S. Cyber Command (USCYBERCOM), a centralized command for ensuring the security of military information systems. USCYBERCOM's responsibilities include operating, securing, and defending DoD networks, supporting military operations, and conducting military cyberspace operations. USCYBERCOM is a subordinate of the U.S. Strategic Command (USSTRATCOM), one of 10 unified commands under the DoD with members from all four military services. As with traditional power, cyber warfare capabilities are only one component of a broad arsenal of economic, diplomatic, and political tools available to the federal government to combat threats to national security.

Intelligence

The U.S. intelligence community is developing its capacity for cyber espionage. For example, the National Security Agency (NSA) is responsible for foreign signals intelligence. Through these activities, the agency develops its capabilities to intercept and analyze electronic communication. The NSA has expertise in cryptography including both methods for employing strong encryption and performing cryptanalysis. There are 17 different agencies and organizations in the U.S. intelligence community responsible for gathering information, according to Intelligence.gov. They include Air Force Intelligence, Army Intelligence, Central Intelligence Agency, Coast

Guard Intelligence, Defense Intelligence Agency, Department of Energy, Department of Homeland Security, Department of State, Department of the Treasury, Drug Enforcement Administration, Federal Bureau of Investigation, Marine Corps Intelligence, National Geospatial-Intelligence Agency, National Reconnaissance Office, National Security Agency, Navy Intelligence, and the Office of the Director of National Intelligence.

Homeland Security

The U.S. Department of Homeland Security (DHS) is tasked with protecting the United States from domestic emergencies, such as acts of terrorism and natural disasters. In recent years, its mission has expanded to include protecting the nation's critical infrastructure from cyber attacks to ensure continuity of services essential to the government and economy. Critical infrastructure includes telecommunications, energy, banking and finance, transportation, water supply systems, and emergency services supplied both by the private and the public sectors. This mission is carried out by the National Cybersecurity Division (NCSD), a division within DHS. NCSD sponsors various programs to carry out its mission including the National Cyberspace Response System to respond to cyber incidents; the Federal Network Security branch, which focuses on developing and improving solutions that solve common enterprise-wide technological needs in federal agencies; and the Cyber-Risk Management program, which seeks to help agencies better assess and reduce risk in their infrastructure. As part of the Cyber-Risk Management programs, DHS conducts the biennial Cyber-Storm exercises to test emergency response capabilities for cyber incidents, promotes a software assurance program to minimize software vulnerabilities, and holds events in conjunction with the annual National Cybersecurity Awareness month.

The National Cyberspace Response System includes a number of important programs to help coordinate responses to cyber incidents. For example, DHS operates the Cyber Cop Portal to facilitate information sharing for investigators anywhere in the world working on cybercrime cases. The largest of these projects is the U.S. Computer Emergency Readiness Team (US-CERT), the principal organization responsible for defending the nonmilitary federal systems from cyber attacks. US-CERT also has primary responsibility for fostering collaboration and information sharing between the federal government, state and local governments, the private and nonprofit sectors, and other countries. US-CERT monitors and maintains a database of cybersecurity threats and vulnerabilities and makes this data available in a variety of formats for both technical and nontechnical users, such as 'average consumers. US-CERT also publishes a variety of documents to educate consumers on good information security practices to protect their personal information and stay safe online.

Law Enforcement

Cybercrime is on the rise. Cybercrimes include hacking, fraud, extortion, corporate theft, identity theft, money laundering, trafficking in illegal goods, harassment, and violation of intellectual property rights. Although security awareness training can help protect individuals from cybercrimes, it is not failsafe, and even educated consumers can become victims of cybercrime. Multiple federal organizations, in addition to state and local authorities, have law enforcement authority for cybercrime; however, the Department of Justice (DOJ) and the Federal Bureau of Investigation (FBI) are the principal agencies responsible for investigating and prosecuting cybercrime. Other organizations, such as the Bureau of Alcohol, Tobacco, Firearms, and Explosives (ATF) and the Drug Enforcement Administration (DEA), are responsible for certain crimes that use the Internet as a platform, such as illegal online sales of firearms and drugs.

Because the Internet has no borders, a particular problem with cybercrime is the difficulty of establishing jurisdiction for law enforcement. To make it easier for victims of cybercrimes to get help, the FBI, the Bureau of Justice Assistance, and the National White Collar Crime Center partnered to create the Internet Crime Complaint Center (IC3). The IC3 provides a single destination for collecting data on Internet-related crimes and referring them to the proper authority. The 2009 Internet crime report found that IC3 received over 330,000 complaints, an increase of more than 20% over the previous year. The total reported dollar loss in 2009 was $559 million.

Commerce

The information economy is a principal driver of economic activity in the United States and internationally. According to analysis by the Information Technology and Innovation Foundation, a technology think tank, the Internet contributes approximately $1.5 trillion to the global economy annually. Businesses rely on the free flow of information for commerce. They need to communicate securely over reliable networks and store information securely on computers. Consumers meanwhile must have confidence that the Internet is secure to engage in online commerce.

Various agencies have cybersecurity responsibilities with implications for the national economy. The Securities and Exchange Commission (SEC) and the Federal Deposit Insurance Corporation (FDIC) both operate important information systems that are vital to the health of our nation's financial network. However, the Department of Commerce is the chief federal entity responsible for advancing commercial interests in the United States and for ensuring that cybersecurity spurs, rather than hinders, economic growth. The two principal organizations responsible for cybersecurity work at the Department of Commerce are the National Telecommunications and Information Administration (NTIA) and the National Institute of Standards and Technology (NIST).

NTIA is leading government efforts to review and implement new networking technology, such as IPv6 and DNSSEC, intended to create a more secure Internet infrastructure. NIST is the primary federal agency responsible for developing information security standards and best practices for nonnational security systems and providing agencies with general technical assistance to improve their security policies and practices. These include the Federal Information Processing Standards (FIPS) publications that define mandatory implementations of security technologies such as digital signatures and encryption standards and the Special Publication (800 Series) that include recommended guidelines for agencies to use for both specific technologies (e.g., Bluetooth security), specific procedures (e.g., assessing security controls), and specific policies (e.g., contingency planning). NIST manages and operates a number of federal cybersecurity resources including the National Software Reference Library that maintains forensic digital signatures of software and the National Vulnerability Database, a repository of vulnerability data used for automated vulnerability management.

Organizational and Policy Issues

The federal government must develop robust cybersecurity policies that protect national and economic security, and balance these needs against issues such as personal privacy and civil liberties. Over the past few decades, the federal government's response has evolved as conditions have changed, and these issues are still debated today.

A Policy History of Cybersecurity

Various laws and regulations govern federal activities in cyberspace. In addition, the federal government has produced various high-level policy documents and presidential directives intended to guide national cybersecurity efforts. Many information and communication policies, such as accessibility or privacy, do not necessarily relate directly to cybersecurity; however, they may affect the availability and use of these systems. Understanding cybersecurity depends on understanding the history that has brought us to where we are today. What follows is a discussion of major policy initiatives that have influenced cybersecurity since the early 1980s, when the modern computing and Internet era began.

Military and Intelligence

As with much of IT, cybersecurity initially grew out of military and intelligence efforts. The Department of Defense and the Central Intelligence Agency have long held an interest in protecting communication from interception or manipulation and information systems from unauthorized access. Even though activities to advance cybersecurity have increased in recent years, the broad goals of federal efforts in this area have remained the same for decades. In 1984, President Reagan issued National Security Decision Directive Number 145 (NSDD-145) declaring that a "comprehensive and coordinated approach must be taken to protect the government's telecommunications and automated information systems against current and projected threats." The Directive outlined four objectives for improving cybersecurity: (1) developing a capability to assess threats and vulnerabilities and implement effective countermeasures; (2) developing a technical knowledge base both within government and the private sector; (3) applying government resources more effectively and encouraging private sector efforts; and (4) supporting other policy objectives to enhance cybersecurity.

The Directive gave oversight for implementing these objectives to a steering committee composed of senior-level government members, including the Secretary of State, the Secretary of the Treasury, the Secretary of Defense, the Attorney General, the Director of the Office of Management and Budget, and the Director of Central Intelligence. Notably NSDD-145 established the Secretary of Defense generally, and the Director of the National Security Agency specifically, as the principal agents responsible for developing and implementing the necessary security programs, research, and standards for improving cybersecurity not just for the Department of Defense, but for the entire federal government. NSDD-145 also specified additional responsibilities for the Department of Commerce, which was directed to issue Federal Information Processing Standards for the security of information systems.

Cybersecurity may have its roots in the Department of Defense, but just as the Internet has evolved from a defense network into a commercial network, so too has cybersecurity changed to the point that it is no longer dominated by the military.

Cybercrime

Much of the initial federal cybersecurity policy outside of the military focused on cybercrime and law enforcement issues. The Computer Fraud and Abuse Act of 1986 (CFAA), for example, created criminal penalties for unauthorized access to information systems. Unauthorized access is defined to mean not only access to a computer without authorization but also access to information on a computer that exceeds authorized access (e.g., an FBI agent using his or her credentials to obtain information from a computer system that the agent is not entitled to use). Specifically CFAA criminalized the following:

- Unauthorized access to a computer system containing restricted government information with the intent to harm the United States or to benefit a foreign nation
- Unauthorized access to a computer system to obtain financial records
- Unauthorized access to a computer system exclusively used by the government or disruption of government use of a computer system that is not exclusively used by the government
- Use of a government computer system to commit fraud
- Unauthorized use of a government computer that results in alterations, damages, or destruction of the system or prevents authorized use of the system
- Buying or selling passwords or related information to enable unauthorized access to a computer system affecting interstate or foreign commerce or used by the government

CFAA also granted the U.S. Secret Service the nonexclusive authority to investigate offenses committed under the Act. Two years later, Robert Morris, a Cornell student, unleashed the Morris worm, one of the first major self-propagating viruses. The Morris worm spread rapidly across ARPANET, the Internet's predecessor, infecting approximately 10% of the connected systems and causing an economic loss of millions of dollars, according to an article on the "Security of the Internet" (1997) in *The Froehlich/Kent Encyclopedia of Telecommunications*. According to the same source, the severity and impact of the worm prompted the Defense Advanced Research Projects Agency to fund the Computer Emergency Response Team (CERT) Coordination Center to track and respond to these types of incidents. Morris was eventually charged and convicted of violating the CFAA.

Electronic Surveillance

The proliferation of IT introduced the need for new government regulations protecting privacy in electronic communications. The Foreign Intelligence Surveillance Act of 1978 (FISA) was created in response to concerns that the Fourth Amendment rights of Americans were at risk from domestic surveillance operations and that the federal government's authority to use electronic surveillance to combat terrorism was at risk. The purpose of FISA was to provide government oversight of domestic surveillance of foreign individuals in the United States while still protecting national security. Under FISA, the federal government could authorize electronic surveillance without a court order for up to 1 year as long as the U.S. Attorney General could certify that U.S. citizens would not likely be subjected to surveillance. FISA also outlines procedures for obtaining authority to use pen registers and trap-and-trace devices to monitor incoming and outgoing communications in foreign intelligence investigations. These devices allow investigators to collect address information for electronic communication, such as the source and destination of communications, but not the message itself. For example, a pen register records the numbers dialed on a particular telephone while a trap-and-trace device records what numbers called a particular telephone.

The Electronic Communications Privacy Act (ECPA) of 1986 created new legal protections for the privacy of electronic data communications by creating civil and criminal penalties for unauthorized interception of electronic communications. ECPA also defined requirements for government access to electronic communication, both in transit and in storage, for law enforcement purposes and foreign counterintelligence investigations. The law outlines specific conditions necessary for a government investigator to gain access to electronic communications, such as a warrant or court order, and defines recordkeeping requirements for service providers, such as maintaining backups of subpoenaed data. One notable problem with ECPA is that electronic data in storage, specifically data stored for over 180 days, is treated differently than data in transit. Investigators must satisfy stricter requirements to gain access to electronic communications in transit, such as providing probable cause to obtain a search warrant. The bar is lower for data in storage and investigators can more readily gain access using a subpoena. ECPA also created a provision governing the use of pen registers and trap-and-trace devices (the "Pen/Trap statute"). ECPA's requirements did not substantially alter the existing electronic surveillance permissions created by FISA.

A further expansion of electronic surveillance occurred in 1994 when President Clinton signed into law the Communications Assistance for Law Enforcement Act (CALEA) that mandated that telecommunications providers, including wireless carriers, comply with government requests for electronic surveillance, including site location data for cell phones. Importantly, CALEA specifically excluded the Internet from its requirements. In addition, CALEA does not require the service provider to be able to decrypt the communications, or enable the government to decrypt the communications, if it does not possess the key. CALEA was created in response to technical and administrative challenges law enforcement faced in acquiring wiretaps in a timely manner. CALEA has provided the legal framework for modern surveillance systems such as the FBI's Digital Collection System Network (DCSNet) that allows agents to easily intercept voice and text communication over traditional telephony networks.

Information Technology (IT) Management and Risk Management

In the 1990s, government recognized the need to modernize IT practices and adapt to the growing threat of having insecure computer systems. The Clinger-Cohen Act (originally more aptly named the "Information Technology Management Reform Act"), passed in 1996, was created to reform the way the federal government designed, acquired, used, operated, and managed IT resources. Most notably the Clinger-Cohen Act assigned the Director of the Office of Management and Budget (OMB) responsibility for improving the acquisition, use, and disposal of information technology by, for example, establishing best practices for IT acquisition, overseeing the development of standards in cooperation with NIST, and monitoring and reviewing the budget of IT projects. The Act also directs all federal agencies to take certain steps to modernize their IT process by designating a chief information officer (CIO) responsible for IT acquisition and management. Following the passage of the Clinger-Cohen Act, agency heads formed a Federal CIOs Council to develop best practices and standards across agencies. Initially an informal group, Congress later established the council as an organization within the executive branch, consisting of CIOs and deputy CIOs across many federal government executive agencies.

One of the most important moves to improve cybersecurity across the entire federal government was the passage of the E-Government

Act of 2002. The Act established a broad framework intended to promote the development and use of e-government services and processes to make the federal government more efficient and to increase opportunities for citizens to engage with the government. The Act directed all federal government agencies to develop performance metrics to demonstrate progress toward implementing e-government solutions. One of the most substantive changes brought about by the Act was the creation of the Office of Electronic Government in the OMB whose department head would be the de facto CIO of the federal government responsible for managing technology investments, improving information security, ensuring privacy, and developing enterprise architecture across the federal government.

A key part of the E-Government Act is Title III, also known as the Federal Information Security Management Act (FISMA). The purpose of FISMA is to define a comprehensive framework for information security controls at federal agencies including effective management and governance, the development of information security standards and best practices, and proper oversight. FISMA is technology neutral and does not include prescriptive requirements for specific technologies, but instead leaves the selection of IT solutions to individual agencies. FISMA tasks the National Institute of Standards and Technology (NIST), with cooperation from the defense and intelligence communities, to be responsible for developing the security standards implemented at civil agencies. In addition, policy makers recognized the value of market-driven technologies; FISMA encourages the use of commercially developed information security solutions.

The precursor to FISMA was the Computer Security Act of 1987. The purpose of the Act was to establish minimum standards for federal computer systems. Specifically the Act assigned the National Bureau of Standards (now NIST) the responsibility for developing, in cooperation with the NSA, the technical, management, physical, and administrative standards and guidelines needed to assure cost-effective security and privacy for federal information systems. The Computer Security Act also required agencies to establish security plans for all federal computer systems containing sensitive information and mandated security training for all users of federal IT systems.

Homeland Security

After the terrorist attacks on September 11, 2001, Congress passed the USA PATRIOT Act that modified aspects of ECPA, FISA, and CFAA. Although the focus of the law was not on cybersecurity, it contained many amendments to strengthen federal cybersecurity efforts to improve national security and facilitate federal law enforcement activities. The most important of the amendments were contained in Title 2 of the Act, which modified and expanded the government authority to conduct electronic surveillance. For example, the PATRIOT Act expanded the ability of law enforcement to use pen registers and trap-and-trace devices to monitor Internet communications. The Act also increased the amount of information that a law enforcement agent could compel a service provider to disclose about their customers to include information such as network IP addresses and billing information. In addition, the Act granted service providers the ability to voluntarily disclose private communications if they believe it is an emergency situation that could result in physical harm to others.

Civil liberties groups have argued that the PATRIOT Act gives the federal government too much power in the name of national security at the expense of individual rights and personal privacy. Section 217 of the PATRIOT Act is one such example. This section includes a provision that allows law enforcement officials to intercept electronic communication from a "computer trespasser" if they receive authorization from the owner or operator of the computer system in question. The purpose of the provision is to provide private sector computer system owners and operators the ability to call on law enforcement to help monitor and respond to cyber attacks, especially those on critical infrastructure. However, this provision illustrates the difficult nature of balancing law enforcement with individual rights: under this law, government has the authority to monitor private communications of individuals on a computer system without any judicial approval and potentially without any judicial oversight. Although the purpose is to monitor trespassers, or those engaged in unauthorized activity, the term is defined loosely and could be used to broadly monitor the online activities of individuals.

Other important sections in the Act include strengthening criminal laws against terrorism, which contains a provision about deterring and preventing cyber terrorism and developing enhanced cybersecurity forensic capabilities. The Act also calls for the Secret Service to create a national network of task forces to prevent, detect, and investigate electronic crimes, including potential attacks against critical infrastructure and financial systems. Even though the PATRIOT Act expanded government authority to pursue cyber criminals threatening national security, some feel it did it at the expense of civil liberties.

The Homeland Security Act of 2002 (HSA) implemented widespread organizational changes throughout the federal government, most notably creating the Department of Homeland Security (DHS) as a new cabinet-level department. The HSA created within DHS a Directorate for Information Analysis and Infrastructure Protection responsible for, among other things, developing a comprehensive plan to secure critical infrastructure and related systems. Many functions and centers relating to cybersecurity previously run out of other departments were transferred to DHS including the Federal Computer Incident Response Center at the General Services Administration and the National Infrastructure Protection Center at the FBI. The Secretary of DHS was made responsible for developing a national plan for securing critical infrastructure, developing and coordinating emergency response for attacks on critical information systems, working with both the public and private sectors to provide warnings on information security risks, and performing and funding cybersecurity-related research and development.

Federal Resources and Leadership

Although legislation has shaped much of the cybersecurity agenda over the past few years, federal efforts have not been driven entirely by Congress. Even though the position of White House Cybersecurity Coordinator is new and—for the first time—a senior-level official in the White House is officially responsible for advising the president on cybersecurity issues, many past policies governing information security were also set by the highest levels of the executive branch.

In 1998, President Clinton issued Presidential Decision Directive 63 (PDD-63) setting a national goal of securing America from attacks against its critical infrastructure within 5 years. As noted in the directive, "any interruptions or manipulations of these critical functions must be brief, infrequent, manageable, geographically isolated and minimally detrimental to the welfare of the United States." The directive called for forming public–private partnerships to help reduce vulnerabilities and designated sector-specific lead agencies to be the primary liaison to work with the private sector on securing critical infrastructure. To support the private sector in improving cybersecurity, the federal government pledged to assist with periodic risk assessments of critical infrastructure, help identify best practices, and develop better ways to respond to computer crime.

PDD-63 also required the government to conduct an assessment of critical infrastructure, in particular the federal government's assets, and to prepare a plan on how to protect the United States from cyber attacks. In response to this requirement, President Clinton's White House released the "National Plan for Information Systems Protection" in 2000. The Plan was the first step in the United States toward a comprehensive review of cybersecurity issues and challenges facing the federal government and made clear the necessity of improving cybersecurity to protect the nation's economic and national security in the information age.

The George W. Bush Administration continued to develop a comprehensive plan for cybersecurity. In 2003, DHS released the "National Strategy to Secure Cyberspace" as part of the "National Strategy for Homeland Security." The document combined both high-level thinking about improving cybersecurity for the nation and specific recommendations the government could take to reduce security risks. The strategy defined three strategic objectives: prevent cyber attacks against critical infrastructure; reduce vulnerability to cyber attacks; and minimize damage and recovery time from cyber attacks that do occur. To achieve this, the strategy outlined broad national priorities that focus on improving information collection, analysis and sharing, reducing threats and vulnerabilities, improving security awareness and training, securing government information systems, and developing a system of international cooperation for cybersecurity.

After the September 11, 2001, terrorist attacks, the U.S. government began to embrace a more methodological approach to national security by creating a structured framework by which to identify, catalogue, and respond to threats to the homeland. An example of this is Homeland Security Presidential Directive-7 (HSPD-7), issued in December 2003, in which DHS instructed all federal departments and agencies to identify, prioritize, and protect critical infrastructure from terrorist attack. For each sector, such as energy or agriculture, DHS has directed that a lead agency continue to assume primary responsibility for coordinating critical infrastructure protection between the public and private sectors. These lead agencies must develop sector-specific risk management plans using the risk management framework defined in the National Infrastructure Protection Plan, a policy framework created by DHS.

HSPD-7 applied this rigorous approach to cybersecurity, a key component of critical infrastructure in virtually every sector. The Department of Commerce, for example, was ordered to coordinate the security of IT products and services necessary to meet homeland security requirements with the private sector, the Office of Science and Technology Policy was directed to coordinate interagency research and development for critical infrastructure, and the Office of Management and Budget was instructed to implement government-wide standards for information security at federal agencies.

DHS continues to implement various programs to improve federal network security, although some efforts have not been made public. In January 2008, DHS issued HSPD-23, a classified directive that came out of a presidential request for an interagency review of cybersecurity threats to the United States and how best to defend against them. HSPD-23 established the Comprehensive National Cybersecurity Initiative (CNCI) with the goals of reducing vulnerabilities, protecting federal resources, and better anticipating threats. CNCI has created multiple interagency working groups including the National Cyber Study Group to coordinate CNCI's activities, the Communications Security and Cyber Policy Coordinating Committee, tasked with implementing recommendations and presenting findings to the White House, and the Joint Interagency Cyber Task Force, responsible for monitoring federal projects and coordinating between the intelligence and nonintelligence communities.

Although many details of CNCI are classified, the Obama Administration has released information about 12 initiatives. They include coordinating cybersecurity research and development across the government, connecting agencies to increase government-wide situational awareness, increasing the security of classified networks, expanding cybersecurity education through training and personnel development, and better securing the global supply chain for IT. One important strategic effort has been the Trusted Internet Connections (TIC) initiative outlined in OMB Memorandum M-08-05 in November 2007 and which continues as part of the CNCI. The goal of the initiative is to reduce the total number of external network connections in the federal government by consolidating them into a centralized solution by using preapproved network services.

This will allow DHS to better implement cross-agency network security monitoring. For example, by identifying, cataloging, and consolidating the number of Internet access points, DHS can more reliably implement solutions to analyze network traffic for the malicious or potentially malicious activity on federal networks. DHS has implemented some of this through its EINSTEIN network intrusion detection systems. EINSTEIN 1 provided basic network monitoring and could detect anomalies on the network. EINSTEIN 2 provided significantly enhanced capabilities as it can automatically analyze network packets for specific signatures of malicious content and report threats to US-CERT in real time. The next generation of this technology, EINSTEIN 3, which DHS began pilot testing in 2010, will provide more advanced real-time packet inspection and identification. It will also be capable of detecting and responding to attacks, such as by automatically generating threat signatures. These types of systems are useful for responding to "zero day" exploits that attack vulnerabilities previously unknown to users. EINSTEIN 3 will also be designed to support enhanced information sharing between DHS, civilian agencies, and the intelligence community while still maintaining appropriate safeguards to protect the privacy of communications.

In late 2010, the Obama Administration directed a 60-day comprehensive review to reassess U.S. policies and practices for cybersecurity. The resulting Cyberspace Policy Review, guided heavily by recommendations from the nonprofit Center for Strategic and International Studies' (CSIS) report to the president, recognized previous efforts but called for renewed federal leadership and accountability for improving cybersecurity. The Cyberspace Policy Review called for a national awareness campaign to educate Americans about the importance of action, increased efforts to partner with stakeholders abroad and in the private sector, better information to guide cybersecurity planning and response, and better defined performance metrics for improving the security of critical infrastructure. Most notably, it advocated for stronger senior-level leadership and authority on these issues from the White House. The proposal also included more forward-looking proposals such as appointing a privacy and civil liberties official to the National Security Council's cybersecurity directorate, building identity management solutions, and focusing research and development efforts on "game-changing" technologies that can greatly improve overall security. The Obama Administration announced that efforts begun under the CNCI will be continued under its updated national cybersecurity strategy.

Private Sector Coordination

The private sector has an important role to play in supporting federal cybersecurity efforts. From power to transportation to information and communications technology, national security depends on many services provided by the private sector. In fact, according to the Government Accountability Office, approximately 85% of critical infrastructure is owned and operated by private organizations. Although the federal government is not directly responsible for securing this infrastructure, it does have oversight, for example, by setting security standards or audit requirements, for these sectors. But this oversight must be managed carefully as the federal government is not necessarily best placed to evaluate the risks of systems beyond its purview. To ensure the security of critical infrastructure, the federal government must partner and work with the private sector. For example, the National Security Agency is developing the classified "Perfect Citizen" project that would involve deploying sensors to monitor private sector networks of critical infrastructure to detect anomalous activity.

A key challenge the government faces with the private sector is how to enable effective information sharing. Companies may be reluctant to share data about attacks because of how that may impact their business or they may lack an incentive to share information in a timely manner. Conversely, government agencies may not be able or willing to quickly share intelligence with the right people at the right time. To address these issues, the government has formed the Government Coordinating Councils (GCC), an interagency government counterpart with representatives from the federal, state, and local levels, to partner with the Sector Coordinating Councils (SCC), a self-governed group of industry representatives. In addition, the private sector collaborates through various Information Sharing and Analysis Centers (ISACs). ISACs exist for many sectors including communication, electric, financial services, and surface transportation. ISACs help protect critical infrastructure by sharing threat data across sectors and providing the federal government with intelligence on known threats, vulnerabilities, and incidents. Each sector can create its own rules to facilitate data sharing, such as keeping information classified or making the threat information anonymous. Despite these improvements, information sharing remains a challenge because the private sector hesitates to disclose proprietary information that gives them a competitive advantage. Likewise, the public sector cannot always share information in a timely manner because of restrictions that prevent the government from giving individualized treatment to companies or sharing information that is either classified or has not gone through a strict review process. As a result, according to the Government Accountability Office, policy makers must find additional areas for reform to create the necessary conditions for successful information-sharing arrangements.

Federal Cybersecurity Agenda: Emerging Policy Issues

The federal government will likely take on an even greater role in managing cybersecurity issues in the years ahead. First, it will continue to expand its role as coordinator of national cybersecurity: developing information security standards and best practices, facilitating information sharing and pursuing cybersecurity-related research and development. Second, as the federal government increasingly adopts and funds e-government solutions, for everything from electronic health care records to intelligent transportation systems to a nationwide public safety network, it will become more actively involved in building, operating, certifying, and maintaining information systems critical to our national economy and security. For example, the 2009 Stimulus Act included over $25 billion for health information technology, including a nationwide network of electronic health records and health information exchanges. The National Coordinator for Health IT at the Department of Health and Human Services is now responsible for setting the security requirements for health information systems that it will certify. Similarly, the federal government allocated approximately $3.4 billion in stimulus funding for the smart grid, an effort to modernize the power grid using two-way communication and sensors. The Department of Energy and the Federal Energy Regulatory Commission must assess and make recommendations on best practices for smart grid components such as smart meters to ensure the security and reliability of the electric grid. Total federal spending on cybersecurity will most likely rise from approximately $8 billion in 2010 to $10 billion in 2015, as reported by *PC World* and *Information Week*, two industry publications.

The issue areas discussed below are emerging as important policy issues for cybersecurity.

Electronic Surveillance

Most of the efforts by law enforcement to perform Internet-based surveillance, such as the FBI's Carnivore program that involved deploying packet-sniffing servers to Internet Service Providers (ISPs) to monitor e-mail and other Internet-based communication, have received a public backlash spurred on by civil liberties group. Now law enforcement fears that the increasing security capabilities of modern communications networks and devices will make them impenetrable to government surveillance. In particular, many communications providers are beginning to offer security architectures that utilize end-to-end encryption so that no third party, including the service provider, can intercept or decrypt private communications. This has created tension between service providers who seek to offer the highest level of security possible to their customers and governments that would prefer to restrict the use of this technology. The conflict has been evident both in restrictions placed on the use of certain technologies and on the ability of businesses to export certain technologies to other countries.

A high-profile example occurred in 1993 when the NSA developed the Clipper chip, which was a hardware-based cryptographic tool for telecommunications devices that implemented a key escrow system intended to allow law enforcement to be able to access its communications. Although the Clipper chip faced public backlash and was not widely adopted, the underlying issue has not receded. Debate continues as to whether and to what extent government should use technology mandates to weaken commercial security offerings in order to gain access to sensitive information for law enforcement or counterterrorism purposes. For example, until the late 1990s the United States had export restrictions for cryptographic protocols, although many of these have now been lifted.

In 2010, India, the United Arab Emirates, and Saudi Arabia all made requests that Research In Motion (RIM), the manufacturer of the popular Blackberry smart phones, make changes to their service offering so that government investigators can access the private communications of its customers. RIM refused to comply with this request, even under threat of having to cease operations in these countries. The Obama Administration announced its intent to update CALEA to require Internet-based communications providers, such as RIM, Skype, Facebook, and others, to allow law enforcement to be able to comply with wiretap orders. Such a requirement, if implemented, would likely require substantial revisions in how some of these systems work as their design often precludes interception and decryption of transmissions by anyone, including the service providers.

Differences between the United States and other Countries

Differences between the U.S. approach to cybersecurity and that of other countries have long been apparent. For example, the Bush-era "National Strategy to Secure Cyberspace" revealed a marked difference in the U.S. government's perspective on cybersecurity compared to the one outlined in 2001 by the European Commission entitled "Network and Information Security: Proposal for a European Policy Approach." Whereas the U.S. government stated that its principal goal was to protect critical infrastructure from cyber attacks, the EC focused more broadly on creating a dependable computing and networking environment and protecting privacy. The EC proposal also indicated that it was worried by the fact that they were losing control of information security to foreign companies, many in the United States. For example, with regard to secure e-mail, the report complained that "access for European users depends on the export control policy of the United States." To remedy this situation, the proposal suggested standardizing the security practices of organizations in the European Union's member states in an effort to both act as role models for European businesses and to improve their market power. In addition, the European proposal recommended a targeted research program to develop strong encryption products equivalent in security to what was commercially available. This would have the desired effect of promoting the development of security products within Europe that were not subject to the export restrictions of the United States.

Differences between the two regions continue with the U.S. government more likely to support security technologies that increase their ability to investigate cyber crimes and terrorism, whereas the European Union may tilt the scale more toward protecting the privacy of citizens.

Efforts to address cybersecurity at an international level often reveal differences between countries generally. Since 1998, for example, Russia has called for an international arms control treaty for cyber warfare at the United Nations and other international forums. This proposal has been routinely rejected by officials in the United States, although their tone softened in 2010, according to a story in *The Wall Street Journal* (Gorman, 2010). Given the likelihood that cyber and information warfare will be a significant part of future military conflicts, cyber disarmament has important strategic consequences for many countries. It is also important in terms of defining foreign relations, as international norms have not yet been defined for what types of cyber activities constitute acts of aggression. Creating international cybersecurity peace treaties may require changes in Internet governance that promote stronger control by national governments.

Policy makers need to remember that cybersecurity is not a domestic issue and the federal government must engage with partners abroad. The United States currently does not have a formal policy or framework for working with foreign partners on cybersecurity issues. Most of the efforts to date have focused on collaborating on international cybercrime and law enforcement issues.

Identification and Authentication

One important challenge that many organizations face is how to manage electronic identities for users, organizations, and devices. The government must maintain the necessary controls to properly authenticate and authorize users to use federal networks and systems. DHS issued Homeland Security Presidential Directive 12 (HSPD-12) in 2004 that called for a common identification standard for all federal employees and contractors. Previously, the federal government lacked a government-wide standard on the requirements for identification used to access secure government information systems and facilities. HSPD-12 directed NIST to develop a robust federal standard for secure identification that can authenticate individuals electronically. In addition, the directive required all agencies to implement the standard for all federal systems and facilities.

   Identity management is also important for activities such as accessing electronic health records, sending secure e-mail, accessing government services, and banking online. In June 2010 the Obama Administration released the "National Strategy for Trust Identities in Cyberspace" that provided a long-term vision to create a trusted identity system. The purpose of the system is to secure online transactions and better identify and authenticate online users. Although the policy statement does not mandate specific technology, it does highlight the need for strong, interoperable credentials. Currently the United States lags countries such as Estonia that have created a robust electronic ID system for its citizens to use for everything from paying taxes to voting online.

Research, Education, and Training

Many government proposals call for research and development to improve security technology to keep pace with new challenges that are constantly emerging. For example, the "National Strategy to Secure Cyberspace" (2003), calls for the national research agenda to be prioritized to support technology that would improve the security of cyberspace across all sectors. Although much of the publicly funded cybersecurity research comes out of the National Science Foundation (NSF), other organizations, such as the National Institute of Standards and Technology (NIST), the national laboratories and federally funded research and development centers, and the various intelligence agencies fund and sponsor information security research. For example, the Office of Science and Technology Policy (OSTP), with oversight for coordinating research and developing technology to secure critical infrastructure, has been tasked with creating short-, medium-, and long-term recommendations to improve cybersecurity. This includes improving the security of networking protocols on the Internet and the security of supervisory control and data acquisition (SCADA) systems used to monitor and control industrial facilities like factories, power plants, and refineries.

Only recently has the value of research to cybersecurity begun to be appreciated by the federal government, although more work in this area remains. Congress passed the Cybersecurity Research and Development Act in 2002 to increase the amount of funding made available for both applied and academic research in information security. The Act directed the National Science Foundation, in cooperation with other agencies such as NIST and OSTP, to fund research in areas such as cryptography, computer forensics, reliable IT infrastructure, privacy, network security architecture, vulnerability assessments, wireless security, and emerging threats. In addition to providing research grants, the Act also authorized NSF funding to establish multidisciplinary Centers for Computer and Network Security Research at universities throughout the country.

The federal government has long recognized the need to hire and retain well-qualified information security professionals. In 2000 Richard Clarke, the National Coordinator for Security, Infrastructure Protection, and Counter-Terrorism for President Clinton wrote in the *National Plan for Information Systems Protection* that "the most urgently needed, the hardest to acquire, and the sine qua non for all else that we will do, is a cadre of trained computer science/information technology (IT) specialists." In response, the government created a multipronged effort to train and recruit federal IT security personnel. These efforts included completing an occupational study for IT positions in the federal government, training existing federal employees and providing continuing education, creating a security awareness training program for all federal employees, creating a scholarship for service programs to recruit undergraduate and graduate students into federal service, and recruiting high school students to federal employment through federal internship and summer work programs.

The Cybersecurity Research and Development Act also provided funding to improve the cybersecurity workforce. Faced with a limited supply of qualified candidates and heavy competition for recruitment from the private sector, workforce issues have been a challenge for the federal government. To increase the quality and quantity of cybersecurity professionals, the Act authorized grant funding to universities to improve their curriculum and educational opportunities in this area. In addition, it created a competitive grant program for students pursuing graduate degrees in computer or network security to train both future cybersecurity professionals and faculty.

Reforming Current Risk Management Practices

Critics of FISMA argue that its compliance requirements force agencies into a paper-pushing exercise that yields few tangible improvements in the overall cybersecurity posture of the organization. Agencies were previously required to submit reports quarterly. Most of these data submissions came as individual spreadsheets or copies of internal security assessment reports. The Obama administration, led by former federal Chief Information Officer Vivek Kundra, advocated for security programs that continuously and automatically monitor federal systems and networks. In April 2010, the Office of Management and Budget released M-10-15, a memo outlining new FISMA reporting requirements for all federal agencies. These included requirements to report data feeds directly from security management tools, provide responses to a set of questions on the security posture of the agency, and respond to agency-specific follow-up interview questions. The new memo also requires agencies to begin reporting this new data on a monthly basis beginning in January 2011.

The federal CIO also created "CyberScope," an online reporting tool to facilitate data collection and reporting. CyberScope allows any of the more than 600 different users from the federal agencies to submit data on their security and privacy programs using a secure web interface. Part of the goal of the CyberScope initiative is to reduce the reporting costs for cybersecurity so more resources can be directed to securing systems rather than compliance. OMB estimates that FISMA's certification and accreditation process costs the federal government $1.3 billion annually. Automation should help reduce these expenditures. In addition, the OMB (Streufert, 2009) is planning to collect data to establish better performance metrics for cybersecurity investments.

Another goal of collecting data electronically through CyberScope is to more easily facilitate automated analysis of cybersecurity risk assessments, as have been achieved at some model agencies such as the Department of State. The data collected through this program will eventually be fed into a federal cybersecurity dashboard that will provide government leaders with practical intelligence on the state of cybersecurity both government-wide and at individual agencies. The goal of these efforts to streamline data collection and create more automated cybersecurity analytics tools is to drastically reduce the timeframe to collect data, identify threats, and implement remedies.

Conclusion

Cybersecurity remains uncharted territory. While significant progress has been made, one of the core underlying issues is that organizations still cannot accurately measure risk. Without a clear measure of risk, appropriate mitigation strategies cannot be taken. And without an accurate measurement of risk, good security practices often go unrewarded while bad security practices go unpunished. In the current environment, consumers are more likely to purchase a product based on the reputation of the vendor rather than on the level of security the product actually provides. Developing an improved understanding of risk will help put market forces to work by encouraging the private sector to develop better cybersecurity products and reward innovation.

In regard to cybersecurity, the federal government is clearly ahead of where it was a few decades ago. Today, agencies understand the importance of risk management and have dedicated significant resources to secure government information systems, including hiring and training information security professionals, developing security policies and procedures, and providing user education. But problems with implementation persist at many agencies. As the federal government takes on more responsibility to develop strong cybersecurity practices internally and in the private sector, this problem may increase.

In addition, the threat landscape is changing and government must adopt flexible policies to address these challenges. Although the initial reaction in government is sometimes to simply prohibit disruptive new technologies, like mobile phones or social networking sites, that break existing security models, a long-term prohibition on progress is not possible or advisable. Instead, public sector managers should seek creative solutions that balance productivity and convenience with the appropriate level of security. Future federal cybersecurity efforts must address emerging threats based on the changing nature of information technology such as the growth of cloud computing, a ubiquitous mobile Internet, and the emergence of the "Internet of Things." For example, what new risks will emerge once IPv6 is more widely deployed and every device on the planet, including weapons, has an IP address?

Many policy debates remain unresolved. One of the central questions is whether cybersecurity should fall principally under the domain of the Department of Defense or the Department of Homeland Security. Although the military, intelligence, and homeland security agencies would all prefer to have greater control over cybersecurity, a strong case could be made for locating the majority of the cybersecurity policymaking in the Department of Commerce: long-term, information security will only improve through market-driven innovation that benefits government, businesses, and consumers. Cybersecurity is an arms race between the good guys and the bad guys; to prevail, the government should renew its commitment to funding cybersecurity research and development. Moreover, most IT products have the same security profile regardless of whether the user is in government or the private sector. The same is true within government where the distinction and requirements between intelligence and nonintelligence systems do not differ substantially.

More broadly, efforts should continue to update a coordinated strategic plan to secure cyberspace and mitigate the threats to national security, ensure reliable systems, foster innovation, and protect citizens. The United States should continue to build a coordinated response to cybersecurity threats, both between the public and private sectors and between the United States and foreign partners. Cybersecurity does not start or end at the border, but instead requires a global framework for monitoring, detecting, and responding to cyber incidents.

Many challenges and uncertainties remain, but one thing is clear: more work remains to be done.

References

"2009 Internet Crime Report," Internet Crime Complaint Center (IC3), 2009, http://www.ic3.gov/media/annualreport/2009_IC3Report.pdf.

Atkinson, R. D., S. Ezell, S. M. Andes, D. Castro, and R. Bennett, "25 Years After .com," (The Information Technology and Innovation Foundation, Washington, DC: 2010), http://www.itif.org/files/2010-25-years.pdf.

"CDW-G Federal Cybersecurity Report: Danger on the Front Lines," November 2009, CDW Government, Inc. http://webobjects.cdw.com/webobjects/media/pdf/Newsroom/2009-CDWG-Federal-Cybersecurity-Report-1109.pdf.

Computer Security Act of 1987, http://csrc.nist.gov/groups/SMA/ispab/documents/csa_87.txt.

"Critical Infrastructure Protection: Key Private and Public Cyber Expectations Need to Be Consistently Addressed," GAO-10-628, Government Accountability Office, July 2010.

"Critical Infrastructure Protection: Progress Coordinating Government and Private Sectors Efforts Varies by Sectors' Characteristics," GAO-07-39, Government Accountability Office, October 2006, http://www.gao.gov/new.items/d0739.pdf.

"Cybersecurity: Progress Made But Challenges Remain in Defining and Coordinating the Comprehensive National Initiative," GAO-10-338.

Cyberspace Policy Review, http://www.whitehouse.gov/assets/documents/Cyberspace_Policy_Review_final.pdf.

"FY 2010 Reporting Instructions for the Federal Information Security Management Act and Agency Privacy Management," April 21, 2010, OMB, http://www.whitehouse.gov/sites/default/files/omb/assets/memoranda_2010/m10-15.pdf.

Gorman, S., "U.S. Backs Talks on Cyber Warfare," June 4, 2010, *Wall Street Journal*, http://online.wsj.com/article/SB10001424052748703340904575284964215965730.html.

Hildreth, S. A., "Cyberwarfare," Congressional Research Service, June 19, 2001.

http://www.pcworld.com/article/174241/study_us_govt_cybersecurity_spending_to_grow_significantly.html

http://www.informationweek.com/news/government/security/showArticle.jhtml?articleID=224000297.

Lynn III,W.J.,"Defending a New Domain,"Foreign Affairs, September/October 2010, http://www.foreignaffairs.com/articles/66552/william-j-lynn-iii/defending-a-new-domain.

"National Plan for Information Systems Protection," 2000, 5, http://www.fas.org/irp/offdocs/pdd/CIP-plan.pdf.

"National Security Decision Directive Number 145," September 17, 1984, http://www.fas.org/irp/offdocs/nsdd145.htm.

"Network and Information Security: Proposal for a European Policy Approach," Commission of the European Communities, June 6, 2001, http://www.justice.gov/criminal/cybercrime/intl/netsec_comm.pdf.

Presidential Decision Directive/NSC-63 Critical Infrastructure Protection, May 22, 1998, http://www.fas.org/irp/offdocs/pdd/pdd-63.htm.

"Security of the Internet," in *The Froehlich/Kent Encyclopedia of Telecommunications* vol. 15. Marcel Dekker, New York, 1997, 231–255. Available at: http://www.cert.org/encyc_article/tocencyc.html.

"Seventeen Agencies and Organizations United Under One Goal,"Intelligence.gov (accessed August 1, 2010).

Streufert, J., "Measure More, Spend Less on the Way to Better Security," November 12, 2009, http://csrc.nist.gov/groups/SMA/ispab/documents/minutes/2009-12/metrics_jstreufert.pdf.

"Telework 2010: Telework in the Federal Government," FedScoop, 2010, http://www.fedscoop.com/pdf/telework-2010.pdf.

The National Strategy to Secure Cyberspace, 2003.

7

EUROPEAN CYBERSECURITY POLICY*

NEIL ROBINSON

Contents

---

* Noting as an illustration of how fast things can change in this area, in the months since this was written, the European Commission released a new communication on critical information infrastructure protection—"Achievements and Next Steps: Toward Global Cyber Security" (COM 163).

Introduction

Half of all European growth in productivity is currently driven by
information and communications technology (ICT) and this trend is
expected to accelerate, according to the Digital Agenda, the European
Union (EU) strategy on how to leverage technology to support economic growth. But the Digital Agenda also identifies the unintended
consequences of a digital economy: spam accounts for 80% to 90%
of all e-mails in circulation globally, identity theft and online fraud
both continue to grow, and there are increasingly complex types of
cyberspace threats that are often motivated by financial purposes.
According to EurActiv, an online information provider dedicated to
EU affairs, in early 2010 the European Commission estimated that
the costs of cybercrime for the EU are €750 billion annually, greater
than the costs of drug trafficking and roughly equivalent to 1% of
global gross domestic product (GDP). As a result, the Digital Agenda
highlights the need for further EU action in regard to Internet trust
and security, one of seven policy priority areas for the region.

Protecting cyberspace is a complex task as it bestrides multiple
public policy domains, including criminal justice, technology, standardization, cooperation, research and development, and market regulation. Cybersecurity also requires active participation of a
range of stakeholders across the public and private sectors, as well as

individuals. But addressing the challenge of cybersecurity in the EU, a community of over 600 million people in 27 different countries is especially complicated as various organizations and institutions at the national and regional levels make policy efforts difficult to harmonize. The main European institutions with respect to understanding EU policy, however, are the European Commission (EC), Council of Ministers (Council of the European Union), European Network and Information Security Agency (ENISA), and the European Police Agency (Europol). The EC is represented by the European Parliament, which also represents the views of European citizens and holds the executive power (often referred to as "Guardian of the Treaties"). The Council of Ministers represents governments and is the main decision-making authority while organizations such as ENISA and Europol are separate agencies or institutions.

In addressing cybersecurity, European Community Communication 251 (2006) adopted what it termed a "three-pronged approach" that covers

- Specific measures relating to Network and Information Security (NIS), defined by the EC as "the ability of a network or an information system to resist, at a given level of confidence, accidental events or malicious actions that compromise the availability, authenticity, integrity and confidentiality of stored or transmitted data and the related services offered by or accessible via these networks and systems"
- The regulatory framework for electronic communications
- The fight against cybercrime

European cybersecurity policy focuses on the domains of network and information security and cybercrime. Crucially, due to the complex historical, geopolitical, and institutional construct of the EU and member states, military responses to cybersecurity are not dealt with. This is an area of competence that remains outside of the purview of the EU. Other organizations, specifically the North Atlantic Treaty Organization (NATO), have been more active in this area with the formation of the Co-operative Cyber-Defence Centre of Excellence in Estonia and inclusion of defense against cyber attack as part of NATO's New Strategic Concept at the Lisbon Summit in November 2010. The military aspects of addressing cybersecurity are seen as increasingly important with the

United States, United Kingdom, France, Germany, and Sweden all working on doctrine for how to deploy military force in cyberspace.

This chapter will first describe relevant European organizations involved in cybersecurity, followed by details on various *normative* (i.e., rules that set out what ought to happen) EU laws and regulations. Although EU law, action plans, initiatives, and communications account for one side of the story, it is increasingly noted that the key to successfully tackling cybersecurity is partnership and a strong implementation of initiatives. Partnership, dialogue, multilateralism, and multistakeholder approaches are now constant characteristics of EU policy in the field of cybersecurity. The weight being given to proposing new laws compared to strengthening implementation is perhaps most starkly observed in the EU's Digital Agenda. Out of the 100 actions proposed, only 31 are legislative (i.e., revolve around the drafting or modification of EU legislation).

Institutions

This section provides an overview of the main organizations with respect to the formulation of European cyberspace policy. The main executive and legislative institutions are described along with a summary of what was until late 2009 a unique "pillar structure" to policy areas in the EU, which is of significant impact with respect to cybersecurity policy.

The European Commission: "Engine-Room" of European Union Policy

Roughly analogous to a national-level civil service, the European Commission (EC) is an apolitical executive body responsible for much of the preparation, implementation, and monitoring of European policy. The European Commission proposes legislation that is then submitted to the Council of Ministers and European Parliament for approval. The EC is composed of a number of Directorates-General (DGs), the European equivalent of U.S. Secretaries, with responsibilities for various policy areas, or portfolios. For purposes of this chapter, the main portfolios for cybersecurity are the DG Information Society and Media and the DG Home Affairs.

DG Information Society and Media is primarily technically orientated and concerned with the use of ICTs across the public and private sectors, as well as citizen usage. Its portfolio includes telecommunications regulation, promoting the uptake of ICT in society for economic and social benefits and regulatory policy governing the ICT market. It is also responsible for a considerable applied technical and scientific research and development (R&D) budget. In relation to cybersecurity, DG Information Society and Media includes policy desks looking at Network and Information Security (NIS). The work is mainly of a technical nature, for example, investigating security risks inherent in specific technologies, use of risk management to promote Critical Infrastructure Protection (CIP), or whether the market for ICT security products and services is sufficiently vibrant. The DG is also concerned with user awareness regarding cyberspace risks and digital literacy education and training.

The second DG of relevance is DG Home Affairs, which with respect to cybersecurity has responsibility for two significant policy areas, namely cybercrime and critical infrastructure protection. In the cybercrime area, the DG monitors the implementation of rules and policies using criminal law to address the misuse of cyberspace. With regard to critical infrastructure protection the DG introduces measures to improve the resilience and protection of national and European critical infrastructure, including for the ICT sector. The EC continue to note that the consequences of damage to infrastructures across two or more member states provides a clear rationale for EU-level intervention.

The EC also plays an active role in international discussions, such as at the Organization for Economic Cooperation and Development (OECD), Council of Europe, and the United Nations. For example, according to Communication 181, the EU made an especially strong case for the availability, reliability, and security of networks and information at the UN-organized World Summit on the Information Society (WSIS) in Tunis in 2005. This furthered the policy debate regarding the need to continue the fight against cybercrime and spam while protecting privacy and freedom of expression. The need for a common international understanding of NIS was also identified at this meeting, as was the importance of collecting and sharing security-related information and best practices regarding countermeasures.

The European Council of Ministers: National Governments

The second major institution of importance in European policy regarding cybersecurity is the Council of the European Union, also known as the Council of Ministers. Every 6 months, an EU member state assumes the role of the presidency of the Council on a rotating basis. The Council is the major decision-making body of the European Union. It is made up of 27 ministers (one for each member state) who represent different national ministries depending on the specific policy being discussed (e.g., agriculture, police, criminal justice, etc.). The Council effectively represents the relevant department(s) in each member state with specific responsibility for particular issues. The member state in charge of the rotating presidency has a degree of latitude about which issues are going to be of interest, called "policy priorities." The priorities are important as they inject added policy impetus to selected issues. In 2009, for example, the Czech Presidency supported a major conference on Critical Information Infrastructure Protection, due in no small part to a sustained cyber attack that Estonia suffered a year earlier.

The European Network and Information Security Agency: Middleware of European Cybersecurity Policy

Unlike the EC or the Council, the European Network and Information Security Agency (ENISA) is a European Community agency of the EU. This means it has a greater degree of independence in its activities than, for example, the EC that must negotiate with member states to get policies implemented.

Based in Crete, Greece, ENISA is an intermediary or "policy middleware" between the EU, specifically the European Commission and member states, and the private sector. Effective information security, it was recognized, can contribute toward the smooth functioning of the EU's internal market.* Hence, ENISA's mission is to foster a

---

* Regulation (EC) No 460/2004 of the European Parliament and of the Council of March 10, 2004, establishing the European Network and Information Security Agency. A "European Community agency" is a body set up by the EU to carry out a specific technical, scientific, or management task within the "Community domain" ("first pillar") of the EU. These agencies are not provided for in the treaties. Instead, each one is set up by an individual piece of legislation that specifies the task of that particular agency.

culture of network and information security for the benefit of citizens, consumers, and public and private sector organizations alike. Although its specific role is under review as of this writing in early 2011, ENISA currently acts both as a Centre of Excellence for NIS, with its "customers" being the European Commission and EU member states, and to further cooperation with the business community in order to help the private sector address cybersecurity.

ENISA achieves its objectives by undertaking a variety of tasks, mainly revolving around the provision of advice and assistance to the European Commission and member states on addressing security-related issues in hardware and software; collecting and analyzing data on security incidents in Europe and emerging risks; promoting risk assessment and risk management methods; and raising awareness and stimulating cooperation between public and private sector actors, such as the development of public–private partnerships (PPPs) in this area.

ENISA is headed by an executive director and has a management board and a Permanent Stakeholders Group (PSG) consisting of representatives from relevant groups such as ICT industry, user organizations, and academic experts in cyberspace. In regard to NIS, ENISA is currently undertaking three major areas of work:

- Supporting policy cooperation between member states in the European Forum for Member States (EFMS) and the European Public–Private Partnership for Resilience (EP3R)
- Providing expertise and assistance regarding the implementation of the security measures in the revised Regulatory package for Telecommunications
- Contributing to cybersecurity preparedness exercises and provision of technical support for the establishment of a Computer Emergency Response Team (CERT) for the EU institutions and a European-wide network of CERTs

When an evaluation of ENISA was carried out in 2007, Communication 285 noted that although significant problems existed with the agency, there were positive aspects of its operation despite limited resources.

Given the expiry of ENISA's official remit in March 2009, a regulation to extend the existing legal mandate and budget of ENISA until 2012 was adopted by the European Council and the Parliament in September 2008, according to Regulation 1007. At that time, the then Commissioner for DG Information Society and Media, Mrs. Viviane Reding, called upon both the Council and the European Parliament to open an "intense debate on Europe's approach to network security and how to deal with cyber attacks" and that the future role of ENISA should be included in these deliberations. ENISA's legal mandate is thus undergoing change and, as of early 2011, its tasks and objectives are likely to evolve further.

At the end of September 2010, the EC made public a proposal to strengthen and modernize ENISA. The EC hopes that by giving ENISA a broader range of tasks, the EU, member states, and the private sector will be better supported in the development of their capabilities to prevent, detect, and respond to cybersecurity challenges. In effect, the proposal contains two legal initiatives: a relatively uncontroversial recommendation to extend its current legal mandate and budget by a year and a half but also a new legal mandate assigning ENISA important new areas of responsibility, greater flexibility, and increased budget. This unusual approach recognizes the need for debate among the Council and the Parliament but risks a legal vacuum if the new mandate is not formally adopted before the current one expires in 2012.

The proposed terms mean that ENISA will become the catalyst for a more coordinated European fight against cybercrime by including representatives from the law enforcement community, judiciary, and European data protection and privacy commissioners. This constitutes a major step forward as it brings together (at least operationally) the discrete and largely separate policy portfolios of DG Information Society and DG Home Affairs. Some characteristics of this new set of roles include

- Greater flexibility, adaptability, and capability to focus on emerging issues relating to cybersecurity
- Better alignment of the Agency to the EU regulatory process, providing countries and institutions with assistance and advice
- Action by the Agency in taking into account the network and information security aspects of the fight against cybercrime

- Strengthened governance structure through a stronger supervisory role of the Management Board, in which the EU Member States and the European Commission are represented
- Simplification of procedures to improve efficiency
- Gradual increase of the Agency's financial and human resources

The 2010 proposal indicates that ENISA would assume a broader range of tasks to permit a more dynamic response to the changing requirements of risks in cyberspace. Such tasks include regular assessments on the state of NIS in Europe and the provision of assistance to the EU and member states in promoting the use of risk management and good security practices and standards for electronic products, systems, and services.

Europol—Criminal Intelligence Regarding Cybercrime

With a remit to collect and analyze criminal activity regarding organized transnational crime affecting member states, the role of Europol, the European Policing Organization set up in 1999 in The Hague, cannot be ignored. In June 2010 a meeting was held at Europol Headquarters where it was decided to establish the European Union Cybercrime Task Force. This meeting was attended by representatives from law enforcement cybercrime units from across the member states and also officials from Eurojust (an EU agency supporting judicial cooperation across the Union) and the European Commission. Participants discussed operational and strategic issues on cybercrime investigations, prosecutions, and cross-border cooperation as well as information exchange, case studies, new criminal trends, criminal modus operandi, legal constraints, and the role of the private sector as well as provision of police and criminal justice training.

As a result of this meeting, the subsequently established European Cybercrime Platform includes the Internet Crime Reporting System (ICROS), the Analysis Work File (AWF), a support system for crimes related to the Internet, and an Expert Forum that hosts technical data and police training. The intent of the European Cybercrime Platform, as described by Europol's 2010 to 2014 Strategy, is for it to serve as a reporting point, receiving national-level reports and statistics about the prevalence of cyber-crime in each member state and aggregating them to find trends. Ultimately, it is hoped that the European Cybercrime Platform will be part of a proposed European Cybercrime Center, which was first described in the Conclusions of the Spanish Presidency in April 2010. Specifically, it was proposed as part of a strategy to cope more effectively with crimes committed by means of electronic networks. An essential element of the facilitation of information in this regard would be undertaken by the European Cybercrime Platform, as described above. Longer-term actions for the Center proposed by the Council in April included

- Ratification by the European Union of the Council of Europe Cybercrime Convention
- Improvement of training standards of law enforcement and those in the criminal justice system to better deal with cyber-crime investigations
- Encouragement of information sharing between police authorities of the member states
- An assessment of the fight against cybercrime in the EU and member states in order to achieve a better understanding of trends and developments
- Adoption of a common approach in respect to international collaboration, for example, regarding revocation of Domain Name and Internet Protocol (IP) addresses
- Promotion of harmonization of different contact points, such as those of the G8 Hi-Tech Crime community and Interpol

The Council asked the European Commission to draw up a feasibility study on the possibility of the establishment of the European Cyber Crime Center to carry out these activities. It asked that this feasibility study should include arrangements for budgeting and whether it should be located within Europol.

In late 2010, Europol was known to be working on a first version of a threat assessment regarding cybercrime known as iOCTA (Internet facilitated organized crime threat assessment). As of early 2011, no further details have yet been released regarding this assessment, but the analytical capabilities involved are relevant in the establishment of any forthcoming European Cyber Crime Center. Coincidentally,

Europol was assigned the status of a full EU agency in 2010, meaning it has increased powers to request the provision of criminal intelligence from member states but also subject to increased budgetary control by the European Parliament.

The (Former) Pillars of European Policymaking and the New Structure

This section concludes by summarizing the unique pillar structure of the EU, which up until recently saw different sets of rules apply to different policies relating to cybersecurity, depending upon whether they were concerned with matters in the "Internal Market" or "Police and Criminal Justice Co-operation."

Until the entry into force of the Treaty of the EU (TEU) and Treaty of the Functioning of the EU (TFEU) in December 2009, EU policy was based on a "pillar" structure, the result of the evolution of heavily negotiated compromises based in the origins of the European Project in the European Coal and Steel Community (ECSC). The "First Pillar" (the Internal Market) provided the basis for the creation and imposition of common European regulations across the member states, to propose regulatory intervention in, for example, the areas of competition, private international law, and consumer rights. The objective of such intervention was to remove barriers to free trade within and between the member states. Policy in the "Second Pillar" included areas of EU organizational machinery and the governance of the institutions, such as the powers for the European Court of Auditors. The "Third Pillar" was an area of EU competence in which, formerly, power was placed in an Intergovernmental Council of the EU. This was because policies relating to interior affairs (such as criminal justice, law enforcement, and so on) was not originally seen as an area of specific EU competence (i.e., that warranted direct EU intervention using consistent European-wide rules) due to broad differences between legal, cultural, and social norms in the member states. However, this has now changed under the Treaty of the European Union (the Lisbon Treaty). Title V of the Treaty of the Functioning of the European Union (TFEU) that entered into force on December 1, 2009, brings these areas back into the competence of the EU, under an Area for Freedom, Security and Justice (AFSJ):

The Union shall constitute an area of freedom, security and justice with respect for fundamental rights and the different legal systems and traditions of the Member States.

In practice, this means that legislation in this area can now be adopted by a smaller majority (two-thirds) of the European Council and the European Parliament and it is no longer possible for a single country to block a proposal. Furthermore, in monitoring the implementation of EU law, the European Commission will have greater powers to refer cases of noncompliance of the member states to the European Court of Justice.

Nonetheless, in order to place the different policy initiatives in their appropriate context, an appreciation of the pillar structure is important because the TFEU remains relatively recent and most policy initiatives in this area are a result of this unique arrangement.

Instruments: Normative Law and Policy

A number of European policy initiatives on cybersecurity have been launched over the last 10 years. They take the form of non-binding Communications, Action Plans, and Strategies, or legislation, such as Framework Decisions, Directives, or directly binding Regulations. But they generally stem from a wider context of the formulation of strategies setting out how Europe can make the most of ICTs in economic and societal growth. These may be part of much broader plans describing strategic global-level objectives for Europe.

The Digital Agenda initiative, for example, aims to provide sustainable economic and societal benefits from a single digital market. It is the first of seven "flagship initiatives" to be released, making up the overarching Europe 2020 strategy. Europe 2020 is about three things: "smart, sustainable and inclusive growth." The Digital Agenda for Europe is a horizontal initiative and lays out key actions in seven areas regarding how Europe can maximize the benefits of ICTs. These are a vibrant digital single market, interoperability and standards, trust and security, fast and ultrafast Internet access, research and innovation, enhancing digital literacy and skills, and finally ICT-enabled benefits for EU society.

Given that lack of security and trust is seen as a major barrier to the widespread uptake of ICTs by European citizens, it is also an obstacle to growth. For example, a consumer survey conducted by the UK's Office of Fair Trading (OFT) in 2009 identified that a third of Internet users are not shopping online with the lack of trust being identified as the biggest reason. The two most relevant policy areas in this regard are Network and Information Security (NIS) and the fight against cybercrime. This section looks at the salient initiatives and policies in both areas.

Network and Information Security (NIS) Policy

The *Network and Information Security: Proposal for a European Policy Approach* was a response to a request from the European Council, in March 2001, for the development of "a comprehensive strategy on security of electronic networks including practical implementing rules." The initiative set out seven main policy efforts and indicated how NIS policy initiatives relate to two other important domains: the existing telecommunications and data protection regulatory framework and policy concerning cybercrime. The Communication proposed a number of measures:

- Raise awareness through the launch of public information and education campaigns as well as promotion of best practices
- Strengthen Computer Emergency Response Teams (CERTs) to establish a European Warning and Information System and subsequent examination of how to organize data collection, analysis, and planning of predictive responses to emerging cybersecurity threats
- Promote funding of cybersecurity research and development support within the EU's official scientific research funding
- Further facilitate market-based mechanisms to support standardization and certification including the acceleration of work on interoperability, support for electronic signatures, and further development of the next generation of IP technology (IPv6)

- Establish an inventory of legal measures regarding cybersecurity taken by member states in accordance with EU law, and propose legislation on cybercrime
- Promote effective and interoperable security solutions in e-government and e-procurement activities and incorporate e-signatures in any future e-government activities
- Reinforce international dialogue on NIS

Strategy for a Safe and Secure Information Society 2006

In the *Strategy for a Safe and Secure Information Society: Dialogue, Partnership and Empowerment*, the European Commission presented its ideas for how risks to the emerging information society would be addressed. The strategy identified that NIS represented a complex policy challenge requiring cooperation and coordination between the public and private sectors. In addition to a widespread culture of security, the strategy argued that a secure information society must also be based on enhancing NIS. A dynamic and integrated approach was proposed based on dialogue, partnership, and empowerment. According to the strategy, this would be an open and inclusive multi-stakeholder dialogue across the public and private sectors.

The strategy proposed to benchmark national NIS-related policies and identify best practices to improve awareness among small and medium-sized enterprises (SMEs) and citizens. This strategy also urged governments, the private sector, and research and academia involved to participate in a structured multistakeholder debate focusing on the need to strike "an appropriate societal balance between security and the protection of fundamental rights" (p. 8).

ENISA, meanwhile, was asked to develop a partnership with member states and other relevant parties and to develop an appropriate data collection framework to enable the collection of useful data on cybersecurity risks and vulnerabilities. Member states and the research community were also invited to join in a strategic partnership together to ensure that data on the ICT security industry was available in addition to evolving market trends for ICT security products and services. ENISA was also asked to examine the feasibility of a European Information Sharing and Alert System to support a more effective response to threats to information infrastructures.

The Commission recommended that the member states participate in proposed benchmarking activities; promote, in close cooperation with ENISA, awareness-raising campaigns on the benefits of security; leverage the e-government services to communicate and promote good security practices; and stimulate the development of NIS programs as part of higher education curricula. The private sector was invited to, among other things, develop an appropriate definition of responsibilities for software producers and Internet Service Providers (ISPs) in relation to the provision of adequate and reliable and auditable levels of security; promote diversity, openness, interoperability, usability, and competition as key drivers for security; stimulate the deployment of security-enhancing products, processes, and services to prevent and fight ID theft and other "privacy intrusive" attacks; disseminate good security practices across a range of relevant organizations (e.g., SMEs or network operators); provide training programs for security personnel; work toward affordable security certification schemes for products, processes, and services that address EU-specific needs; and, involve the insurance sector for the development of appropriate risk management tools and methods to tackle ICT-related risks and foster a culture of risk management in organizations and businesses (in particular SMEs).

The European Council endorsed this strategy, publishing its Resolution on the Strategy (2007/ C68/01).

European Programme on Critical Infrastructure Protection

European policy concerning Critical Infrastructure Protection (CIP) is based on the 2007 European Programme on Critical Infrastructure Protection (EPCIP). The purpose of this program, like the Stockholm Programme (see below) in the context of the former Third Pillar, was to set out key actions that Europe needed to take in respect to the protection of critical infrastructures, of which cyberspace is generally regarded as but one example. EPCIP focuses on motivated attacks as well as on the implications of accidents and natural disasters. The Programme has three main tasks: first, the creation of broad measures across all CIP areas; second, the protection of European critical infrastructures and reduction of their vulnerability; and third, the establishment of a national framework to assist EU countries in the protection of their National Critical Infrastructures. The EPCIP program includes a number of associated proposed European rules and regulations, the most important of which include setting up a procedure for identifying and designating European critical infrastructure in addition to developing a common approach to assessing the need to protect such infrastructure (to be implemented by a proposed EU Directive on identification of European critical infrastructures); actions to establish a Critical Infrastructure Warning Network (CIWN); Critical Infrastructure Protection expert groups at EU level and the establishment of information-sharing processes and identification and analysis of interdependencies.

Communication on Critical Information Infrastructure Protection (CIIP) 2009

March 2009 saw the publication of a Communication from the European Commission on Critical Information Infrastructure Protection (CIIP): COM 2009 (149). The objectives were to protect Europe from large-scale cyber attacks and disruptions, promote a culture of security and resilience, and tackle cyber attacks and disruptions from a systematic perspective. The means outlined in the strategy included enhancement of the CIIP preparedness and response capability in the EU, promotion of the adoption of adequate and consistent levels of preventative, detection, emergency, and recovery measures in the member states and foster international cooperation, particularly on Internet stability and resilience. The proposed approach to achieve the objectives was fourfold: to build on national and private sector initiatives, engage the public and private sectors, adopt an all-hazards approach (including natural events and manmade accidents as well as cyber attack) and remain multilateral, open, and inclusive.

In addition to the threat posed by cyber attacks, this Communication identified the role of cyberspace in European infrastructure security and its associated vulnerabilities. The Communication also had a number of more specific objectives, namely the fostering of cooperation and exchange of good policy practices between member states, development of a European-level public–private partnership on the security and resilience of Critical Information Infrastructures; enhancement of incident response capability across the EU; promotion of national and pan-European–level exercises on simulated large-scale network security incidents; and finally, the reinforcement of international cooperation on global issues, specifically resilience and stability of the Internet. The action plan that accompanied this Communication was thus made up of several strands: preparedness and prevention, detection and response, mitigation and recovery, and international cooperation. Finally, the Communication set out objectives to establish criteria to identify European Critical Infrastructures in the ICT sector.

The subsequent *Council Resolution on a collaborative European approach to Network and Information security* [2009/C 321/01] formally adopted the approach described in the Communication on CIIP alongside calling for further development of ENISA into a more efficient body and increasing its available resources.

European Public Private Partnership for Resilience (EP3R)

As described in the Communication on Critical Information Infrastructure Protection in 2009 the European Public Private Partnership for Resilience (EP3R) was created following a Resolution from the European Council on *A collaborative European approach to Network and Information Security*. According to a nonpaper on EP3R, this endorsed a multistakeholder approach to cybersecurity, the main objectives of which are

- Provide a platform for sharing information and policy practices in order to foster a common understanding of the economic and market dimensions of security and resilience in the context of CIIP as well as on the roles and responsibilities of public and private stakeholders
- Discuss public policy priorities, objectives, and measures with a view to define appropriate conditions and socioeconomic incentives to improve the coherence and coordination of policies for security and resilience in Europe
- Identify and promote the adoption of good baseline practices for security and resilience, with a view to pursue minimum security and resilience standards and coordinated risk assessment approaches

EP3R is based on four key principles:

- Complementarity: EP3R should build upon, complement, and leverage the existing national public–private initiatives while respecting national responsibility
- Trust: EP3R should provide the structure, processes, and environment for trusted collaboration, including the protection of sensitive information from disclosure
- Value: emphasis on exchanges between public and private sector participants and providing value for both governments and industry. EP3R should aim to deliver concrete results
- Openness: open to all stakeholders contributing to the security and resilience of CIIPs, balancing the need for a high degree of representation with the potential for a higher number of participants to lower the level of trust

Nonetheless, private sector participants involved in this process identified that the necessity to establish practical and appropriate structures, rules, and processes for E3PR would play an important role in its effectiveness.

European Forum for Member States

The European Forum for Member States (EFMS) is a counterpart to the EP3R and was another part of the Action Plan implementing the Communication on CIIP from March 2009. EFMS and the EP3R are meant to be complementary. The EFMS is meant to include representatives of national public authorities with responsibility for NIS and CIIP policy in their respective country. The objective and basic principles revolve around the sharing of information and good policy practices on security and resilience of Critical Information Infrastructures between Member States. As such, it is only open to official government representatives.

Revised Regulatory Framework for Telecommunications 2009 (Framework Directive)

As a result of an Amending Act to the *2002 Directive on a Common Regulatory Framework for Electronic Communications and Services*, a new set of rules governing telecommunications were adopted in late 2009. The Amending Act creates a consistent pan-European policy on telecommunications infrastructures, measures to prohibit market dominance and discrimination and the protection of consumers. The Act contained a set of obligations relating to NIS for providers of public e-communications networks. These rules were contained within a new chapter on Security and Integrity of Networks that requires that providers take measures around three domains: implement measures to ensure a level of security appropriate to the risks, prevent and minimize the impact of security incidents on users and connected networks, and finally ensure the continuity of supply of services.

This act goes on to introduce a "breach notification" law in article 13a. This means that providers must provide notification of information security breaches having significant impact on operations and the Competent National Authority, usually the communications regulator in each member state, must inform other EU authorities, ENISA, and the public when appropriate (e.g., if the breach involved customers' personal data). Relevant national governmental agencies are now also required to submit a yearly report to the European Commission and ENISA. The European Commission also reserves the right, after having taken the advice of ENISA, to adopt appropriate "technical implementing measures" to harmonize the implementation of rules in the previous paragraphs, according to article 13a. Article 13b lays out enhanced powers of each Competent Regulatory Authority to monitor and enforce implementation of these rules.

The breach notification obligation received considerable criticism from the European Data Protection Supervisor (EDPS). The EDPS argued that restricting the obligation to providers of electronic communications services missed the point because other organizations, such as "providers of information society services" broadly defined, are more likely to put personal data of individuals at risk and hence breach notification. It also argued that the misuse of personal data would decrease by incentivizing firms rather than penalizing them.

Public Consultation on Future of European Network and Information Security Policy, 2009

At the request of the European Council and European Parliament and in the context of the extension of the mandate of ENISA described previously, between November 2008 and January 2009 the European Commission organized a public consultation on the future of European NIS policy. This received 596 contributions ranging from governmental and public bodies, private citizens, industry associations, individual companies, and academic institutions. Of the more significant comments by respondents to the consultation, the importance of a more coordinated approach was recognized, as was the need to undertake any policy in the context of global cooperation taking advantage of transnational organizations such as the OECD and United Nations. The responses also highlighted the importance of information exchange between relevant organizations in the public and private sectors. ENISA was generally regarded as having a great deal of support as well as links between Computer Emergency Response Teams (CERTs) across Europe.

Chapter on Trust and Security in the Digital Agenda for Europe 2010

NIS and CIIP were identified as secondary objectives within the single chapter on Trust and Security in the 2010 Digital Agenda for Europe (COM 2010(245)). Beginning with the assumption that establishing trust is of utmost importance if the benefits of the Digital Agenda are to be fully exploited, the Chapter on Trust and Security went on to say that "Europeans will not embrace technology they do not trust: the digital age is neither 'big brother' nor 'cyber wild west'" (p. 16).

The Digital Agenda proposed two key actions for the European Commission to undertake. The first included measures aimed at achieving "a reinforced and high level" of NIS, covering the modernization of ENISA, measures to enable faster reactions in the event of cyber attacks and establishing a CERT for EU institutions. The second, by 2010, was to introduce measures to combat cyber attacks against information systems (described below as proposals for a new Framework Directive on attacks against information systems) and the creation of related rules on jurisdiction in cyberspace at European and international levels by 2013. Other actions proposed for European policy makers include

- Establish a European cybercrime platform, to deliver a coherent approach to cybercrime across the European Union by 2012.
- Examine the feasibility of the creation of a European cyber-crime center by 2011.
- Work with global organizations in the public and private sector across the digital and physical domains to conduct internationally coordinated actions against computer-based crime and security attacks.
- Support EU-wide cybersecurity preparedness exercises, starting in 2010.
- Explore the extension of security breach notification provisions in the context of the modernization of the European legal framework regarding personal data protection (currently as described above, breach notifications only apply to providers of e-communications services rather than more broadly "information society service providers").
- Disseminate guidance on how the new telecommunications regulatory framework will apply in the context of the European legal framework regarding privacy and personal data protection (as some have argued that the obligations imposed upon telecommunications providers in respect of NIS may be at odds with their obligations under European law regarding privacy and personal data protection).
- Support the establishment of national reporting points for illegal online content (hotlines) and awareness campaigns on online safety for children as well as foster a multistakeholder dialogue and self-regulation of European and global service providers (e.g., social networking platforms) in regard to the use of such services by minors.

To support the Digital Agenda, member states were asked to

- Establish a well-functioning network of CERTs at the national level covering all of Europe.

- Carry out large-scale attack simulation and test mitigation strategies, in cooperation with the European Commission, starting in 2010.
- Fully implement hotlines for the reporting of offensive and harmful online content including the organization of awareness campaigns on online safety for children, teaching programs for online safety in schools, and encouragement for providers of online services to implement self-regulatory measures regarding online safety for children by 2013.
- Set up or adapt national alert platforms to the European Cyber Crime Platform (ECCP) by 2012.

Policy Responses to Cybercrime

In 2001 the European Commission published a Communication on Creating a Safer Information Society by Improving the Security of Information Infrastructures and Combating Computer-related Crime (COM 2000 (890). It followed a 1998 study presented by the EC at the Tampere Summit of the European Council known as the COMCRIME report. The 2001 Communication concluded that high-tech crime should be included in efforts to agree on common definitions and sanctions for various forms of cross-border crime. The 2001 Communication proposed a number of measures including further introduction of criminal law in the area of high-tech crime. The promotion of specialized computer crime police units was also raised, as was the support for technical training for law enforcement. Finally, this Communication identified the intent to establish an EU forum including law enforcement, service providers, telecommunications operators, data protection authorities, and other interested parties. This forum would have, as its aim, the enhancement of mutual understanding and cooperation at EU level as well as raising awareness of risks relating to online criminal activity, the identification of effective tools and procedures to combat computer crime and the encouragement of further development of early warning and crisis management mechanisms.

European Council Framework Decision on Attacks
against Information Systems, 2005

In 2005 the Framework Decision on Attacks against Information Systems (2005/222/JHA) was published. Broadly, this document sought to approximate, into European law, the Council of Europe Budapest Convention on Cybercrime No. 185 (see below). The stated objective of this Framework Decision was to improve cooperation between judicial and other competent authorities via the approximation of rules relating to criminal law across the member states in the area of attacks against information systems. This was deemed to be the most effective response to address the threat of attacks against information and computer systems.

The Framework Decision was intended to build upon the work performed by other international organizations, such as the Council of Europe's Convention on Cybercrime. Definitions between these two are synchronized to a great extent. Three central criminal offenses are elaborated in the Framework Decision: illegal access to information systems (article 2), illegal system interference (article 3), and illegal data interference (article 4). Member states were required to make provision for such offenses to be punished. The criminal act was defined as having to be intentional. Punishment was required for instigating, aiding, abetting, and attempting to commit any of the offenses listed. Member states were required to transpose the decision within a period of 2 years. In 2008 a report on the implementation of 2005/222/JHA was released by the European Commission. It concluded that a "relatively satisfying degree of implementation" had been achieved despite the fact that transposition of the Framework Decision was still not complete. The European Commission invited those seven member states that, at the time, had not yet communicated their transposition (brought into applicable national law the Framework Decision) to resolve the issue.* Every member state was asked to review their legislation to better suppress attacks against information systems, and the Commission also indicated that given the evolution of cybercrime it was considering new measures as well as

---

* Malta, Poland, Slovakia, and Spain did not respond to the request for information, and the answers from Ireland, Greece, and the United Kingdom were deemed as not possible to allow a review of their level of implementation.

promoting the use of the Council of Europe and Group of 8 Nations (G8) network of contact points to rapidly react to threats involving advanced technology.

Communication from the Commission: Toward a General Policy on the Fight against Cybercrime, 2007

The EU's current general policy governing cybercrime is described in a Communication from the Commission released in 2007. This initiative aimed to achieve a number of objectives relating to establishing policies and harmonizing member state approaches to cybercrime. The policy advocated for the

- Establishment of national cooperation between police and law enforcement authorities regarding cybercrime, starting with the establishment of a high-level expert meeting in 2007 and the possibility of a central EU-level cybercrime point of contact
- Increasing financial support for initiatives aimed at improving training for police and law enforcement regarding dealing with cybercrime cases
- Assistance to public authorities in setting up more effective measures and the allocation of sufficient resources
- Supporting research in this field
- Creation of a conference bringing together law enforcement and the private sector to promote closer cooperation
- Launching public–private sector actions to raise awareness of costs and dangers posed by cybercrime
- Further promoting international cooperation
- Taking action to encourage the ratification of the Council of Europe's Budapest Convention 185 on Cybercrime by the Member States
- Taking action in conjunction with the member states to prevent and fight coordinated and large-scale attacks against national information infrastructures

This communication also noted that measures were needed to address traditional forms of crime facilitated by electronic networks. As a result, it proposed an examination of relevant legislation with a view to the drafting of specific legislation against identity theft, improvement of techniques used to fight fraud and illegal trade on the Internet, and further support for specific sectoral measures such as fighting fraud of noncash means of payment. Other objectives were proposed in respect of illegal content including incitement to terrorism or online pedophilia. Member states were encouraged to devote more resources to disrupting these activities, conclude agreements between them, and improve dialogue regarding procedures to ensure the swift removal of such content once it was reported. The Communication also noted the Commission intended to assess progress on the implementation of these actions and report in due course to the Council and Parliament.

The Stockholm Programme and Associated Commission Action Plan Implementing the Stockholm Programme

The 2009 Stockholm Programme, adopted by the European Council on December 10 to 11, 2009, promotes policies to ensure network and information security and faster EU reactions in the event of cyber attacks. It called for both a modernized ENISA and a Directive on attacks against information systems (see above). The European Commission Action Plan Implementing the Stockholm Programme was adopted in mid-2010. The Stockholm Programme and its associated Action Plan represent the next multiannual strategic work program to deliver "an Area of Freedom, Security and Justice" across the EU. It is hoped that it will build upon polices established in the predecessor Tampere (2000 to 2005) and Hague (2005 to 2010) Programmes. These initiatives reflect a renewed focus upon the citizen and aims to set out how security policies may be designed to better take account of fundamental rights. The Stockholm Programme contains a number of actions in respect to cybersecurity, mostly revolving around legal instruments regarding cybercrime and critical infrastructure protection.

Proposal for a Directive on Attacks against Information Systems, Repealing Framework Decision 2005/222/JHA, 2010

At the end of September 2010 the European Commission released its proposal for a Framework Directive on Attacks against Information

Systems, specifically dedicated to addressing the threat from botnets. This would amend the 2005 Framework Decision on Attacks
against Information Systems. New legislation is needed, according to the European Commission, because of the rising number of
attacks against information systems across Europe, and the previously
unknown large-scale and dangerous nature of these attacks that have
affected the information systems of banks, the public sector, and even
the military such as with the cyber attacks against Estonia, Georgia,
and the recent retaliation against Paypal, MasterCard, and Visa in
the context of the WikiLeaks case. The 2008 Implementation Report
on the 2005 Framework Decision underlined the emergence of such
threats because botnets remained outside the direct focus of the original legislation. A new Directive would also be able to take advantage of the opportunity presented by the entry into force of the TEU
and TFEU in 2009 to establish new legislation within the AFSJ, as
described earlier. The Proposed Directive will thus retain the current
provisions of the 2005 Framework Decision but now include penal-
ization of tools, such as malicious software or unrightfully obtained
computer passwords, to commit the previously criminalized offenses.
It also introduces criteria regarding aggravating circumstances under
which the minimum penalty of imprisonment is extended. The proposed new Directive would introduce illegal interception of information systems as a criminal offense, bringing European law into
alignment with the Budapest Convention, and improve criminal justice and police cooperation across Europe by strengthening the network of 24/7 contact points by setting a time criteria for responding to
urgent requests. Member states will be required to collect basic statistical data on cybercrimes and the proposed Directive also raises maximum terms of imprisonment of at least 2 years for various offenses,
raising the level of criminal penalties of offenses committed under
aggravating circumstances to a maximum term of at least 5 years.

Examples of Member State Initiatives

Although there is a noted plethora of rules, regulations, and initiatives
at the European level, much of the success or failure of these policies
of course rests with member states and industry, who are responsible
to a greater or lesser degree for the successful implementation of these

different initiatives. In addition, member states must deal with military responses to cybersecurity as this remains substantially outside of the purview of the EU and is more a matter of NATO membership. Although distinguishing the difference between cybercrime, cyber terrorism, and cyber war is difficult, much of what is discussed above generally relates to the nonmilitary responses to risks in cyberspace.

The difficulty of implementation of these laws and regulations described above is not necessarily restricted to cybersecurity policies, however. How to improve the implementation of European law is a constant perennial concern of policy makers in Brussels regardless of the policy domain. Notwithstanding this, there are a number of ways that the extensive policies and laws can be implemented by member states. This may vary from direct transposition of EU legislation, to member states following guidance and best practice agreed and discussed at the EU level. At its most basic level (and again depending upon the specific legislative form), member states must implement or transpose European legislation into their own national law. Depending on the type of European instrument this may be done with varying degrees of consistency to the original text. For example, a Regulation is directly binding upon member states, whereas a Framework Directive can be transposed with varying degrees of latitude. Law must be implemented usually within a certain time frame. In addition, the European institutions have the opportunity, where they consider that legislation is a blunt instrument, to support or facilitate other "softer" measures such as the provision of guidance or the sharing of best practice, aimed at improving policy responses to certain issues without necessarily getting out the rule book. Some of the most common ways to achieve this are by the participation of member state national representatives (e.g., from law enforcement or cabinet-level national security communities) in working groups or forums hosted by the European Commission. In this aspect, the Commission plays the role as facilitator or enabler of a platform for the improvement of the implementation of EU policy.

The remainder of this section illustrates how three EU member states approached these issues in regard to cybersecurity. In 2009 the United Kingdom published its National Cyber-Security Strategy that is due to be updated at the end of 2011. In early 2011 France and the Netherlands followed suit with the release of their respective cyber-security strategies. The publication of these national strategies was welcomed by ENISA that had previously articulated the need for a holistic approach to addressing cybersecurity through the sharing of information, implementation of good practices and national exercises, as well as the establishment of national CERTs and improvement of cooperation between national CERTs across Europe to combat national, pan-European, or even global incidents and threats. Speaking at the first Critical Information Infrastructure Protection International Conference in Madrid in February 2010, ENISA's Executive Director, Dr. Udo Helmbrecht, stressed the importance of holistic national strategies that should also form an integral part of an overall EU cybersecurity strategy.

In France, ANSSI (Agence Nationale de la Sécurité des Systèmes d'Information) was established in July 2009 as an agency charged with addressing the challenges faced by cybersecurity. The formation of this agency grew out of the French White Paper on Defence and National Security, published in 2008, which identified cyber attacks as one of the main threats to the national territory. The prevention and reaction to cyber attacks were also identified as major priorities in the organization of national security. The agency is attached to the Secretary General for National Defence and replaces the Central Directorate for Information System Security (DCSSI) and is also assigned a wider mission than its predecessor.

The missions of ANSSI are to

- Establish detection and early warning mechanisms for cyber attacks via a stronger operational center, working on a round-the-clock basis and having operational monitoring function for sensitive government networks. The center should also be able to implement appropriate defense mechanisms.
- Reduce vulnerabilities by the establishment of criteria for trusted products and services across the public and private sector.
- Provide advice and intellectual support to government entities and operators of critical infrastructure.
- Administer and manage awareness raising and communication schemes aimed at companies and the wider public to keep them informed about information security threats and related means of protection.

The United Kingdom has a wealth of agencies and organizations involved in its policy approach to cybersecurity. In mid 2009, the Office of Cyber Security (OCS) was revealed, as was the Cyber Security Operations Centre (CSOC) based at the electronic intelligence agency GCHQ. These were described in the "Cyber Security Strategy of the United Kingdom safety, security and resilience in cyber space." Subsequent to the change of administration in May 2010, the OCS was renamed the Office of Cyber Security and Information Assurance (OCSIA), perhaps reflecting a merged mandate to address policy aspects of information assurance, formerly within the remit of the UK Cabinet Office and Central Sponsor for Information Assurance (CSIA). OCSIA and CSOC are charged with taking forward the National Cyber Security strategy and its associated implementation program. The Cyber Security Strategy outlined that in order to address the complex challenges of cybersecurity, a comprehensive approach across government, all organizations and public and international partners must play a role. The strategy is based on a three-pronged approach of reducing risk, exploiting opportunities, and improving knowledge, capabilities, and decision making to support securing the UK's advantage in cyberspace:

- Reducing risk by
  - Reducing the threat of cyber operations by reducing an adversary's motivation and capability
  - Reducing the vulnerability of UK interests to cyber operations
  - Reducing the impact of cyber operations on UK interests
- Exploiting opportunities and knowledge by
  - Gathering intelligence on threat actors
  - Promoting support for UK policies
  - Intervening against adversaries
- Improving knowledge and awareness by
  - Developing doctrine and policy
  - Developing governance and decision making
- Enhancing technical and human capabilities

The OCSIA is the main policy lead for cybersecurity in the United Kingdom and sits within the Cabinet Office. As well as working alongside government departments, such as the Home Office, Ministry of Defence, GCHQ, Communications Electronic Security Group

(CESG), Centre for the Protection of the National Infrastructure (CPNI), and department of Business, Innovation, and Skills (BIS), it supports the Security Minister and helps determine priorities for action in relation to securing cyberspace. OCSIA provides strategic direction and coordinates government action relating to cybersecurity across the United Kingdom. This cross-government program is composed of the following elements:

- Safe, secure, and resilient systems
- Policy, doctrine, legal, and regulatory issues
- Awareness and culture change
- Skills and education
- Technical capabilities and research and development
- Exploitation
- International engagement
- Governance, roles, and responsibilities

The other main organization of note in the United Kingdom is the Centre for the Protection of the National Infrastructure (CPNI). CPNI is responsible for the provision of integrated protective security advice to reduce the vulnerability of the Critical National Infrastructure (CNI) in both the public and private sectors. As such, CPNI has to use "softer" regulatory means to encourage private sector owner-operators of Critical Infrastructure to take their security seriously. Its mandate covers physical, personnel, and electronic security. CPNI is an interdepartmental organization and uses resources from industry, academia, and other government departments and agencies, chiefly the intelligence community, Ministry of Defence, Home Office, and the Serious and Organised Crime Agency.

There are a number of other relevant agencies and government departments worthy of mention, however, including the Serious and Organised Crime Agency (SOCA) that deals with computer crime, identity theft and investigation, and intelligence gathering on cybercrime and the Communications and Electronics Security Group (CESG) which, as the "National technical authority for Information Assurance" provides advice on accreditation of products and services and, via its CLAS Checkmark Scheme, the standard-based framework for cybersecurity consultants.

By contrast, in the Netherlands, the responsibility for cybersecurity rests across both the Ministry of Economic Affairs (MinEZ), which has the job of policy coordination for the use of ICT and is the national point of contact for IT security in general. The Ministry of Interior and Kingdom Relations (MinBZK) is responsible for the security of governmental IT systems and services and also leads efforts to protect the Critical National Infrastructure of the Netherlands.

The National Cyber Security Strategy (NCSS) "Success through cooperation" was released in 2011 and sets out a number of actions lines and priority activities identified by the Dutch Cabinet. As well as laying out that the Netherlands should adopt an integral approach across the public and private sectors, the strategy also required that an adequate and topical threat and risk analysis would be conducted. Furthermore, the strategy outlined that the resilience of Dutch ICT networks would need to be reinforced as well as improvements to the response capacity to deflect ICT disruptions and cyber attacks. Investigation and prosecution of cybercrimes would be intensified. Finally, the Netherlands indicated that it would stimulate research and education into cybersecurity.

The National Infrastructure against Cyber Crime (NICC) was set up modeled on the forerunner to the UK's CPNI, the National Infrastructure Security Co-ordination Centre (NISCC). NICC has as its objectives the bringing together of the public and private sector to exchange information, best practices, and experience in fighting cybercrime. Its focus on cybercrime is thus distinct from CNI (see below). NICC has established information exchange points that receive reports from national intelligence or CERTs (Computer Emergency Response Teams). Plans are underway to establish NICC as a permanent organizational unit within the Dutch Government. NICC is very much based on cooperation models with different sectors and the integration of existing initiatives. NICC's activities include acting as a central contact point; undertaking duties of a reporting point; watching cybersecurity trends; performing monitoring and detection activities; distributing information and undertaking education, warning, development, and knowledge-sharing activities; and finally, surveillance and prevention and termination of cybercrime risks.

NAVI (the National Advisory Centre on Critical Infrastructure) acts to connect government and business to support the protection of the critical physical and digital infrastructure. It issues guidance to those involved in the critical infrastructure requesting advice about protection against malicious disruption.

In many of these approaches, the importance of international cooperation (at the European or global level) is identified and work-streams or specific initiatives developed along these lines. For example, via the representation on the permanent stakeholders group of ENISA and by participation in the pan-European exercises, national governments interact with European policy initiatives. Furthermore, bilateral discussions often take place between countries with shared or similar approaches (e.g., between the United Kingdom and the Netherlands).

Despite this, the multitude of different entities responsible for European "cybersecurity" policy with their wide range of institutional history, focus, and mandate, not to mention the complexity of the different types of instrument (each with different impacts) create a complex environment for member states to understand and in some cases can lead to the fragmentation of links, with some of the less mature countries being unable to understand the bigger picture of who is responsible for what at the European level.

Conclusions

European cybersecurity policy is a maze of communications, conclusions, directives, and regulations. This chapter has provided an overview of relevant EU policy instruments and their substantive content as they relate to the protection of cyberspace.

However, what remains to be seen is the extent to which these normative laws will be effectively implemented: a key concern with any EU-level policy-making effort is that while laws and initiatives and programs may be prepared by the different EU institutions described above, it is at the member state level where the effect is felt in addressing these complex risks, ultimately helping to exploit the economic and social benefits of cyberspace.

Aside from this, the complexity of how Europe addresses these issues is further increased by the different institutional approaches of the organizations involved in public policy in this area, as described above. Experts, academics, and researchers generally agree that successfully addressing risks posed in cyberspace requires a concerted effort between the private sector, business, governments, and the general public. Individuals as private citizens need to keep home computers patched and up to date, as do businesses. Industry, as a provider of security products and services, must also work to make these more secure by reducing bugs and software flaws that can be exploited. Finally, governments have a job to support awareness campaigns, provide advice and guidance, intervene as a last resort where there has been "market failure" to properly address these issues and where cybersecurity takes on the character of a national-level threat, instigate appropriate measures to reduce the threat.

Although it is fair to say that things do move slowly in European policy making, the last 4 years have seen more activity in specific areas relating to cybersecurity. This includes a more sophisticated appreciation at the European policy level of the importance of nonregulatory measures to help the private sector improve levels of security (e.g., by the provision of nonbinding guidance and sharing of best practice) and in specific areas (e.g., exercises and trusted information sharing). However, the different character of each of the policy entities involved in cybersecurity (ranging from the technology market orientated DG Information Society, to the legally DG Home Affairs and agencies like Europol and ENISA) serves to complicate matters further and render this policy landscape somewhat opaque. It should therefore be hoped that the formation of common platforms such as the EU Cybercrime Platform helps to bring a degree of outward-facing coherence to these efforts.

References

Communication from the Commission to the Council, the European Parliament, the European Economic and Social Committee and the Committee of the Regions. "A Strategy for a Secure Information Society—Dialogue, partnership and empowerment" [COM (2006) 251 final].

Communication from the Commission to the Council, the European Parliament, the European Economic and Social Committee and the Committee of the Regions of 6 June 2001: "Network and Information Security: Proposal for a European Policy Approach" [COM (2001) 298 final—not published in the Official Journal].

Communication from the Commission of 12 December 2006 on a European Programme for Critical Infrastructure Protection [COM (2006) 786].

Communication of the European Commission on Critical Information Infrastructure Protection—"Protecting Europe from large scale cyber-attacks and disruptions: Enhancing preparedness, security and resilience."

Communication from the Commission to the European Parliament and the Council on the evaluation of the European Network and Information Security Agency (ENISA), [COM/2007/285].

Communication from the Commission to the European Parliament, the Council and the Committee of the Regions of 22 May 2007—Towards a general policy on the fight against cyber crime: [COM (2007) 267].

Communications from the Commission to the Council, the European Parliament, the European Economic and Social Committee, and the Committee of the Regions. "Strategy for a Secure Information Society–Dialogue, partnership and empowerment" [COM (2006) 251 final].

Cooperative Cyber Defence Centre of Excellence (CCD COE).

Council of Europe ETS No. 185 Convention on cybercrime (Budapest Convention).

Council Resolution on a collaborative approach to Network and Information Security (2009/321/01) 2009.

Creating a Safer Information Society by Improving the Security of Information Infrastructures and Combating Computer-Related Crime COM 2000 (890) 2001.

Directive 2002/21/EC of the European Parliament and of the Council of 7 March 2002 on a common regulatory framework for electronic communications networks and services ("Framework Directive") [See amending acts].

http://www.euractiv.com/en/infosociety/eu-establish-cybercrime-agency-news-486715.

Lynn, W., III. Defending a New Domain Subtitle: The Pentagon's Cyber-strategy; *Foreign Affairs* Vol. 89, No. 5; September–October 2010.

NATO News: NATO Adopts New Strategic Concept (November 19, 2010). http://www.nato.int/cps/en/natolive/news_68172.htm.

Non Paper on Establishment of a European Public-Private Partnership for Resilience (EP3R).

Reding, V. Intervention during the Plenary Session of European Parliament on 2 September 2008.

Regulation (EC) No. 1007/2008 of the European Parliament and of the Council of 24 September 2008 amending Regulation (EC) No. 460/2004 establishing the European Network and Information Security Agency as regards its duration, OJ L 293 of 31.10.2008.

Report from the Commission to the Council based on Article 12 of the Council Framework Decision of 24 February 2005 on attacks against information systems, COM (2008) 448.

Strategy for a Safe and Secure Information Society: Dialogue, Partnership and Empowerment COM (2006) 251 final.

Towards a global partnership in the Information Society: Follow-up to the Tunis Phase of the World Summit on the Information Society (WSIS), COM (2006) 181 final of 27.4.2006.

8

A LOCAL CYBERSECURITY APPROACH

The Case of Catalonia

IGNACIO ALAMILLO DOMINGO AND AGUSTÍ CERRILLO-I-MARTÍNEZ

Contents

Introduction

The global character of cybersecurity requires coordination and cooperation at different territorial levels in the implementation of policies. Although cybersecurity generally transcends state borders, local governments can also make relevant contributions to promote policies that contribute to achieving overall objectives. Because of their proximity to people, for example, local governments can develop tools that respond to local needs in a more effective way than national, regional, or global solutions.*

Establishment of local policy can also be a tool for tackling a variety of related issues to the development of the information society and the use of information and communication technologies (ICTs), such as consumer protection, the fight against crime, public health, and education.

The use of local policy is especially noticeable in decentralized states, which by their nature must adopt a different organizational solution to cybersecurity. Taking the Spanish region of Catalonia as an example, this chapter shows how such development can be tailored to effectively apply, supplement, and reinforce national (Spanish), regional (European Union, EU), and international (International Telecommunications Union, ITU) policies.

The chapter is divided into three parts. It begins with an assessment of relevant global, regional, and national cybersecurity policies, followed by an analysis of how the local Catalan plan supplements them. The chapter concludes by providing ideas about the role that subnational security policies can have within a global framework.

Global, Regional, and National Policies Relevant to Catalonia

The information society has become a global platform for the free circulation of information, ideas, and knowledge. But according to the International Telecommunications Union (ITU) and the United Nations (UN) World Summits on the Information Society (2003–2005), the information society also faces challenges, such as cybersecurity, a notion reflected again in the ITU/UN World Information Society 2007 Report: Beyond WSIS.

This section provides an overview of the global, regional, and national policies relevant to the development of a local cybersecurity policy for Catalonia, in particular the cooperation with other territorial entities.

---

* Throughout this chapter, and consistent with the volume, local governments will be referred to as subnational entities that have significant levels of autonomy like Autonomous Communities in Spain, regions in Italy, or Länder in Germany.

Global Cybersecurity Policy at the World
Summit on the Information Society

The Declaration of Principles of the World Summit on the Information Society of Geneva, of May 12, 2004, reaffirmed the desire to build a people-centered, inclusive, and development-oriented information society where everyone can create, access, utilize, and share information and knowledge premised on the purposes and principles of the Charter of the United Nations and respecting fully and upholding the Universal Declaration of Human Rights.

For example, section 19 of the Declaration of the Principles of the World Summit on the Information Society declared confidence and security in the use of ICTs as a key principle of an inclusive information society. Specifically, section B.5 of the Declaration indicates the need to strengthen the trust framework, including information security and network security, authentication, privacy, and consumer protection, as a prerequisite for the development of the information society and for building confidence among users of ICTs, promoting, according to section 35, "a global culture of cybersecurity needs."

Sections 36 and 37 of the Declaration also indicated that support is needed for actions directed to "prevent the potential use of ICTs for purposes that are inconsistent with the objectives of maintaining international stability and security, and may adversely affect the integrity of the infrastructure within States, to the detriment of their security," with a strong focus on criminal and terrorist purposes, and spam.

Section 59 deals with cybercrime, which notes that "All actors in the information society should take appropriate actions and preventive measures, as determined by law, against abusive uses of ICTs, such as illegal and other acts motivated by racism, racial discrimination, xenophobia, and related intolerance, hatred, violence, all forms of child abuse, including pedophilia and child pornography, and trafficking in, and exploitation of, human beings."

Further, the Tunis Commitment of June 28, 2006, underlines the importance of the security, continuity, and stability of the Internet, and the need to protect Internet and other ICT networks against threats and in their vulnerabilities. The Tunis Commitment also identifies Internet security and protection as one of the elements that must form part of public policies of the governance of the Internet.

From the agenda of the Geneva Declaration and its subsequent follow-up in the Tunis Commitment comes the detailed activity of the International Telecommunications Union in matters of cybersecurity with the following principal objectives, as quoted from line C.5 of the Action Plan:

1. Promote cooperation among the governments at the United Nations and with all stakeholders at other appropriate working groups to enhance user confidence, build trust, and protect both data and network integrity; consider existing and potential threats to ICTs; and address other information security and network security issues.

2. Governments, in cooperation with the private sector, should prevent, detect, and respond to cybercrime and misuse of ICTs by developing guidelines that take into account ongoing efforts in these areas; considering legislation that allows for effective investigation and prosecution of misuse; promoting effective mutual assistance efforts; strengthening institutional support at the international level for preventing, detecting, and recovering from such incidents; and encouraging education and raising awareness.

3. Governments, and other stakeholders, should actively promote user education and awareness about online privacy and the means of protecting privacy.

4. Take appropriate action on spam at national and international levels.

5. Encourage the domestic assessment of national law with a view to overcoming any obstacles to the effective use of electronic documents and transactions including electronic means of authentication.

6. Further strengthen the trust and security framework with complementary and mutually reinforcing initiatives in the fields of security in the use of ICTs, with initiatives or guidelines with respect to rights to privacy, data, and consumer protection.

7. Share good practices in the field of information security and network security and encourage their use by all parties concerned.

8. Invite interested countries to set up focal points for real-time incident handling and response, and develop a cooperative network between these focal points for sharing information and technologies on incident response.
9. Encourage further development of secure and reliable applications to facilitate online transactions.
10. Encourage interested countries to contribute actively to the ongoing UN activities to build confidence and security in the use of ICTs.

The objectives set at the international level are broad but form the basis for country activities in accordance with the regional context (in our case, the European Union), both of which will have to be taken into account when defining national and local cybersecurity policies. In addition, as noted, the achievement of objectives in this area is based on the adoption of instruments for cooperation between all actors to ensure coordination among them. This is particularly important for decentralized states where central and local governments will work according to the distribution of powers among them as we will see later in the case of Spain.

Regional Cybersecurity Policy in the European Union

The European Union covers cybersecurity through a variety of initiatives, including these three:

- Specific security measures for networks and information systems, including the creation of the European Network and Information Security Agency (ENISA) created by Regulation (EC) No. 460/2004 of the European Parliament and of the Council of March 10, 2004, and the establishment of the Network and Information Security Steering Group (NISSG).
- Through regulations governing electronic communications and, specifically, the Directive 2002/58/EC of the European Parliament and of the Council of July 12, 2002, concerning the processing of personal data and the protection of privacy in the electronic communications sector.

- Fight against cybercrime, including the regulation of member states' laws on child pornography offenses, substantive criminal law in the field of high-tech crime, and the application of the principle of mutual recognition to pretrial orders associated with cybercrime investigations involving more than one member state.

The European Union has also established specific actions that, in a supplementary way, deal with the problem of ICT security through research and development programs, the "Safer Internet" program, and involvement in international forums that tackle these questions, such as the Organization for Economic Cooperation and Development (OECD), Council of Europe, and the United Nations.

The Communication from the Commission "The role of e-Government for Europe's future," COM (2003) 567 of September 29, 2003, recognized that it is only possible to offer public services within an environment in which there is confidence, an environment that must always guarantee secure interaction for companies and for the general public and interoperability.

In more general terms, the Communication from the Commission "Challenges for the European Information Society beyond 2005," COM (2004) 757 of November 19, 2004, identifies the need to establish policies relating to the use of information and communications technology to cover gaps in the public services, including identity management issues; the insufficient degree of security and dependability of the networks; and the difficulty of being able to send signed electronically documents in the context of telematics procedures, especially in relation to small- and medium-sized enterprises (SMEs).

In "i2010. A European information society for growth and employment," COM (2005) 229 of June 1, 2005, a strategic framework, called i2010, was proposed to promote an open and competitive digital economy and backing information and communication technology as a stimulus to inclusion and quality of life.

One of the pillars on which this strategic framework is based is the construction of a Single European Information Space that is specifically developed in the Communication from the Commission "A strategy for a Secure Information Society—Dialogue, partnership and empowerment," COM (2006) 251 of May 31, 2006, and in the strategic framework of i2010.

This Communication recognizes that security is a challenge to everyone, including the public authorities, which must deal with the security of their systems, not only to protect information in the public sector but also to give an example of good practices to others.

In this context, the Commission invited the member states to take, among others, the following actions: promoting awareness campaigns on the virtues, benefits, and advantages associated with the adoption of effective technology, practices, and behavior in relation with security; promoting the deployment of e-government services designed to communicate and encourage good security practices, which could later be extended to other sectors; and fighting identity theft and other attacks against privacy.

Later, in the same context, there is the Communication from the Commission "On Fighting span, spyware and malicious software," COM (2006) 688 of November 15, 2006, which identifies lines of action to combat these threats to security. Notably, member states and competent authorities are called upon to lay down clear lines of responsibility for national agencies involved in fighting spam, and ensure effective coordination between competent authorities.

The European Union also has tackled the question of protecting critical information infrastructures in, for example, the Communication by the Commission "Critical Infrastructure Protection in the fight against terrorism," COM (2004) 702 of October 20, 2004, the Green Paper on a European Programme for Critical Infrastructure Protection, COM (2005) 576 of November 17, 2005, and the Council Directive 2008/114/EC of December 8, 2008 on the identification and designation of European critical infrastructures and the assessment of the need to improve their protection.

Through some of these various instruments and related efforts, the European Union has materialized some of the objectives established at the international level. They are implemented through organizations at the regional level but also by the European Union member states. However, the European Union has not provided direct intervention of local governments in these policies, leaving this decision in the hands of each member state. Nonetheless, local governments should take into account all these principles and policies when they develop their own cybersecurity policies.

National Cybersecurity Policy in Spain

In Spain, there are various cybersecurity policies, primarily Plan Avanza and Plan Avanza 2. The Plan Avanza, led by the Ministry of Industry, Tourism and Trade, through the State Telecommunications and the Information Society Secretariat, is one of the more important instruments in relation to the Spanish strategy for information security and was in effect between 2006 and 2010.

The Plan Avanza was structured in four large areas of action, one of which is called "New Digital Context" and, in reference to the line of security and confidence ("e-Confidence"), had the following objectives:

- To increase the degree of awareness, training, and sensitization of the public, companies, and Public Administrations in matters of information and communication technology security. In this way, it seeks to reduce the number of companies with over 10 workers with access to the Internet which have security problems, placing this at 10% by 2010, and increasing the number of individuals who take specific security precautions; specifically, in 2010, 60% of private individuals should have installed antivirus software.
- To stimulate the use of digital identity, considering that by 2010, 100% of the general public with identification cards will have a single, effective, and practical identifier that can be used intensively in all ambits.
- To stimulate the incorporation of security into organizations as a critical factor to increase their competitiveness, developing the necessary security infrastructures and promoting the adoption of better practices, especially the information security certificate. By 2010, 95% of companies with more than 10 workers will have applied security precautions.
- To develop an effective infrastructure for the execution of the national policy on information security, coordinating the various agents and actions, carrying out continuous monitoring of the state of information security, and coordinating international representation in matters of ICT security.

The measures envisaged in the Plan Avanza to achieve these objectives included circulation, communication, and dissemination of awareness campaigns; development of a network of security centers and the creation of a computer security incidents response team (CSIRT); promotion of innovation of security technology; stimulus to the installation of digital identity and electronic signature; promotion of certificates of security, products, services, and processes; extension of the better practices associated with security and self-regulation; and actions for information security and confidence, including the creation of an Information Security Committee, with the participation of Ministries and the Public Administrations competent in matters of information security, as well as the private sector, carrying out tasks of coordination among the various agents, promoting mechanisms of national and international cooperation, creating discussion areas, and disseminating and understanding better practices in matters of information security; and developing metrics and methodologies for the evaluation of e-Confidence indicators, making studies on advances in matters of the use of security technology by the various segments of users (the public, companies, homes, etc.).

When the OECD analyzed Plan Avanza it found that the plan played an important role in contributing to positive results toward progress in advancing the country's information society, improving security, and protecting consumers' rights. OECD also observed that stakeholders are increasingly active, and more and more regional and local governments are seeking support from the Plan.

For its part, the Plan Avanza 2, covering 2011 through 2015, continues developing the line of e-Confidence. It focuses on achieving several objectives that will contribute to overcoming the challenges related to spreading trustworthy ICT among citizens and enterprises, strengthening the protection of privacy in the network and for children, continuing the fight against online fraud, and helping in the protection of logical infrastructures, especially through the Communication Technology Institute (INTECO).

Spanish Cybersecurity Organization

In addition to Plan Avanza 2, the Spanish government created several bodies that will be in charge of it (INTECO; Red.es; Cryptology

National Center—Computer Security Indicent Response Team (CCN-CERT) and tackle various cybersecurity aspects.

RedIRIS, is a public entity attached to the Ministry of Industry, Tourism and Trade. It performs the following principal functions:

- Stimulating the development of information security through the execution of programs defined in the Plan Avanza for convergence with Europe and between the autonomous communities
- Analyzing the information society through the Telecommunications and Information Society Observatory
- Offering specific advice and support to the General State Administration
- Managing the registry of ".es" domain names

In matters relating to security in technology and the information society, it was considered necessary to define a strategic plan and model for the introduction of a National Security Centre, which includes starting up a Security Demonstrator Centre for SMEs with the purpose of making tests and comparisons of the various types of security products, serving as a platform of tests and support to other centers such as the Incident Response Centre of the Information Technology and Security Observatory, strengthening the use of information security technology among Spanish SMEs and stimulating international visibility of Spanish technology in information security.

Also, it was considered necessary to carry out research into Internet users for the purpose of preparing a study on user perception and confidence in the network. The idea is to stimulate knowledge and follow-up of the principal indicators and public policies related with information security and confidence, to generate a database for purposes of the analysis and evaluation of security and confidence on a time perspective, and finally to prepare and present reports on matters of security, which would form support for the Administration in making decisions in matters of security.

Also, Red.es manages RedIRIS and participates in INTECO. RedIRIS is the national Research and Development network that provides security services to the scientific community, including the following:

- The RedIRIS (IRIS-CERT) security service, for the purpose of detecting problems affecting network security in the RedIRIS centers, and actions coordinated with these centers in solving the problems. It also has a preventive task, warning of potential problems in time, offering advice to the centers, organizing activities in accordance with them, and other supplementary services
- Public Key Infrastructure services (PKI) for the RedIRIS community, including secure server certificates and grid network certificates
- Access control and authorization services, through the federated authentication sofware (PAPI) software

The Communication Technology Institute (INTECO), promoted by the Ministry of Industry, Tourism and Trade, and with participation by Red.es, is a platform for the development of the Knowledge Society through projects in the field of innovation and technology, including initiatives in technological security, accessibility, and inclusion in the digital society, and communication solutions for individuals and companies.

The activity of INTECO in relation to information security includes the following projects:

- Response Centre for Incidents in Information Technology for SMEs, for the main purpose of achieving a solid development of the Spanish business fabric by providing SMEs with reactive, preventive, and training services in matters of security
- Rapid Antivirus Alert Centre, with the main purpose of stimulating awareness in matters of security, offering alerts, information, free protection tools, and daily security reports on the latest malicious codes appearing in the Network since 2001
- Information Centre for Dissemination of the Security Culture, with the main purpose of
  - Starting up and operating a portal for the dissemination of information in matters of information security
  - Preparing contents and practical guides in matters of information security, in collaboration with relevant agents in this field

- Information Security Observatory, with the main purpose of analyzing, describing, advising, and disseminating the security culture and confidence in the information society, through the generation of specialized knowledge in the subject, and the preparation of recommendations and proposals that allow the definition of valid trends for the taking of decisions in the field of security.

- The Observatory must be a point of reference for the analysis and follow-up of confidence in the information society in Spain, preparing, collecting, summarizing, and systemizing indicators.

- Also it will generate and disseminate specialized knowledge in at least the following key areas of information security: Security of electronic signature and digital identity; measures of protection against information security risks; digital rights management technologies (DRMs); and other available security technology and tools.

The Secretary of State director of the National Intelligence Centre, as director of the National Cryptographic Centre (CCN), is the authority responsible for coordinating the actions of the different bodies of the Administration that use coding methods or procedures, in order to guarantee the security of information technology in this ambit, advising on the coordinated acquisition of cryptographic material and training the specialist administrative personnel in this field.

The director of the CCN is the authority for certification of information technology security (http://www.oc.ccn.cni.es) and the authority on cryptographic certification (http://www.ccn.cni.es). Also, he is in charge of overseeing compliance with the regulation relating to the protection of classified information, in the aspects of information and telecommunications systems, in accordance with article 4.e) and f) of the Act 11/2002, of 6 May.

The National Cryptographic Centre is attached to the National Intelligence Centre, sharing means, procedures, regulations, and resources with it. Within its field of action, the National Cryptographic Centre carries out the following functions:

- Preparing and disseminating standards, instructions, guides, and recommendations to guarantee the security of the Administration's information technology systems and communications. Actions arising from the development of this function will be proportional to the risks affecting the information processed, stored, or transmitted by the systems (http://www.ccn.cni.es)
- Training the specialist personnel of the Administration in the field of security in information and communications technology systems
- Constituting the certification institution of the national scheme of evaluation and certification of information technology security, of application to the products and systems in its field (http://www.oc.ccn.cni.es)
- Evaluating and accrediting the capacity of the coding products and information technology systems, which include the means to code, process, store, or transmit information securely
- Coordinating the promotion, development, obtaining of, acquisition, and putting into exploitation and use of security technology for the systems mentioned above
- Overseeing compliance with the regulations relating to the protection of classified information in its ambit of competence (e.g., NATO security information)
- Establishing the necessary relations and signing the relevant agreements with similar organizations in other States, for the development of the functions mentioned

Within the activities of the CCN, there is CCN-CERT, the Spanish Computer Emergency Response Team, the main purpose of which is to improve the levels of security in information systems in the public authorities of the Spanish State.

The purpose of CCN-CERT is to be the center of alert and response to security incidents, assisting the public authorities to respond more rapidly and efficiently to security threats that affect their information systems, through two broad lines of action:

- The provision of information services, such as alerts regarding new threats

- The undertaking of tasks of research, training, and dissemination of information security

The National Security Scheme, regulated by Law 11/2007, of June 22, of electronic access for the general public to the public services, addressed to public authorities, was approved by Royal Decree 3/2010, of January 8. The aim of the National Security Scheme is to create the conditions necessary to inspire confidence in the use of electronic means, by implementing measures that guarantee the safety of systems, data, communications, and electronic services, thereby allowing citizens and Public Administrations to exercise their rights and comply with their obligations through these methods.

It was prepared in collaboration with all the Public Administrations to which it applies, getting a favorable report from the Permanent Commission of the Higher Council of Electronic Government, the Public Administration Sector Conference, and the National Local Authorities Commission, and being submitted to the preliminary report of the Spanish Data Protection Agency. The National Security Scheme is the main participative process in Spain, and it explicitly considers the feedback of the regions and local authorities.

The Spanish government has driven different public policies and implements several mechanisms to improve the development of information societies in Spain that have a great impact on cybersecurity. In this process, the Spanish government has taken into account local government, but greater participation and coordination will be needed, especially moving forward as more local entities deploy electronic procedures.

The Catalan Plan for Cybersecurity

Spain is organized in territorially autonomous communities that have legislative and executive powers conferred by the Spanish Constitution and the Statute of Autonomy.

There are currently 17 regions in Spain, one of which is Catalonia, home to about 7.5 million people constituting 16% of the Spanish population. The Generalitat of Catalonia is the institution created in 1977 in which the self-government of Catalonia is politically organized.

The Statute of Autonomy passed in 2006 gives the Generalitat of Catalonia the powers that enable it to carry out self-government.

Powers of the Generalitat of Catalonia in the Field of Information Security

In 2004, the Catalan government (Generalitat of Catalonia) established a new security policy that aims to protect the information systems used by the government and its departments and the bodies that depend on them.

It is organized by the Telecommunications and Information Technology Centre and supplemented by the Information Security Office, a unit attached to the area of quality, security, and relations with suppliers, which is in charge of watching over the establishment of regulations and standards of security, making a preventive analysis of security problems, intervening in support of corporate systems, and responding, in general, to any need of security put to it.

The main policy is supplemented by initiatives addressed both to corporate protection and to the overall security of specific sectors, such as Order SLT/465/2008, of October 27, which regulates the Information Security Program of the Ministry of Health, which has an undoubted impact on the health sector. Another example are the technological initiatives being led by the general management of the regional police force—the Mossos d'Esquadra—in relation to the fight against all forms of electronic crime, through a specifically specialized unit addressed to improving the capacity of detection and response to crime with a technological base. Finally, there is the important task undertaken, in matters of information security, by the Catalan Certification Agency, a body attached to the Catalan Open Administration Consortium, and the Catalan Data Protection Agency, in the ambits of digital identity and personal data protection, aspects that are intimately related to security.

Because of the various policies and actions in matters of the fight against electronic crime described above, there is a strong need to establish and lead a public action of a global nature in Catalonia, with the collaboration of all the authorities and the private sector, to coordinate and stimulate all the actions directed to combating the problems mentioned above and to be a reference in Spain.

However, Catalonia had suffered a significant time-lag in relation to the public performance in Spain and even compared to other regions, which resulted in the loss of competitiveness and restraining investment in the ICT market. Although some policies and actions have been adopted, ICT security levels were not optimal in Catalonia. In fact, the situation could only be considered successfully treated in a few cases, especially in large public or private organizations, while vulnerabilities remained for most citizens, small and medium enterprises (SMEs), as well as in Public Administrations with fewer resources.

Accordingly, the Catalan government decided to act decisively and urgently to establish a long-lasting political action program to correct this situation, setting a 4-year plan (2009 to 2013), which is currently ongoing.

The Statute of Autonomy of Catalonia is its basic institutional regulations. It defines the rights and obligations of the citizens of Catalonia, the political institutions of the Catalan nationality, their competences and relations with the Spanish State, and the financing of the Government of Catalonia. This law was approved in referendum by the citizens on June 18, 2006, and substitutes the Statute of Sau that dated from 1979. Among other competences, the Statute of Autonomy of Catalonia provides the foundation of the powers of the Generalitat of Catalonia in matters of security in the information society:

- Guarantees the protection of individuals and families, particularly children and youth (Article 40 EAC).
- Obligates public authorities to "ensure the dignity, safety, and full protection of all individuals, especially those who are most vulnerable" (Article 42.3 EAC).
- Guarantees the protection of health, safety, and defense of the rights and legitimate interests of consumers and users (Article 49.1 EA).
- Grants exclusive powers of the Generalitat of Catalonia in matters of consumer affairs, indicating the aspects of consumer training and education, which are particularly important in security of ICT (Article 123 EA).
- Grants executive powers on the administrative regulation of electronic commerce (Article 112.1.a EAC).

- Obligates public authorities to act positively in relation to ICT by providing that "public authorities shall facilitate knowledge of the information society and shall encourage equal access to communication and to information technologies in all areas of life, including the workplace; they shall encourage that these technologies are at the service of people and do not negatively affect their rights, and shall guarantee the provision of services by means of the above-mentioned technologies, in accordance with the principles of universality, continuity and modernization" (Article 53 EAC).
- Grants executive power over electronic communications. This power includes in any case promotion of the existence of a minimum set of universally accessible services and inspection of the shared telecommunications infrastructures and exercise of the corresponding power to sanction. Security of electronic communications networks must be protected, as these networks are the main factor allowing the existence and continuity of the information society (Article 140.7 EAC).

Introducing the Catalan Information Security Centre (CESICAT)

The Catalan plan for ICT security was approved by the Catalan government on March 17, 2009, and aims to guarantee a secure information society in Catalonia for everyone. The Catalan cybersecurity plan is structured around four principal objectives. In order to achieve them and to enhance ICT security in Catalonia, the Telecommunications and Information Society Secretariat (TISS) of the Government of Catalonia created the Catalan Information Security Centre (CESICAT). It is in charge of establishing and monitoring programs under the strategic direction of the Catalan General Directorate of the Information Society, with direct participation of the private sector and civil society. Specifically, CESICAT will implement public policies in ICT security and create a regional business network of support, applications, and services of ICT security, which can become a national and international industrial reference.

CESICAT is incorporated to support and assist the Government of the Generalitat of Catalonia in reaching the objectives of the regional Plan for IT Security in Catalonia.

Its legal structure is a foundation of the public sector of the Generalitat of Catalonia, with the participation of both public sector agencies and private sector companies. The main reasons for believing that the objectives of general interest pursued are best achieved establishing a foundation instead of other forms of public or private are

1. To incorporate many kinds of public and private bodies, without the problems of granting shares in the capital
2. The most appropriate formula for nonprofit initiatives, and not wanting to compete in the market
3. Easier access to grants, and has excellent tax benefits in connection with the public company
4. Strengthens the role of neutral operator, coordinator, and collaborator with the private sector
5. Evolution of founding a center of excellence in management and research

CESICAT manages a program of 16 political action lines over several years (initially from 2009 up to 2013), funded initially from the Catalan Government public budget, but with a financing model that covers the main universal services but that also guarantees its continuity through the provision of some commercial services. CESICAT is highly specialized and small, with about 30 people on staff and a budget of approximately one million euros per year. When responding to cyber incidents, CESICAT uses its own personnel and the regional police, as well as external support from selected contractors.

CESICAT is organized as follows:

1. General management
   This unit is in charge of governance and administration. It is also accountable for the implementation of the regional plan and publishes the following publications:
   - The CESICAT annual report
   - Reports on the state of ICT.cat (a plan to improve competitiveness of ITC companies in Catalonia) security in Catalonia, oriented to provide feedback both to the Catalan government and CESICAT
2. ICT security incident prevention and response unit

This unit is in charge of the following services, in support of the indicated actions:

- Prevention and training in ICT security service that includes the following actions: dissemination of notices and alerts in ICT security, as a form of prevention; security awareness programs; ICT security guides; program for the management of lists of secure configuration of ICT systems; information security courses (Catalan public employees' school, universities, others); practical workshops on tools, methodologies, and others and service of alerts and warnings on ICT security and vulnerabilities

- Vulnerabilities and ICT security incidents response service against service denials, malware, unauthorized access, incorrect use of systems, or combinations of the following: remote assistance (containment, solution, and recovery); local assistance (forensic analysis, containment, solution, and recovery); coordination with third parties; analysis of incidents (in laboratory); and knowledge base of vulnerabilities and response strategies

3. ICT security professional services unit

This unit is in charge of the following services, in support of the indicated actions:

- Preventive analysis in ICT security service in relation with surface, penetration, infrastructure, and best practices

- ICT security consultancy service. In particular, risk analysis, security management programs, and support for the acquisition and management of security infrastructure

- Specialized legal advice in ICT security service like legal aspects of security programs: labor, criminal, administrative, and treatment of electronic evidence (legal aspects of forensic computer systems); legal guidelines and recommendations; and finally, protocols of collaboration with police and bodies responsible for national security and critical infrastructures

CESICAT and the Catalan Cybersecurity Objectives

Establishment of the Catalan Information and Communications Technology (ICT) Security Strategy The first objective was the development of a local information security strategy that supplements national, regional, and global policies. In order to meet this goal, Catalonia developed specific research tools and increased public awareness of threats and vulnerabilities through a multidisciplinary approach with multiple participants on one hand, and a high-level governance structure on the other.

A public model of security in the information society is defined for Catalonia, to address in a holistic manner the challenges posed at all times, operating in contact with all those involved and having a real capacity of response to the problems that may arise, with an information security center as the articulating unit of the regional ICT security plan, making a continuous analysis of risk and overseeing the integrity and continuity of the networks and systems.

But a top-down approach is insufficient. Because government cannot handle the cybersecurity challenge alone, there is a need to involve the private sector and civil society. This can be achieved in a variety of ways, such as the creation of public–private partnerships, development of best practices, and information sharing and participation in shared organizations. CESICAT, for example, is a shared organization with participation from both Catalan governmental bodies and private companies. Further, a government program that aims to improve the computer service offering in Catalonia, TIC.cat, contains a subprogram specifically to promote dialogue with companies that offer security products and services. This effort will align their efforts with those of the government and help the companies be more competitive.

This system leverages existing initiatives and programs, such as the Catalan Public Key Infrastructure system, under the responsibility of the Catalan Certification Agency, and the action of supervisory bodies, including trade, consumption, children and young people, and the police. Collaboration between CESICAT and other public initiatives related to information security is primarily through the Telecommunications and Secretariat of the Generalitat de Catalonia. For example, there have been joint actions between CESICAT and the Catalan Consumer Agency and police in regard to the removal of illegal content affecting the safety of consumers.

CESICAT actions related to objective 1 are as follows:

1. Establishment of a Catalan model of information society security; who's who in information security in Catalonia; dialogue with all the sectors affected and with the bodies involved in each of the sectors, including the Catalan Administrations, the Chambers of Commerce, and companies, through the TIC.CAT plan.
2. Creation and operation of a security incident response team (CSIRT) for Catalonia, addressed to public administrations, universities, companies, and individuals, which will also act as a catalyst for the ICT security community. This team provides reactive services to security incidents, proactive services such as improving awareness, and security quality management services.
3. Continuous analysis of risks that may have an impact on the development of the information society in Catalonia.
4. Provision of managed security services for specific entities and groups, principally the Catalan public sector and SMEs. (Such services include an intrusion detection and prevention service [IDPS], security information and event management [SIEM], and vulnerabilities management service [VMS].)

   Finally, support and promotion for the protection and assurance of the .CAT domain name system and the basic Internet services used by the general public (e-mail, web, ftp, others) when the electronic communication suppliers operate in Catalonia.

Support for the Protection of Critical ICT Infrastructures The second objective aims to protect the elements that form Catalan critical ICT infrastructures, such as computer, energy, water, transportation, financial, telecommunications, and health systems.

The consequences of a cyber attack on critical infrastructures vary. Even though it may not result in any direct victims per se, it could mean the loss of vital infrastructure services with severe consequences.

For example, the loss of telephone service relied upon by the emergency services or leakages of toxic chemicals.

A cyber attack can also cause failures in public services, such as the case of an attack on the public communication services, which support vital services such as e-Health. Some cases to be dealt with are the ICT services of the Government of Catalonia and the Catalan local authorities, the emergency service, and civil protection networks (the single number 112 contacts the Catalan Police, Citizen Advice Agencies, the fire brigade, rural agents, etc.), and the private services that support them.

Although each government department must perform an assessment of their infrastructure to determine what should be classified as critical infrastructure, CESICAT will be able to act as a unit of cybersecurity for all departments, due to the presence of the Catalan police in the CESICAT constituency. The Spanish critical infrastructure protection draft legislation establishes the legal competence referred to the protection of the critical infrastructure upon the Spanish police, but also upon the regional police. This possibility opens an opportunity to regions to cover the full spectrum of cybersecurity issues.

CESICAT actions related to objective 2 are as follows:

> In collaboration with the Catalan police, competent in matters of public security and the protection of critical infrastructures, and in the ambit of the competences of the Government in ICT, CESICAT is starting the following actions:
>
> First, establishment and follow-up of a protection plan for critical government ICT infrastructures, including electronic communications by the authorities, data processing centers, and coordination with Catalan and Spanish agencies, in particular the Catalan Emergencies Centre (CECAT) and the Spanish National Critical Infrastructure Protection Centre
>
> Second, public–private collaboration in relation to critical nongovernmental ICT infrastructures located in Catalan territory, with a catalogue of interdependencies and mutual protection measures

Promotion of a Catalan ICT Business Network   The third objective is the creation of an ICT security business network in Catalonia to supplement the public policies introduced before and stimulate the development of the ICT sector in the security industrial sector, as introduced in this section.

A study on the ICT market in Catalonia, carried out in 2008 by the Information Society Observatory Foundation of Catalonia (FOBSIC), found that there was an insufficient number of companies offering support to Catalan SMEs and citizens, and there was an excessive concentration of the service offered in the Barcelona area, which implied an important lack of support in the rest of Catalonia. Thus, it recommended the stimulation of SMEs in the ICT sector through different actions, including

- Promoting technology and quality certificates for companies in the sector
- Communicating the benefits of certificates, regulations of mandatory compliance in contracting with the administration, and support for training programs
- Creating certification of methodologies and processes in the supply of services

The creation of a network of SMEs promotes ICT security services and protection against cyber incidents. It encourages the development of an ICT security community with special attention to training and certification of professionals, companies, products, and software, including open security software, as well as innovation and research.

The SME network generates ICT business for the region and essentially can serve as a near-shore security expert community for Catalonia. As such, it was located in a technology park in the city of Reus.

CESICAT actions related to the third objective are as follows:

Promotion of a Catalan business fabric with solid ICT security, as a tool of industrial policy for the sector, especially addressed to the SMEs, micro-SMEs, and self-employed professionals acting in the Catalan ICT market

First, creation of a national network of SMEs specialized in ICT security, which supply services of immediate response, coordinated and supported, even financially, by CESICAT

Second, promotion of a software community on ICT security products, based principally on free software under the control of a community of developers, directed by CESICAT, including risk analysis products, security evaluation and follow-up products, coding products, products for parental control over contents, antivirus, antispam, antimalware products, and so forth

Third, promotion of the evaluation and certification, by accredited bodies, of secure software development processes, including, for example, secure web coding (OWASP) or secure software coding

Fourth, promotion of the certification of security processes, by accredited bodies, and especially, of the ISO 27000 security process standards family

Fifth, promotion of training and certification of professionals in ICT security and related disciplines, including security processes based in ISO 27000; security management based, for example, in Certified Information Security Manager (CISM); technical security based in, for example, Certified Information Systems Security Professional (CISSP); business continuity based in Business Continuity Professional Certification (BCP); good ICT government based in Certified in the Governance of Enterprise IT (CGEIT), or ICT audit, based in Certified Information Systems Auditor (CISA) or Control Objectives for IT (COBIT)

Sixth, promotion of the certification of product security based in ISO 15408 Common Criteria, focusing on selection and evaluation of security profiles for the security evaluation of products acquired by the public sector; production of security profiles, with special attention given to products acquired by the Government of Catalonia and the local authorities

Seventh, promotion of research and innovation in ICT security, including the creation of a chair in ICT security in a Catalan University or specialized research center, and fostering joint publications between the university, companies, and CESICAT

Increasing Confidence and Protection of the General Public The fourth objective seeks to improve the confidence and protection of the general public in their use of information technology with special attention given to vulnerable groups, such as children, through awareness and support programs.

Examples of the current activities "A Internet posa-hi seny!" an awareness program targeting youngsters that is conducted through Facebook and features two imaginary roles, Cesc and Cati Cesicat.

This awareness program is based in a Facebook profile, available at http://www.facebook.com/home.php#!/profile.php?id=100000 831630615, which is used by Cati Cesicat to give security advice using the social network.

Another interesting awareness action is based on an online gaming space (http://www.cesicat.cat/cesicat2010), where there are several games designed to teach youngsters to protect themselves.

There is also coordination with relevant agencies in the fight against all forms of computer crime. Some experiences include investigating voice Internet protocol (IP) fraud against small municipalities, in a coordinated action with the Catalan police.

CESICAT actions related to the fourth objective are as follows:

First, education in security and confidence, especially addressed to vulnerable groups, such as children, and the elderly, but also targeting consumers generally. Presence of the principal public and private portals addressed to the Catalan public, and other tools under the Web 2.0 philosophy (e.g., Facebook); publication of guidelines, recommendations, teaching materials; and specific actions, such as awareness campaigns. Concretely, CESICAT has already published several guidelines addressed to public administrations, companies, and citizens, which may be downloaded from the CESICAT webpage, and which are distributed in print at conferences and events organized by the CESICAT regularly directed to different groups.

Also, CESICAT created specific Facebook and Twitter accounts to establish additional relationship models with their communities of interest.

Second, promotion of essential security instruments among the general public, including fostering the use of electronic certificates; vigilance and monitoring tools installed in the computers of the general public, with their consent, for proactive detection of threats; or backup copy tools, coding, and others. Mainly open software tools, CESICAT is currently distributing tools such as Truecrypt, an open-source disk encryption software, or Ovaldi, an open-source local vulnerability assessment scanner.

Conclusions

From a global point of view, the World Summit on the Information Society stated trust and security of ICT as key principles of an inclusive information society. These general principles have subsequently been defined in several assignments developed by the ITU in the area of cybersecurity by promoting cooperation among states and other actors, prevention and response to cybercrime, education, or by strengthening trust and safety.

The European Union has also advanced in this area through specific measures for networks and information systems, regulations on electronic communications, and the fight against cybercrime. It has also insisted that security is a challenge for everyone. Beyond the actions specifically developed by the European Union, it has invited state members to actively take different actions in this area.

At the national level, the Spanish government has adopted several instruments for defining national policy on security technology in order to increase the degree of awareness, training, and sensitization; to stimulate the use of digital identity; to stimulate the incorporation of security into organizations; and to develop an effective infrastructure for the implementation of the national policy of information security. The Spanish government has created different agencies to implement several policies adopted in this field (Red.es, INTECO, CHN).

Finally, we focused our attention on local cybersecurity policy as established by the Government of Catalonia on March 17, 2009. The Generalitat of Catalonia implements its policy through a public foundation. This option allows a transversal approach to cybersecurity through the participation of different bodies of the Generalitat of Catalonia, which represent different areas affected, such as telecommunications, police, universities, enterprises, and e-government. From this perspective, it achieves greater proximity between the cybersecurity policy and the different actors involved and affected.

Finally, the plurality of actors and policies on cybersecurity that we analyzed prove the need to use mechanisms to promote coordination between the different territorial levels and the various political actors that define and implement them. Coordination is necessary to ensure consistency in the development of cybersecurity policies. In this regard, we must remember that the European Commission Communication "On fighting spam, spyware and malicious software," COM (2006) 688 final, calls on Member States and competent authorities to lay down clear lines of Responsibility for national agencies involved in fighting spam, and Ensure effective coordination between competent authorities." Also, in Spain, the Avanza Plan has paid attention to the need to coordinate the various actors and actions.

For example, CESICAT currently has partnerships with various actors involved in cybersecurity. In Spain, CESICAT collaborates with the CCN-CERT, and INTECO entities at the state level are responsible for the security policies of the information presented earlier. At the international level, CESICAT has been integrated into the network of CSIRTs of Forum of Incident Response and Security Teams (FIRST), and is part of the antiphishing working group.

Coordination and collaboration are especially necessary when public authorities want to influence global public goods such as network security in the 21st century, in a context where prevention and time-to-incident are absolutely essential.

References

CESICAT.   http://www.cesicat.cat/Dossier%20Pla%20nacional%20de%20 seguretat%20TIC%20Catalunya%20v2.pdf (accessed December 2010).
CESICAT. (2010). Guia per a l'ús segur de les Xarxes Socials. http://www. cesicat.cat/fitxers/publicacions/Guia%20per%20a%20l%20us%20 segur%20de%20les%20xarxes%20socials.pdf (accessed December 2010).

Communication from the Commission to the Council and the European Parliament—Critical Infrastructure Protection in the fight against terrorism, COM (2004) 702 of October 20, 2004.

Communication from the Commission to the Council, the European Parliament, the European Economic and Social committee and the Committee of the Regions—The Role of eGovernment for Europe's Future, COM (2003) 567 final of September 29, 2003.

Communication from the Commission to the Council, the European Parliament, the European Economic and Social committee and the Committee of the Regions—Challenges for the European Information Society beyond 2005, COM (2004) 757 of November 19, 2004.

Communication from the Commission to the Council, the European Parliament, the European Economic and Social committee and the Committee of the Regions—i2010. A European information society for growth and employment, COM (2005) 229 of June 1, 2005.

Communication from the Commission to the Council, the European Parliament, the European Economic and Social committee and the Committee of the Regions—A strategy for a Secure Information Society—Dialogue, partnership and empowerment, COM (2006) 251 of May 31, 2006.

Communication from the Commission to the Council, the European Parliament, the European Economic and Social committee and the Committee of the Regions—On Fighting span, spyware and malicious software, COM (2006) 688 of November 15, 2006.

Directive 2002/58/EC of the European Parliament and of the Council of 12 July 2002 concerning the processing of personal data and the protection of privacy in the electronic communications sector.

Directive 2008/114/EC of December 8, 2008 on the identification and designation of European critical infrastructures and the assessment of the need to improve their protection.

English version of the National Security Framework in: http://www.csae.map.es/csi/pdf/ENS_SECURITY_ENGLISH_final.pdf (accessed December 2010).

Green Paper on a European Programme for Critical Infrastructure Protection, COM (2005) 576 of November 17, 2005.

OECD. (2009). Information Society Strategies: From Design to Implementation. The case of Spain's Plan Avanza. Working paper for the workshop: "Common Challenges and Shared Solutions: Good Governance in Information Society Strategies, the Spanish Case Study." Madrid, Spain. November 18, 2009. http://www.oecd.org/dataoecd/9/15/44242867.pdf (accessed December 2010).

Plan Avanza. http://www.planavanza.es/InformacionGeneral/Executive/Documents/Resumen_ejecutivo.pdf (accessed December 2010).

Regulation (EC) No 460/2004 of the European Parliament and of the Council of 10 March 2004 establishing the European Network and Information Security Agency.

TIC.cat. http://www.anella.cat/web/tic/portada/-/journal_content/56/25818881/
26235789 (accessed December 2010).

WSIS. http://www.itu.int/wsis/docs/geneva/official/dop.html (accessed December
2010).

9

Securing Government Transparency

Cybersecurity Policy Issues in a Gov 2.0 Environment and Beyond

GREGORY G. CURTIN AND CHARITY C. TRAN

Contents

Introduction

E-government, social media, and Web 2.0/Gov 2.0 (and as important, whatever comes after Gov 2.0) are here to stay, and public sector
agencies at all levels need to figure out how best to deal with it, not
to fight it.

Although this paper specifically focuses on cybersecurity policy
related to social media and Gov 2.0 adoption at the local level, it is
worth recounting this passage from the Federal CIO Council on the
risks associated with social media (italics added):

> The decision to embrace social media technology is a risk-based deci-
> sion, not a technology-based decision. It must be made based on a strong
> business case, supported at the appropriate level for each department or
> agency, considering its mission space, threats, technical capabilities, and
> potential benefits. *The goal of the IT organization should not be to say "No"*

to social media websites and block them completely, but to say "Yes, follow-ing security guidance," with effective and appropriate information assurance security and privacy controls. The decision to authorize access to social media websites is a business decision, and comes from a risk manage-ment process made by the management team with inputs from all play-ers.... The use of social media and the inherent cybersecurity concerns form a complex topic that introduces additional vulnerabilities, targeted by an advanced threat, requiring updated sets of controls. (p. 6)

We focus in this chapter on cybersecurity policy issues related spe-cifically to efforts by governments and public agencies at the local level to become more transparent through the use of Web 2.0 tools (Gov 2.0) and implementation of open data/open government initia-tives. As such, we assume that virtually all agencies are already imple-menting some baseline level of network security, data loss prevention, antivirus, intrusion detection, and so forth, and do not go into any detail on those aspects of cybersecurity.

Cybersecurity and Gov 2.0

The integration of the digital world into the daily lives of citizens has increased user demand for government transparency, information access/availability, and outlets for citizen feedback. President Barack Obama made open government and government transparency a cor-nerstone of the new administration, issuing a seminal Open Data Directive as one of his first official memoranda in January 2009. Governments at all levels have followed suit, slowly at first, but in the second half of 2010 and through 2011 the pace has picked up rapidly. This digital movement—popularly termed "Government 2.0" or sim-ply "Gov 2.0"—was described in 2010 by Mark Drapeau of *O'Reilly Radar*, an online news and information site focusing on emerging technologies, as

[A]bout changing the status quo of government in various ways [includ-ing] but [...] not necessarily limited to: innovation by government, transparency of its processes, collaboration among its members, and participation of citizens. In total, these would constitute a huge trans-formation of government, at any level.

However, as more government entities attempt to meet this growing expectation for government transformation, they must tackle key policy issues, especially regarding the security of publicly available online data and information, and increasingly open communications by public officials and employees to and with members of the public. At the highest level, in his early open government directives, President Obama specifically called for agencies to stop using the general threat of security and privacy as a reason to do nothing as this only would stifle innovation.

One of the key business and policy questions facing public officials considering how best to implement social media is the proper balance between risk management and open government. There is a natural tension between the hallmarks of open government—open data, open access, transparency, and accountability—and the sensitivities of security.

E-Government Services, Open Data Initiatives, and the Social Media Fueled "Gov 2.0"

At the U.S. federal and state government levels, agency chief information officers constantly rate cybersecurity as one of their top concerns. Yet they are also under increasing pressure from all fronts to implement more and better e-government services, develop usable open data resources, and generally support more transparent decision making and communications including implementing vibrant social media initiatives. The pressure is even greater at the local level, where citizens interact daily with a variety of public agencies. In Southern California, this can include multiple municipal governments and their specific departments charged with key public services, public utilities including water and energy, often overlapping public transit agencies, local and regional planning agencies and organizations, community redevelopment agencies, air quality districts and other environmental agencies, public school and community college districts, and countless others. Communications, service delivery, and information technology personnel as well as elected officials struggle daily with balancing the desire, and sometimes the mandate, to provide ever more access to public data and information, and facilitating real dialogue with citizens and constituents, and the very real threats to privacy and security issues. The rise of Gov 2.0 has raised the stakes on both sides of that balance.

Cybersecurity Risks Related to Gov 2.0

As the editor in the introduction to this book notes, cybersecurity can be defined broadly as the vulnerability of computer systems, including Internet websites, against unauthorized access or attack, or the policy measures taken to protect them. The cybersecurity risks in Gov 2.0 also cannot be focalized into one type of concern or category. Gov 2.0/Web 2.0 is inclusive of a number of factors including human actions, concerns related to infrastructure, social expectation, and even crosses over to multiple platforms and interfaces.

Human Error and Carelessness

Especially with social media, the most real security threat may be the inadvertent disclosure of potentially compromising information or data by careless government employees. Much of the allure of social media is its ability to "connect" large numbers of individuals in real time. Real time presents great opportunities for Gov 2.0 including the ability to inform constituents of details as events are occurring and to have open channels that can immediately connect government to what constituents are experiencing. However, real-time response can also result in less time and focus spent on ensuring correct responses and increases the potential that government employees might provide information that has not yet been vetted, may be privy to security concerns, or may even be expressed in a manner that is not appropriate.

Physical Network Access

The incredible growth of social networking and social media sites, services, and applications—thousands and growing exponentially each day—provides numerous new potential entry points for computer networks. This is one of the most basic, and obvious, threats and should not be overlooked.

Malicious Data/Information Mining

Virtually all cell phones made after 2005 in the United States are required by law to include GPS (Global Positioning System) technology. The law, commonly known as E911 (Enhanced 911), was mandated by the Federal Communications Commission (FCC) as a means of ensuring that users who dialed 911 in emergencies could be located within 100 meters of their actual location.

From this legislation and technological implementation, most leading smart phones have the ability to procure geotags that provide latitude and longitude coordinates of the phone and, subsequently, where the phone user is located. The popular social media sites Twitter and Facebook have measures in place to avoid the publishing of geotags by unwitting users, and most smart phones include the ability to turn these settings off. Social media sites specifically focused on photo sharing—such as Flickr and Picasa—do an even better job, by offering geotagging options but not automatically enabling them.

However, one of the major combined benefits of mobile technologies and social media is the sharing of geo-location information. This is often discussed primarily as an online privacy issue, but in the context of local government agencies it can present a very real cybersecurity issue—location of key public assets such as power plants and other important infrastructure, public transit and transportation data, the comings and goings of key public officials, access patterns around key public facilities, and so forth. This can become a potential problem both in the public context—for example, public agency communications personnel providing photos of events, groundbreakings, and so forth. It can also pose a problem as social media is used more and more for enterprise collaboration or distributed communications and fieldwork. Some new public e-government services are actually built around this. Services such as See-Click-Fix, for example, encourage "active citizenship" by offering a variety of platforms for citizens to report their uses/concerns including mobile device options and photo uploads. The military has taken up the effort as young soldiers especially are starting to use social media to communicate with friends and family, the Army website notes that "Geotagging is the process of adding geographical identification to photographs, video, websites and SMS messages. It is the equivalent of adding a 10-digit grid co-ordinate to everything you post on the Internet."

Social Engineering

A large area of cybersecurity vulnerability revolves around what is known as "social engineering." At its most basic, social engineering as a cybersecurity concept involves exploiting the human element of trust that is at the very core of social networking. This is especially troublesome for public agencies as ever higher profile government actors—elected officials, city managers, board and commission members, general managers, communications and public information officers, and so forth—utilize social media to communicate and share information with the public directly, often in real time.

Trend Analysis of Social Media "Conversations"

A booming industry has arisen around social media "listening." For private sector marketing, branding, and public relations, the goal is to collectively assess what consumers are saying or sharing about a product, an event, a specific company, and so forth. By staying abreast of these "trending" conversations, companies can attempt to actively guide and shape them—by fueling positive trends and attempting to dampen negative trends. This is still much more art than science, but the rise of data mining and business intelligence tools that enable users to relate discrete pieces of data and information to each other for predictive analysis has created powerful opportunities for malicious users. These tools can be used, for example, for what are commonly known as "spear phishing" attacks, or to piece together broad knowledge bases about public facilities and infrastructure, internal operations, plans and strategies, and so forth.

Phishing and Spear Phishing

Phishing scams have become a growing scourge across the Internet: who has not seen that now ubiquitous e-mail inquiry or solicitation attempting to get you to click on an apparently legitimate site link to check an account (often bank or other financial accounts), a special offer, or some similar scheme in order to steal usable information such as credit card numbers. Although many of these phishing scams border on the ridiculous and are readily recognizable by even most digital neophytes, many have become increasingly sophisticated and look remarkably similar to the actual accounts and sites that they are masking. With the rise of social media an even more nefarious scam dubbed "spear phishing" has emerged and escalated rapidly. Spear phishing is an attack targeting a specific user or group of users, and attempts to deceive the user into performing an action, such as opening a document or clicking a link, launches an attack. Spear phishers rely on knowing some specific information about their target, such as an event, interest, travel plans, address, current issue, and so forth, and have found social media sites and conversations a treasure trove for finding these critical pieces of information. The popular use of URL shorteners in the social media world has added to the effectiveness of spear phishing as users cannot easily recognize a modified URL of a branded website.

Application Security/Attacks

Web applications have posed serious security vulnerabilities for public agencies for some time, especially with the rise of e-government services over the past five to ten years. In the Gov 2.0 context, two new trends have added to these security concerns: mobile applications and the rise of open application development contests or challenges by government agencies. Although there are current and emerging security standards in place for application development such as the Open Web Applications Security Project (OWASP) guidelines, tracking and enforcing these in the dynamic Gov 2.0 world is becoming increasingly difficult.

Mobile Government Applications

Predictions by virtually every reasonable technology source note that mobile connections to the Internet—smart phones, pads/tablets—will outstrip computer-based connections by around 2013. Symantec, a security company, and others in the industry report that as mobile phones become "smarter" and add new features, applications, data access, and connectivity, they open up entirely new avenues for cyber criminals. The development of mobile applications—stand-alone applications generally available for download from online application "stores" and mobile web applications generally available to any/all mobile users—is one of the richest areas of application development. The opportunities for mobile e-government services and mobile web applications are virtually endless. So, too, is the variability in the quality of mobile application development. In the commercial space, leading app stores, such as iTunes for iPhone-specific applications and the App Market for Android-based applications, screen applications for functionality, but, according to *Wired*, an industry magazine, do not generally assess security vulnerabilities or malware. More flexible mobile web applications that do not have to be distributed by the various app stores and are therefore potentially more widely accessible are prone to the same vulnerabilities as web-based e-government applications and services but include a layer of complexity because of the multitude of mobile handsets and operating systems in the market. Monitoring and management of this development is often beyond the expertise or capacity of local government IT personnel.

Open Applications Development Contests/Challenges

Vivek Kundra, the current Federal Chief Information Officer, launched in 2008 an "Apps for Democracy" contest while he was still the Chief Technology Officer for the District of Columbia. The simple idea was to open key government datasets and tools to the public, and allow companies and individuals to develop their own e-government applications for use by the government. New York City followed suit with its "NYC BigApps" contest, which is now in its own 2.0 version, and numerous other public sector agencies have followed suit since. In Southern California, the City of Anaheim completed its first "The Great Anaheim Apps Challenge," and the Los Angeles County Metropolitan Transportation Authority (Metro) announced in early 2011 its own "Metro Developers Challenge" focusing on transportation-related web and mobile applications using Metro datasets. Although a number of these contests, such as the one offered by Metro, indicate in their rules and guidelines that apps must be free of malware, this request is generally buried, reducing the potential prominence of this concern and not providing details on how apps can or will be screened for malware. Admittedly, the more that rules and structure infiltrate these Gov 2.0 crowdsourcing initiatives, the more likely they will be perceived to be not really open, but some very basic cybersecurity frameworks could go far in avoiding potentially major problems down the line. The potential for malware especially to be built or introduced into such "open" applications is a distinct vulnerability, especially if the contests and the resultant applications see greater usage by members of the public and the agencies.

Social Media Tools

According to a study by the Human Capital Institute and Saba, two human resources consultancies, 66% of all government agencies in the United States currently use some form of social networking. At the local level, a small but fast growing 31% of counties and municipalities utilize social media for external processes and as a more efficient means of engaging stakeholders, especially for feedback.

Symantec, a global leader in security, makes the case in its annual security threat report that the increasing adoption of social media by government agencies increases the risk of cyber attack. They especially point out the use of shortened URLs—an efficiency measure whereby lengthy URLs are shortened especially for microblogging such as Twitter—as being dangerous because they mask the true links behind them. The firm was sounding the alarm particularly for national-level governments and global corporations, and termed the rise of these highly targeted and sophisticated attacks cyber warfare: "Stuxnet and Hydraq, two of the most visible cyber-events of 2010, represented true incidents of *cyber warfare* and have fundamentally changed the threat landscape," said Stephen Trilling, senior vice president of Symantec Security Technology and Response (Stuxnet was a notable attack on nuclear facilities programs; Hydraq was used in an attack on Google.) However, the alarm should be no less loud for the local level.

In a recent study conducted over 4 months by the Georgia Tech Information Security Center (2011), an average of 130 instances of malware were found every day simply by searching for content on popular, "trending" topics via Twitter, Google, Yahoo!, and Bing.

The principal investigator noted that "While the issue of malware on social networking sites and popular search engines is quiet, it is consistent and happens around the clock, all day every day" (p. 7).

External Communications

One of the main drivers for government adoption of social media is its ease of use as an external communication tool. Facebook, Twitter, and blogging platforms can provide online identities that can be easily communicated and "liked" or "followed" by a potentially large number of constituents. In turn, constituents through the same channels can provide responses resulting in a potentially effective two-way channel. But social media as an external communication tool can be problematic due to issues that might arise from the real-time nature of the content, the brevity emphasized in communication, and the public/private division and conflicts that may be difficult to discern when employees and officials are using these tools.

For example, according to *Social Media Today*, an online social media news site, the Red Cross had an incident where an employee accidentally tweeted a personal tweet in their official account. They were able to rectify the situation with humor and turn the potentially embarrassing situation into a public positive, but such an example shows how easy it is that communication mistakes can happen and lines can be crossed when using open communication tools meant for public consumption. This is particularly true when government officials or public officers may have even official Facebook or Twitter accounts readily available, causing them to make known public views in real time that have not been thoroughly considered or worded. Senator Claire McCaskill (D-Mo) had such an incident when she attempted to express her view on the health care debate via Twitter after a long night at the office, resulting in poor word choice to appropriately express her viewpoint, according to an article in the *Huffington Post*.

Internal Collaboration

Social media also opens the doors for internal collaboration opportunities via blogs, wikis, and mash-up interfaces that include social media networks. Used effectively, social media can provide valuable productivity and efficiency tools for employees, often at a very low cost. However, without proper guidelines, monitoring and training these technologies can provide openings for inadvertent security breaches by employees, or worse yet, malicious security breaches.

Initial Defenses: Baseline Technological Controls

In addition to the most critical line of defense which is the human aspect, there are a growing number of accepted technology tools and approaches that if implemented in a strategic and methodical manner can provide a comprehensive safety net of sorts. The following is a sample list that has been adapted from N.Y. State Cybersecurity Guidelines for Social Media, the Federal CIO council, and others.

Universal Resource Locator (URL) and Internet Protocol (IP) Filtering

This is a fairly basic technology that blocks certain websites, parts of websites, or IP addresses identified by users or administrators. This can help protect users who may be redirected to a known malicious site. In addition, for some social networking sites, using URL filters to block the login pages for all but those employees with a business need, allows for access to public information while preventing access to applications and messaging tools that may bypass a State entity's security controls.

Malware Filtering at the Network Perimeter

This technology inspects traffic before it gets into an entity's network to ensure that it does not contain malware and blocks any malware that it finds. This can be implemented as part of a comprehensive screening, intrusion detection, and usage policy framework.

Intrusion Detection/Intrusion Prevention Systems

This technology provides near real-time monitoring and analysis of network activity for potential attacks in progress.

Data Loss Prevention

This technology is designed to detect and prevent the unauthorized use and transmission of confidential information. It should be used at both the desktop and the web gateway to monitor for and block outbound confidential data. With the rise of mobile data usage, this technology needs to keep pace with all data traffic in the network.

Moderating Content

When hosting a State-entity social media site, establish a process that would allow the host to moderate (i.e., preview, accept, reject) content submitted to the site prior to its being posted (i.e., made visible to visitors). This helps the host block content containing malicious links or inappropriate content.

URL Shortening Preview Tools

These tools display the actual URL destination masked by shortened URLs from services such as Google, TinyURL, and Bit.ly. The preview allows users to make informed decisions about links before clicking. Additionally, customized, branded short URLs can be created to increase legitimacy of content and connect the URL to the source sharing information.

Browser with Restricted Privileges

If available, this feature ensures that the browser and its add-ons run with a minimal set of permissions preventing the installation of malicious code.

Web Reputation Services

These services test websites for spam, spyware, scams, and so forth, and use those tests to give safety ratings to help users avoid visiting unsafe sites. For this technology to be most effective, it should be delivered with end-user training on how to interpret and use the ratings.

Policy Development around Social Media

Given the many potential cybersecurity issues indicated thus far, one of the ways in which government can begin to tackle these issues is to develop policy surrounding social media. Social media policy has to consider a number of factors:

- What social networks should be participating in
- What technologies may be required to participate fully in these social networks
- What standard user guides should be followed by staff (and who on staff should be given access)
- What plans are in place if an issue arises whether it is the dissemination of misinformation, the unauthorized use of an account, or one that may derive itself from the technologies utilized
- What visual and textual branding must be included to ensure constituents formally recognize such social networks as official channels of information

Perhaps most apparent in the list above, and especially in discussing specifically the development of policy, is that the human element must be emphasized.

Internal Considerations

With more and more social technologies becoming available, government agencies must decide how to use their resources in this regard and how to communicate with their specific audiences. A number of these implementations may be free or low cost, but there are monetary and time investments made to create and maintain online identities and information channels. Multiple investments increase the attention required to oversee various channels. It is worth understanding what will likely engage the target audiences and if there is adequate staff to maintain such channels appropriately.

Given the human resources and technologies required to be active participants in social media—to not only disseminate information in a timely matter but to also engage with users interacting with social tools—a part of policy should include how to determine which staff should be responsible for such engagement and the structure required to send out information on channels. For example, in situations that require real-time responses, who makes the call to provide this information to social channels and how should this information be worded or available? Having such policy and structures in place reduces the likelihood of miscommunication.

Additionally, social technologies can now include third-party software that enables access to these networks via desktop applications and mobile devices. This software may also be free or low cost, increasing productivity in these channels, but with additional technologies comes an increase in possible security concerns with products and more means of creating mistakes – especially if these tools enable users to add on multiple accounts that may mix up personal and professional participation.

Ultimately, a number of issues can be avoided or reduced if public sector employees are adequately trained and educated in how they should be engaging with constituents through these channels. Users of technology are often the weakest link in the chain as individual actions may be managed but never fully controlled. Human error and carelessness must be an anticipated factor when considering implementation of any technology. Some might argue that this is not acceptable, but mistakes can occur and will likely happen. In a survey with more than 100 technology, media, and telecommunications companies conducted by Deloitte, a consulting firm, in 2008, "human error" was indicated as a top factor in security threats and ran a gamut of issues with human error being cited by 75% of the participants, according to an article in *CIO.com*, an online magazine. By training and educating employees, some potential dangers can be mitigated. Additionally, by developing policy that includes making training materials available and mandatory for staff engaging with social media, government agencies and their staff will also increase awareness and understanding of their goals with social media and pro's and con's with integrating the experience into their organization.

External Considerations

Social media sites are targeted by cyber criminals because they offer an effective means of propagating malicious code to a wide, unsuspecting audience. According to a report from Websense Security

Labs, a leading web security provider, sites that allow user-generated content are among the most active distributors of malicious content, such as worms that can shut down networks, or spyware and keystroke loggers that can compromise data. Many postings to blogs, chat rooms, and message boards are spam or contain malicious links. Because many links on social media sites are in the form of shortened or condensed URLs (e.g., TinyURL, Bit.ly), a user is unable to determine where these links lead, making it easy for criminals to direct an unsuspecting user to malicious sites. The false sense of a trusted community when visiting social media sites increases the likelihood that a user may fall victim to this type of threat. If an employee is using State resources when this occurs (e.g., a work PC), these resources have an increased risk of becoming infected.

Rise of new positions, such as the Chief Digital Information Officer (NYC), or Director of Digital Communications (Metrolink, OCTA) brands web technology and digital solutions as a primary concern with a distinguishable future ahead. By officiating people to oversee policy and implementation of web solutions, it also provides a distinct and public understanding that standards and structure are required in this area and decisions must be made to proceed responsibly.

Adopted, published policies and guidelines are also a signal to citizens, evoking the foundational nature of Gov 2.0 as being a movement to an open, transparent, and "secure" arena. Citizens in a Web 2.0 world expect the integration of such technologies into their interactions with government entities, but there are still underlying concerns of privacy and public information sharing. Providing guidelines and policies can mitigate such concerns and open up for discussion additional needs and expectations of the citizens as development progresses in this area.

Similar to user guidelines for staff, public input should also have its own guidelines to ensure that users understand where their information is going, what is expected of their content, and in what ways their content can be removed, shown, or edited. Guidelines for public input help to shape expectations, facilitate dialogue, and reduce potential issues that may arise from content removal by directly citing guidelines that the user is adhering to with his or her participation. Policy should also be provided for how information is recorded for public record. This is especially important if there is already existing public policy related to the public record that must now accommodate for new technology and communication channels.

Microstudy—A Snapshot of Local Gov 2.0 in Southern California

This discussion is of particular importance at the local level where users are more likely to engage with, have a direct connection with, or be impacted by government information and transparency. The "mega-region" of Southern California is an ideal place to explore this emerging need in local government policy, as it is an expansive region including a rich variety of municipalities, large and small, and government agencies that have daily effects in citizens' lives from policy and utility perspectives.

This is supported by a brief survey conducted by the authors related to local-level government within the Southern California "mega-region." The microstudy explores the following questions within this area:

- Is Gov 2.0 formal policy currently available?
- Are there action plans that may create formal policy regarding Gov 2.0?
- What are the primary concerns of local-level municipality and government agencies about Gov 2.0?
- Are municipalities and agencies engaging in discussion or idea-sharing regarding Gov 2.0 implementation?
- Does social media adoption or mobile implementation impact this discussion?

For the purposes of this microstudy, "formal policy" is defined broadly and should encompass any type of organization-recognized plan or course of action that impacts the organization's procedures.

This survey was structured to generate a snapshot of policy development about Gov 2.0 implementation as well as gauge the level of implementation that is occurring in the sample area of Southern California. A key hypothesis to this survey is that matters of open government and concerns/actions of establishing related policy already existed. The survey was initiated over an approximate 4-month period beginning November 18, 2010, and for the purposes of this chapter, assesses the responses of six local agencies representing a diverse cross section of agency types, sizes, and geographic coverage in Southern California.

Participants were first recruited from a sample of convenience, primarily client association with Civic Resource Group (CRG), the e-government/Gov 2.0 consulting and development firm of which the authors are associated. The primary requirements for survey participation were as follows:

- The participant is affiliated with a public agency or municipality that is within the "mega region" of Southern California.
- The participant is employed in the position of having knowledge related to his or her agency or municipality's web technology implementation and needs, including knowledge of the agency or municipality's policy.

Those contacted were asked to become survey participants or forward the information to the appropriate potential participant within their own agency/municipality. Contacts were also asked to forward this survey to other related agencies and municipalities that fit the requirements.

For the targeted microstudy, the authors reached out to 10 initial contacts seeking participation in this survey. Of these 10, six participants responded to the survey in a timely fashion. The six respondents had the following:

- Three mid-sized cities with populations ranging from 60,000 to 100,000, each located in a different Southern California county
- An independent agency of a large Southern California county serving a population of about 10 million
- A small municipal water agency serving a population of less than 50,000
- A large regional planning organization covering multiple jurisdictions with about 19 million residents

A survey was developed by CRG and was finalized with 19 questions related to the following:

- General demographic information.
- General—Information technology/e-government planning and policy.
- Gov 2.0/open government.
- Social media.
- Mobile technology.

As Gov 2.0 is a relatively new term, a baseline definition was provided at the start of the survey:

> Gov 2.0 is the incorporation of Web 2.0 technologies in the government sector; this can encompass anything from social media integration to data sharing/transparency to online citizen collaboration. This may also be known as Open Government.

An e-mail with a link to a survey was sent out to a list of possible participants by the authors. E-mails were tailored to the specific people contacted. Participants were also asked to forward the survey link to other related contacts. Prior to filling out the survey, the participants were informed that all questions were optional and that the results of the survey would maintain confidential, as no individual or organization would be named in the results.

General—Information Technology/E-Government Planning and Policy

Participants were provided a list of information technology needs and asked to check up to five in terms of importance to their organization. Although there was no one need selected by all participants, two needs were selected by a majority (4 out of 6) of the participants: "automating internal operations/businesses processes" and "providing online services." Figure 9.1 shows all selected responses.

Participants were also asked to rank the importance of specified training categories for IT/E-Government Training Needs. They were also able to indicate and rank a category that was not prespecified. Similar to the ranking of IT Needs, no one category was ranked the most important across all respondents (see Figure 9.2). Two participants provided additional training categories under "Other"—one related to technical training as it related to e-government technologies, and the other related to training in the use of social media.

Of the respondents, five out of six had existing strategic plans for IT/E-Government in one form or another.

Gov 2.0/Open Government

Participants were asked the priority of Gov 2.0 to their organization, revealing mixed responses of two "High Priority," two "Medium

ITEM	PERCENT (%)
Automating internal operations/business processes	66
Providing online services	66
Providing citizens/residents with online participation and input tools	50
Providing more/better information online	50
Upgrading key internal systems (e.g., financial management, human relations)	50
Implementing line of business systems/applications for key services and departments (e.g., Parks and Rec, Public Works, Utilities)	33
Cloud computing for routine operations (e.g., e-mail)	16
Disaster recovery	16
Homeland security—information sharing, emergency communications, community alerts/information dissemination, collaboration, and so forth	16
Information security (cybersecurity)	16
Technology-/e-government-related training	16

Figure 9.1 Importance of technology needs.

Priority," and two "Low Priority" (see Figure 9.3). Only one out of the six participants, however, had made decisions or developed policy specifically related to Gov 2.0 (Figure 9.4) including one that noted his of her organization will be updating social media guidelines in 2011. One of the five respondents who indicated that he or she had no official policy, however, did elaborate that despite no formal policy the technologies of Gov 2.0 were still heavily used. Half of the respondents indicated that the subject of Gov 2.0 policy was something they had discussed with other government agencies.

Social Media

Five survey participants were also users of some type of social media. Figure 9.5 shows a chart of the types of social media used. Participants

TRAINING CATEGORY	RANK 1	RANK 2	RANK 3	RANK 4	RANK 5
E-Government training (planning, managing, and delivering information and services online)	3			1	
General computer/tech training for staff	1	1	2	1	
Information security training (technical, primarily for information technology, IT, staff)	1	1	2		1
Basic information security awareness training for all staff		1	1	2	
Other		1			1

Figure 9.2   Importance of training categories (1 = most important; 5 = least important).

were also able to specify other social media types, and two participants chose to add in a blog that was not included in the initial options.

Participants who responded to affirmatively to using social media were also asked their primary reasons for using social media (Figure 9.6). In addition to the options provided in the survey, they were able to indicate other reasons. Two participants provided additional reasons related to Public Participation/Two-Way Communication Channel with the Community.

Despite the use of social media by a majority of the participants, only one participant had an established policy for social media use either as a separate item or as part of a larger policy. Two indicated in corresponding notes, however, that such a policy was being considered or may be implemented in the near future.

Mobile Development

Almost all participants (five out of six) have considered or are considering mobile development in their IT/Web Planning. Participants

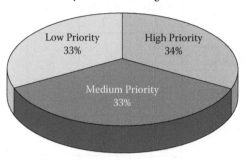

Figure 9.3   Gov 2.0 priority.

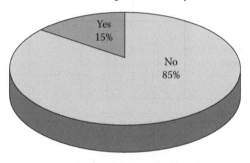

Figure 9.4   Gov 2.0 existing policy.

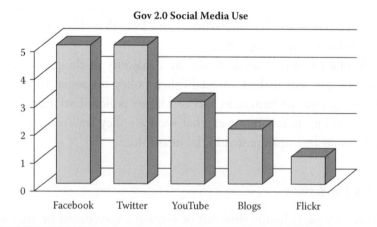

Figure 9.5   Social media use by participants.

PRIMARY REASONS FOR SOCIAL MEDIA USE	COUNT	PERCENT (%)
Popularity of social media tools	4	80
Public expectation of social media access	4	80
Ability to share information easily	3	60
Real-time benefits	3	60
Usefulness of social media as a tool	2	40
Outreach for public participation (two-way communication channel)	2	40

Figure 9.6   Reasons for social media use by participants who use social media.

PRIMARY REASONS FOR MOBILE DEVELOPMENT	COUNT	PERCENT (%)
Access to mobile tools/applications streamlines communication needs	4	80
Increased use/access of smart phones among citizens	4	80
Expected demand of mobile technology	3	60
Mobile mapping technology is beneficial to the purposes of the organization	2	40
Mobile technology provides additional functionality not afforded through other communication options	1	20

Figure 9.7   Reasons for social media use by participants.

were asked to indicate possible reasons for their mobile development. Responses can be seen in Figure 9.7.

Summary Findings

The results of this survey, particularly with its small sample of participants, do not provide a comprehensive review of the Gov 2.0 policy discussion in the mega-region of Southern California, but they do offer a snapshot of what is occurring in the region at the local level. The responses no doubt provide much insight into the questions related to Gov 2.0 that local government practitioners are facing in the region, particularly if the participants can each be seen as separate case studies as opposed to a representative sample.

The question of "Is Gov 2.0 formal policy currently available?" was only confirmed by one survey taker with the other participants leaning more toward working on action plans to create such policy. The existence of formal policy in at least one organization, the medium-to-high priority of Gov 2.0 among the participants, and the discussion of action plans to develop policy support the hypothesis that matters of open government and concerns/actions of establishing related policy currently exist.

The participants had mixed responses to the question of "Are municipalities and agencies engaging in discussion or idea-sharing regarding Gov 2.0 implementation?" Although this small sample size does not relay in any way *how much* discussion is occurring about Gov 2.0, it does reflect that at least some discussion is occurring.

No participant answered the question directly related to primary Gov 2.0 concerns of local-level municipality and government agencies, but some concerns in this area may be discernable from responses in the use of social media and support/plans for mobile development which are ripe areas for Gov 2.0 participation. All participants confirmed support or plans for mobile development, and five out of six respondents were participants of social media. Participants highlighted communication opportunities, public demand/expectation, and citizen use/access as key reasons for their participation in social media and support of mobile development.

Perhaps one of the most crucial pieces of information that supports the importance of Gov 2.0 policy discussion is the estimated populations of the constituents provided by the survey respondents. There were six participants in this survey, but the smallest population/user base estimate provided was around 20,000 and the highest around 19 million. Thus, the discussion of Gov 2.0 policy is an important one to begin to understand. The policies set forth by these municipalities and agencies, particularly in light of their public-oriented reasons for Gov 2.0 participation and development, can and will impact millions of people. From a policy and security perspective, this is even more crucial considering that almost all survey participants already had social media participation, and none were able to definitely say at the time that they had developed policy for its use.

Case Studies

As reflected in the microstudy, development and adoption of formal social media, or Gov 2.0 policies is still low at the local level. It is a relatively new area, and governments are struggling to understand how to best and responsibly manage implementation of Web 2.0 tools for public sector use. Policies can take two general paths—specific policies/guidelines dealing with security issues, or acceptable use policies and guidelines, or the combination of the two. The following case studies show the implementation of the policy at work.

THE CITY OF LONG BEACH—
SOCIAL MEDIA GUIDELINES

In late 2010, the City of Long Beach, a port city of nearly 500,000 located on the coast just south of Los Angeles, developed and published a set of Social Media Guidelines. The City claimed at the time that this was among the first, if not the first, document of its kind to be created and published by a municipal government agency. Although this claim has not been verified, the lack of readily findable social media or Gov 2.0 guidelines or policy-related documents appear to give support to that claim.

The following are some key excerpts from the City of Long Beach Social Media Guidelines. The first is descriptive text that clearly reflects how the City perceives social media tools, the City's use of such tools, and how an employee should understand his or her role when conducting City business within these authorized channels:

> Social media tools are designed to be circulated to a wide audience, many times beyond the initial intended audience. The line between private and public activity has been blurred by these tools and great care should be taken in crafting and sending messages, blog posts or tweets. Any content that you post represents you and the City of Long Beach to the outside world as much as a press release or the City's website does.

Guideline number 4 of the City of Long Beach Social Media Guidelines reflects specifically on ensuring that confidential and proprietary information remain undisclosed, clearly introducing how social channels blur boundaries:

Protecting confidential and proprietary information: Social computing blurs many of the traditional boundaries between internal and external communications. Be thoughtful about what you publish. You must make sure you do not disclose or use City confidential or proprietary information.

Guideline number 7 of the City of Long Beach Social Media Guidelines discusses specifically copyright and intellectual property laws that can be easily infringed upon or violated through online media and specifically addresses that content needs to be generated by staff:

Do not infringe copyrights or violate intellectual property laws. Do not post pictures, videos or other content directly onto City sites that was not taken or created by city employees.

ORANGE COUNTY TRANSPORTATION AUTHORITY (OCTA)—FORMAL DIGITAL COMMUNICATIONS POLICY DEVELOPMENT

The authors were specifically commissioned as web development and communications consultants to develop the formal digital communication policy for the Orange County Transportation Authority (OCTA). What initially began as the development of basic guidelines and how-to's on social media for employees developed into a larger "E-Communications Policy and Guidelines" project.

The E-Communications Policy was directly tied to OCTA's Digital Communications Strategic Action Plan including the application of the Action Plan's four "pillars" of digital communications:

- Web Communications (OCTA's corporate site, public site, and other affiliated project/program websites)
- External e-mail communications
- Mobile communications (OCTA mobile sites, applications, etc.)
- Social media (Facebook, Twitter, YouTube, and other current and future social media tools and networks)

By creating social media as its own "pillar" of information, OCTA's Digital Communications Strategic Action Plan provides social media with not only its own focused place in their digital strategy, but also provides it with the same prominence of more established "pillars" of the traditional web. The addition of mobile communications in this structure shows OCTA's broad understanding and commitment to responsibly implementing current and future technologies. In fact, the E-Communications Policy and Guidelines Summary specifically states:

> The Orange County Transportation Authority ("OCTA") recognizes the importance and public expectation of government transparency and open communications. OCTA's ability to effectively use all forms of electronic communications ("e-communications")—e-mail, web, mobile and social media among others—will be critical for the Authority to successfully communicate information to and connect with the general public.

The E-Communications Policy, however, is moreover focused on mitigating risks and guiding operational needs: "OCTA also understands that the implementation of e-communications comes with certain risks. This document provides a summary of OCTA's efforts to reduce such risks while also providing the necessary guidelines and policies that will assist in clear and concise e-communications."

It also clearly defines specific entities within OCTA that this policy will most likely be effecting in terms of operational needs and strategic value from e-communications technologies, services, and business processes. These entities included Public Outreach and Media Relations, Marketing, Customer Relations and Services, and Project/Program Specific Initiatives.

The creation of an E-Communications Policy also enabled OCTA to make a strategic and internal decision by naming the OCTA External Affairs Division and E-Communications Steering Committee as the specific internal division and committee that would be overseeing e-communications strategy and policy. In doing so, OCTA provides a functional starting point for a formalized process in which policy in this area must be discussed, vetted, and adopted, creating the formalized groundwork for adopting future technologies.

The following is a summary of points that OCTA's E-Communication Policy provides:

- Creating and using a channel given an "official" designation

- Guidelines for users and related policy (e.g., OCTA Code of Conduct Policy and OCTA User Guidelines for E-Communications) that they must follow
- Security compliance with OCTA's Internet Acceptable Use Policy and Electronic Messaging Security Policy
- Privacy concerns
- Records Management
- Disciplinary action

There are also associated policies that provide direction for

- Public comments, such as
  - Procedures for approving public comments
  - Guidelines for removing any comments
  - Guidelines for moderating content
- Recognized/approved channels including usage standards and requirements

Conclusion

Cybersecurity threats are on the rise, and all predictions point to their increasing frequency and levels of sophistication. In the public sector, these risks threaten the take-up of social media and Gov 2.0 by governments and agencies seeking to become more open and transparent. This is especially true at the local level, where local governments and agencies have an even greater pressure on them to engage their constituents directly, and to be as open as possible.

The basic conclusion to be drawn is that governments at all levels, and especially local governments, must continue to adopt, and in fact develop new, Gov 2.0 technologies and strategies in order to remain trusted providers of public services and information. However, governments must do so in a careful, strategic manner, with the policies, guidelines, technological tools, and training in place to defend against cybersecurity threats.

Part of this careful and strategic approach involves making clear business decisions about the value of specific Gov 2.0/social media tools and initiatives. By assessing the potential risks of specific initiatives or long-term strategies, proper planning and resources can be allocated to implement and manage them. Figure 9.8 provides a high-level framework for this kind of assessment.

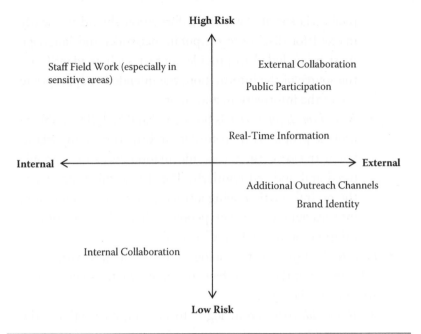

Figure 9.8 Potential risk assessment in Gov 2.0 participation.

While signing up for a social media account and providing users with information (or asking for their feedback) may appear straightforward and easy, the decision for a government agency to participate in Web 2.0 technology and trends bring up a number of risks and issues, as illustrated by Figure 9.8.

- *High risks:* Ultimately, the actions of people are the greatest risk that Gov 2.0 participation must bear.
  - *Public Participation* must be met with policies that ensure that the agencies articulate clearly responsibilities, disclaimers, and policies that enable them to monitor/remove content.
  - *External Collaboration* requires safe measures to ensure that public contributions adequately match the needs and desires of the agencies/organizations. The policies provided in Public Participation must apply here as well, and how participants are providing information must be assessed and analyzed for all possible security risks prior to implementation.
  - Staff Participation must be met with policies as well—staff must understand how they should communicate to the

public via social channels. Information should be clearly marked for disclosure on public networks and language must be included to provide context such as identifying the source of the information, the intended or appropriate use of the information, and so on.

- *Real-Time Information* is both good and bad. Being able to provide people with up-to-date information is important, but at the same time, this information needs to be monitored and updated regularly. The risk of this type of on-the-go information being available increases when taking into account that other people will likely share official information in "real time" as well.

- *Low Risks*: Gov 2.0 technologies and strategies with lower risks are often those that have increased controls before they are open to the public:

  - *Brand Identity*: From logos to naming conventions, the brand identity of the organization must extend through Web 2.0 channels *before* it is implemented.

  - *Additional Outreach Channels*: There are numerous tools in the social web and Gov 2.0 must make conscious decisions about what tools to use. Despite the zero to low cost of signing up for accounts, these channels require staff and staff time, and there is a risk in choosing to participate in channels that will not be beneficial to the organization.

- *Internal Collaboration:* Gov 2.0 opens many doors for internal collaboration and communication, but this, too, has potential risks including the difficulties that may arise in attempting to manage many internal channels, and the misuse or abuse by employees.

As with any new technologies, business models, and services, governments tend to lag well behind the private sector in their adoption. This has also been the case with social media and Web 2.0. Governments are poised, however, to accelerate their implementation of these technologies and strategies, and in fact shape them into an emerging platform—Gov 2.0—developed specifically around the needs of the public sector. Local governments and agencies can be the leaders in this development, and in so doing become more open, transparent, and accountable. Cybersecurity threats new and old will always face the users and advancers of new technologies. Fear of these threats should not stifle innovation but rather stimulate the kind of sound preparations, responses, and new technologies to protect the public good.

References

CIO Council's Guidelines for Secure Use of Social Media by Federal Departments and Agencies: http://www.cio.gov/documents_details.cfm/uid/1F4378B4-2170-9AD7-F2A2B098D3F954EE/structure/Information%20Technology/category/IT%20Security-Privacy.

CIO Magazine—Human error tops the list of Security Threats: http://www.cio.com/article/179802/Human_Error_Tops_the_List_of_Security_Threats.

CommuniquPR—Be prepared for human error in social media: http://www.communiquepr.com/blog/?p=2192.

Department of the Army: http://www.army.mil.

Drapeau, M. (2010). What does Government 2.0 look like? *O'Reilly Radar.* Retrieved from http://radar.oreilly.com/2010/05/what-does-government-20-look-l.html.

Federal Communications Commission: http://www.fcc.gov/pshs/services/911-services/enhanced911/.

Georgia Tech Information Security Center. Emerging Cyber Threats Report, 2011.

Huffington Post: http://www.huffingtonpost.com/2009/07/21/mccaskills-twitter-mistak_n_241699.html.

Human Capital Institute and Saba, "Social Networking in Government: Opportunities and Challenges," January 2010.

ICMA, *PM Magazine*: http://webapps.icma.org/pm/9109/public/cover2.cfm.

Information Week: http://www.informationweek.com/news/government/state-local/showArticle.jhtml?articleID=225400061.

Ionology, Local Government and Social Media: http://www.ionology.com/blog/is-local-government-ready-for-social-media/.

Metro Developer Challenge: http://developer.metro.net/developer-challenge/official-rules/.

New York State Office of Cyber Security and Critical Infrastructure Coordination, "Cyber Security Guideline G10-001: Secure Use of Social Media," May 10, 2010.

New York Times: http://opinionator.blogs.nytimes.com/2010/11/25/the-public-square-goes-mobile/.

PC Magazine, "Human Error" Causes Timbir Server Breach: http:/eventsof2011.com/tech/human-error-causes-tumbir-server-breach-pc-magazine.

Politics Daily: http://www.politicsdaily.com/2011/03/12/are-social-media-the-future-of-local-government/.

Secure Use of Social Media, Cyber Security Guideline G10-001, New York State, Office of Cyber Security and Critical Infrastructure Coordination, May 10, 2010.

Social Media and Web 2.0 in Government: http://www.howto.gov/social-media.

Social Media Today: http://socialmediatoday.com/kanter/271724/lessons-red-cross-twitter-mistakes-and-how-handle-them.

The Vulnerability of Data: http://socialmediaclub.org/blogs/social-media-observer/vulnerability-data.

Waxler, C. CIOs Struggle with Social Media's Security Risks, *Public CIO*, February 11, 2011.

Wired, "Android Market Apps Hit with Malware": http://www.wired.com/threatlevel/2011/03/android-malware/.

10

THE CIVILIAN CYBER INCIDENT RESPONSE POLICIES OF THE U.S. FEDERAL GOVERNMENT

CHRIS BRONK

Contents

Introduction

Cyber, in certain circles one does not even need to append "security" to the term, is a topic of burgeoning interest for several reasons. First, ubiquitous and mobile computing coupled with the movement toward digital formats and the low cost of reproduction has resulted in government fear for loss of information control. This is a problem both in regard to personally identifiable information (PII) of public sector employees and those served by them as well as confidentiality of records not meant for public consumption, exemplified by the intelligence reports posted by WikiLeaks. Second, information technology (IT) has changed the way government works and has become a massive component of public sector budgets. According to the Federal IT Dashboard, the federal government spent $81.9 billion on IT in fiscal year 2010. Third, securing information systems is costly. According to the Office of Management and Budget (OMB), the Department of Homeland Security holds a 2011 budget of more than $350 million for its cybersecurity directorate while the National Security Agency spends upwards of $1 billion on securing the systems of the Department of Defense (DoD) alone, according to the 2011 budget request and reports in *Information Week* (Hoover, 2010), an industry publication. As funding increases, the cybersecurity agenda in Washington will continue to rise in political importance.

But despite all this spending, government computer systems remain vulnerable. For example, three-quarters (75%) of 217 senior-level IT executives at U.S. federal organizations said they experienced one or more data breach incidents in the prior year, according to a 2009 survey conducted by the Ponemon Institute, a consultancy. How to respond to such cyber incidents, whether major data breaches or potentially crippling attacks launched against pieces of critical infrastructure, such as the power grid or telecommunications system, is a major challenge. The global digital interconnection and reliance on networked computers will lead to unanticipated externalities, prompting serious thought about the current state of cyber incident response for government organizations. Two major events in 2010 illustrate this new security era. First, to the dismay of officials around the world, WikiLeaks, an online nonprofit organization, demonstrated the potential unintended consequences of massive digital information compromise by posting thousands of U.S. government reporting cables and raw intelligence reports on the Internet for anyone to view. Second, the reported execution of Stuxnet, a malicious computer worm targeting an Iranian uranium enrichment facility at Natanz, exemplified that it is possible to accomplish physical damage using the Internet.

In order to help public sector managers gain a better operational understanding of their cyber environment, the first part of this chapter provides an overview of the civilian U.S. federal government cyber incident response challenges and reviews relevant policies, including requirements of the Federal Information Security Management Act (FISMA) and guidance from the National Institute for Standards and Technology (NIST) and other civilian agencies. The second part discusses the issue of a national cyber incident response policy, with emphasis on the draft National Cyber Incident Response Plan (NCIRP) and the issues present in mounting an effective response to the sorts of events within the domain of possibility, both known and unknown.

The Cyber Incident Conundrum

A cyber attack will generally render three possible results: (1) a denial of availability to information, (2) a compromise of confidentiality of information, or (3) a subversion of the integrity of information. Denial of availability may be undertaken to protest a particular policy or government service. Thieves may profit from confidential information. Altering government documents may sow confusion or obstruct lawful activity. Typically, we would see these as criminal acts. And there is general agreement that cybercrime is a growing problem. However, differentiating between criminal acts, mere electronic hooliganism, or serious threats to national security is not always apparent as a cyber attack is detected or unfolds.

In coping with cybersecurity, public sector managers must connect government policy with the technical vocabulary of computing and information security. In any real-world incident scenario, the primary issue for the information manager is simply to make the unauthorized activity stop. This necessitates asking what policy has been enacted to aid systems managers in achieving this. Mitigation is at the heart of any incident response and has been incorporated into the policy directives adopted by the U.S. government in the last decade, but less is known of the response process.

Responding to cyber incidents is a dynamic activity as they vary tremendously in impact and scope. For example, some incidents can be seen immediately, such as when systems are knocked offline, but for others this may not be the case, as breaches can continue for periods of great length without discovery. For the IT manager, whether a systems administrator, division head, or chief information officer (CIO), the issue of how to respond should cover a number of questions:

- Is the incident ongoing or has activity ceased?
- Have the culpable parties and technologies been located?
- Should notice of the incident, as currently understood, be passed to higher authority?
- Should vendors of affected technologies or those providing other services be contacted?
- Is it necessary to report the incident to law enforcement?
- Does the incident indicate a wider pattern of activity?

Although this list of considerations is by no means exhaustive, it represents the sort of thinking embodied in the organizational triage that is and will continue to be required in responding to incidents in which digital resources are compromised. Mitigation of incidents increasingly involves elements beyond technology. This provides an important insight for incident response: prevention is often painfully simple in hindsight. For example, according to the 2010 Data Breach Investigations Report from Verizon, an American telecommunications firm, 85% of confirmed data breaches were not deemed highly difficult and 96% of them could have been avoided through simple or intermediate controls.

Civilian Response Policies

Early manifestation of government's desire to secure digital resources can be traced to research by organizations such as SRI International and MITRE by Bell and LaPadula (1973) on behalf of the Department of Defense on computer security, which eventually grew into policy through publication of the Trusted Computer

Security Evaluation Criteria (TCSEC), which dates to 1983. These works largely focused on how to protect information resources through system design. This remains a point of emphasis for computer security, as policy guidance still largely covers prevention of incidents rather than a response to them.

At a time when former generals and top-level government officials, such as William Lynn (2010), the Deputy Secretary of Defense, warn of potentially massive disruptions to critical infrastructures, such as power and water provision, the U.S. government appears woefully behind in securing its own computer systems as well as those it depends upon, which are held by other public and private stakeholders. But arguments that federal systems are either hopelessly vulnerable or amply protected are both flawed. With a middle ground somewhere between those poles as our starting point, reevaluating strategy of response to improve incident management is required. This is largely because existing policy has not been linked to any improvement in either vulnerability mitigation or enhanced incident response capabilities. The information security strategy for the classified systems of the military and intelligence services will largely take place out of public view and is not considered in the purview of this chapter. Thus, high-level policy consideration is largely directed at the Federal Information Security Management Act (FISMA) of 2002 that dictates security policy for unclassified information systems.

The Policy Umbrella: The Federal Information Security Management Act (FISMA)

In 2002, FISMA instituted government-wide directions for federal agencies to secure their information systems. It mandated that agencies would send reports to the Office of Management and Budget (OMB) and then receive feedback regarding performance. The process, grossly simplified, involves (1) creating an inventory of systems, (2) categorizing information on the systems and determining its importance, (3) conducting risk assessment, (4) creating a security plan, (5) certifying and accrediting systems, and (6) engaging in continuous monitoring of systems. With FISMA, OMB, in theory, could deny an agency funding if it failed to take adequate measures to secure its computer systems.

But FISMA did not solve the government's information security problems. To an outside observer, such as security specialist Wm. Arthur Conklin (2008), it seems that much or even most federal activity on the security of information systems emphasizes preparedness and an understanding of systems operations rather than proper incident response. FISMA put the task of implementing the law's provisions upon the agencies themselves, with OMB standing as a reviewer of reporting. A recurring question of those responsible for information systems security in government agencies was what bearing the paperwork process of FISMA, primarily the ongoing need to certify and accredit systems as secure, had on the actual information security posture of those systems.

To a computer engineer or systems administrator focusing on the security of systems, the idea that an annual review or multiyear certification would say much of anything about systems security is incomprehensible as threats continuously evolve. A properly certified system may become vulnerable at any time. Accreditation does not provide a guarantee of trouble-free operation but rather offers a basic level of certainty that the system is operating in a manner that security practitioners would find acceptable.

Despite this, federal agencies' systems security offices and the firms they contract to produce the reporting to comply with the law expend considerable effort in filling out certification and accreditation (C&A) reporting templates as a part of the FISMA process. In 2010, there has been increased push back on how to meet the FISMA mandate. In May, NASA's deputy CIO for IT security, Jerry Davis, argued in an agency-wide memorandum that the fiscal year 2010 FISMA instructions from OMB were, "clear regarding a shift away from cumbersome and expensive C&A paperwork processes, in favor of a value-driven, risk-based approach to systems security" (p. 1). What is unclear, however, is exactly how such an approach to cybersecurity would be undertaken. There may be a consensus that the certification and accreditation machine that FISMA has become is undesirable or even perhaps counterproductive, but the alternatives are unknown.

Managing Incidents: Guidance from Government

Moving beneath the umbrella that FISMA represents, the U.S. government has also produced significant guidance on how to prepare for information security incidents. The National Institute for Standards and Technology (NIST) within the Department of Commerce is tasked with translating the vision encapsulated within FISMA into binding standards called the Federal Information Processing Standards (FIPS) and recommendations (Special Publications). In a role defined by the OMB's Circular A-130, NIST standards and guidance produced by its Computer Security Division are applied to all federal information systems transmitting unclassified information (see Table 10.1). There are currently 14 NIST FIPS, largely providing guidance regarding cryptography. Much longer is the list of Special Publications, more than 120 including appendices and revisions.

FIPS requirements are mandatory, whereas the Special Publications are more granular guidelines providing practical "how-to" advice on computer security. A handful of the NIST guidance publications cover remedies regarding malware or forensics, but only one, Special Publication 800-61: Computer Security Incident Handling Guide, tackles the issue of how an agency should respond to a major computer

Table 10.1   Assignment of Information Security Responsibilities under Circular A-130

AGENCY	RESPONSIBILITY
Department of Commerce	Develop and issue standards guidance
	Provide computer security awareness
	Offer security planning guidance
	Coordinate agency incident response
	Evaluate new information technologies
Department of Defense	Provide technical advice and assistance
	Evaluate vulnerabilities and emerging technologies
Department of Justice	Provide guidance on legal remedies
	Coordinate with law enforcement on incidents
	Pursue legal action in the wake of security incidents
General Services Administration	Provide guidance on security in information technology (IT) acquisition
	Facilitate contracting for security products
	Provide security services to federal agencies
Office of Personnel Management	Update and maintain training for awareness and practice

Source: U.S. Office of Management and Budget, Circular A-130.

security event. What SP 800-61 covers in detail are the general forms of incident that take place: (1) denial of service, (2) malicious code, (3) unauthorized access, (4) inappropriate usage, and (5) multiple components, acknowledging that lines between incident forms may be blurred. These distinctions, while still largely valid, must evolve with the increased sophistication of attacks that target specific resources or actors by multiple mechanisms. SP 800-61 also offers a four-step cycle for incident response: (1) preparation; (2) detection and analysis; (3) containment, eradication, and recovery; and (4) postincident activity. These steps provide the structure for the current civilian U.S. federal government workflow of incident response as discussed below.

Step 1: Preparation

The first step involves the drafting of policy and identifying resources for incident response. Preparation typically means maintaining systems with no vulnerabilities, or at least as few as possible. In regard to response after a threat has exploited a vulnerability to produce an incident, this is the component of guidance that suggests the formation of an incident or emergency response team. Also involved in this component are mechanisms to escalate response to an incident as necessary. Everything that might be needed to overcome an incident, from human capital to replacement hardware, is covered by this phase of incident response. The emphasis in preparation is in building the foundation for a rapidly scalable activity involving staff who may not hold intimate knowledge of affected systems. Technical documentation of network information, data formats, system policies, and expected operational baselines are vital in incident response.

Step 2: Detection and Analysis

Analyzing systems operations to detect incidents emphasizes the capacity to identify departure from the norm in system function. This can be fairly simple to detect, as in the case of a denial of service attack in which many users as well as the system manager(s) observe dysfunction, or quite hard, as when an authorized user spirits away data or a camouflaged Trojan awaits instructions to perform its function.

Baselines for system function are pivotal in detection. Rules should be established for system function, and when those rules are violated, alarms should sound. As such, this component of incident response has been a heavily technical effort. Networks are guarded by intrusion detection systems, hosted by antivirus software, and so on. The problem is that new incidents are occurring rapidly and the code base on which organizational information systems function needs to constantly evolve.

Step 3: Containment, Eradication, and Recovery

The third step encompasses the often ugly business of repairing damaged systems and returning them to trouble-free operation. It is both a science and an art. Evidence is typically collected and determining the source of the attack is desirous but not always possible. There can be conflicting needs in closing the door on a vulnerability. Improving the chances of successful prosecution may necessitate collection of additional evidence; however, system operators and other stakeholders may want only for the vulnerability to be mitigated and a return to normal operation.

Step 4: Postincident Activity

Finally, in the postincident phase, emphasis is placed on learning lessons of what occurred and incorporating those into future IT management decisions. This may include determining the costs incurred and assessing the level of harm to the organization and its systems. Of course, some incidents are easier to put a price tag on than others. An hour of downtime on a revenue-generating website has a different cost than the leak of sensitive or classified reports. This variation goes largely unconsidered in NIST guidance today.

U.S. Computer Emergency Readiness Team (US-CERT)

Also mentioned in SP 800-61 is the role of the U.S. Computer Emergency Readiness Team (US-CERT), a group within the Department of Homeland Security (DHS). US-CERT is a coordinating body for cybersecurity incident response and awareness for the

U.S. federal government. It publishes known vulnerabilities and is designated to aid agencies in their response to security incidents; however, its products appear somewhat comparable to other vulnerability reporting from industry, and it is unclear to what degree US-CERT renders assistance beyond the boundaries of DHS. Reporting of activity from US-CERT is thin. The December 2010 activity report is typical of US-CERT's public communications. It documents software security vulnerabilities and widely known e-mail phishing scams but provides no hint of what major response activities it might have engaged in during the period in which WikiLeaks and Stuxnet were front-page news.

But rendering assistance in major incidents is what US-CERT is supposed to do. According to federal law, when a computer security incident is discovered by a federal civilian agency, commonly referred to as a dot-gov entity in federal IT circles, it must be reported to US-CERT. This fulfills a FISMA (2011) requirement for federal agencies on "notifying and consulting with the Federal information security incident center," in the event of a security incident, and stands as the point of exchange when an incident migrates from an agency issue to an item to be addressed by an interagency process. This is where federal guidance becomes more complicated, as is evinced within national-level plans to cope with major cyber incidents.

Constructing National Policy for Cyber Incident Response

The development of national cyber incident response policy occurring in the civilian agencies of the federal government is largely handled by DHS. In December 2003, Homeland Security Presidential Directive 7 (2011) tasked the department with responsibilities to "maintain an organization to serve as a focal point for the security of cyberspace." DHS responded with the publication of its December 2004 National Response Plan (NRP), which superseded response planning prepared by the Federal Emergency Management Agency (FEMA) during the Clinton Administration. The 2004 NRP (Bush, 2004) included a component addressing response to a major cyber attack, the Cyber Incident Annex. In 2008, the NRP was superseded by the newly enacted National Response Framework; however, as of early

2011 a successor document to the Cyber Incident Annex has yet to be released.

The 2004 Cyber Incident Annex is a highly compact piece of policy guidance for the federal government. It catalogues the agencies to be involved in cyber incident response, identifies policy authorities, and provides a concept of operations for government regarding a non-military cyber incident. As unclassified, public guidance for the community of responders to a cyber incident, it provides only the barest of instructions regarding which offices in government to contact and when to do so in case of an emergency. Two issues raised in the 2004 Annex remain problematic. First is the limited size of pooled expertise on cyber incident response and the capacity for responders to meet a crisis. The second has to do with coordination with the private sector. As the Annex's authors (Bush, 2004, p. CYB-5) opined, "Cyberspace is largely owned and operated by the private sector; therefore, the authority of the Federal Government to exert control over activities in cyberspace is limited." In the Obama Administration's revisiting of a response plan, these items remain the two most complicated.

Currently Planned Efforts

As of early 2011, the Obama Administration's National Cyber Incident Response Plan (NCIRP) remains a draft. The plan represents an attempt to build upon the White House's 2009 Cyberspace Policy Review, spearheaded by Melissa Hathaway, which recommended preparation of a "cybersecurity incident response plan." Part of a near-term action plan, the NCIRP was prepared by the DHS to serve as a more concrete set of guidance for the United States to work from in the event of a major cyber incident affecting the information systems of the government. NCIRP differentiates between various levels of risk and response with a set of shelves, the National Cyber Risk Alert Levels (NCRAL) (Table 10.2).

Designed to steer resources and activate communications channels in response to a major cyber event, NCIRP is linked to the updated iteration of the NRP, now dubbed the National Response Framework (NRF) (Department of Homeland Security, 2008). Overseen by the Federal Emergency Management Agency (FEMA), the NRF is a self-described guide to an all-hazard response by the nation and provides

Table 10.2 National Cyber Risk Alert Levels

LEVEL	LABEL	DESCRIPTION OF RISK	LEVEL OF RESPONSE
1	Severe	Highly disruptive levels of consequences are occurring or imminent	Response functions are overwhelmed, and top-level national executive authorities and engagements are essential; exercise of mutual aid agreements and federal/nonfederal assistance is essential
2	Substantial	Observed or imminent degradation of critical functions with a moderate to significant level of consequences, possibly coupled with indicators of higher levels of consequences impending	Surged posture becomes indefinitely necessary, rather than only temporarily; the Department of Homeland Security Secretary is engaged, and appropriate designation of authorities and activation of federal capabilities such as the Cyber Unified Coordination Group (UCG) take place; other similar nonfederal incident response mechanisms are engaged
3	Elevated	Early indications of, or the potential for but no indicators of, moderate to severe levels of consequences	Upward shift in precautionary measures occurs; responding entities are capable of managing incidents/events within the parameters of normal, or slightly enhanced, operational posture
4	Guarded	Baseline of risk acceptance	Baseline operations, regular information sharing, exercise of processes and procedures, reporting and mitigation strategy continue without undue disruption or resource allocation

Source: National Cyber Incident Response Plan, Interim Version (NCIRP), Department of Homeland Security, September 2010, p. 3.

guidance on how the different layers of government, from federal to local, as well as nongovernmental organizations (NGOs) and the private sector should respond to disaster events.

Largely predicated to serve as the blueprint for an enormous cyber event that has yet to take place, the self-declared purpose of NCIRP is to provide a comprehensive "strategic framework for operational roles, responsibilities, and actions to prepare for, respond to, and begin to coordinate recovery from a cyber incident" (p. 1). NCIRP is important as it is a national plan, not merely one to cover the agencies of the U.S. federal government. Specifically, NCIRP's framework covers all levels of government, from international to local, as well as purveyors and users of IT in the private sector. The document covers four components: (1) a national concept of operations, (2) the organization of the National Cybersecurity and Communications Integration Center, (3) an outline of the incident response cycle, and (4) the roles and responsibilities that cut across federal agencies and other stakeholders in the national cybersecurity enterprise. Each component will be reviewed in turn.

Concept of Operations

According to NCIRP (2010), successful response to a cyber incident depends on effective communication and "requires close coordination across traditional boundaries and requires the development of a robust common operational picture as a foundational element" (p. 3). There is a concern for incident response in regard to communication of information from classified resources inside government and proprietary information held by industry. What the NCIRP will depend upon is a capacity for centralized coordination and decentralized execution. Through its National Cybersecurity and Communications Integration Center (NCCIC), DHS will serve as a hub for response but will need to marshal resources from the Executive Office of the President; Departments of Defense, Justice and State; other Sector Specific Agencies (i.e., Department of Energy for electricity issues); state, local, tribal, and territorial governments, the private sector; and NGOs. In practice this likely means that personnel (analysts, engineers, forensics experts, and others) will be seconded to the NCCIC to cope with a crisis. There may, however, be an issue with such a strategy if many of the stakeholders are also responding to the same crisis.

With the number of participants large in an NCIRP response, the federal government is placed in a position where it should accept that there will be an enormous capacity for leadership discretion in the improvisation of those charged with managing it. Further, according to NCIRP, "The authorities and capabilities of each entity often must change in size, scope and complexity as situations evolve." In the concept of operations, DHS is identified in two capacities, as a supported organization, a role in which it would serve as the lead civilian agency for incident response, and as a supporting organization. In regard to the latter, in a major incident response, lead agency authority may shift to the DoD, but until then, DHS's coordinating bodies would hold the role of shaping incident response. Finally, NCIRP acknowledges that, "As incidents become more complex, incorporating cyber and physical effects, more agencies and organizations may need to become involved" (p. 10).

The Response Center

At the heart of any cyber incident response is the National Cybersecurity and Communications Integration Center. Designed to tackle both day-to-day activities as well as manage more significant incident responses, the NCCIC will be the nerve center of civilian response to major cybersecurity incidents. An amalgamation of the U.S. Computer Emergency Readiness Team (US-CERT), National Coordinating Center for Telecommunications (NCC), and the National Cybersecurity Center (NCSC), the NCCIC also includes input from DHS's Intelligence and Analysis office and, "private sector partners," according to a 2009 press release from DHS. Ostensibly what this input adds up to is large quantities of information regarding security incidents and potential options for response. In mandate, NCCIC is to produce guidance for consumers across government and provide information publicly to those concerned with cyber incident response. This translates to the provision of guidance on security vulnerabilities similar to that provided by industry players such as Symantec and McAfee.

Among the issues of concern for the NCCIC is the capacity to scale up to meet the demand of coordinating the diverse set of actors involved in incident response. Just as the Pentagon grappled with all manner of interservice communications and organizational issues as it pushed the military toward a concept of "jointness" in its operations, so too will there be a need to cover these problems among the set of stakeholders, both public and private, that will be charged with responding to a major cyber event. What DHS will need to consider is how it will create a shared information picture with the command centers of other organizations. For instance, how can the NCCIC develop the capacity to see the situation in network operations centers such as Verizon's in Virginia or AT&T's in New Jersey when such a need arises? Codifying such relationships will not be easy, but will be necessary so that bonds of trust between U.S. government officials and professionals in the telecom sector will exist when something goes wrong.

The Response Cycle

One item given great consideration in the period between publication of the 2004 Cyber Incident Annex and the drafting of NCIRP is demarcating the phases of incident response. In NCIRP, the response cycle is broken down into five phases: (1) prevent and protect (i.e., ordinary day-to-day monitoring and operations), (2) detect, (3) analyze, (4) respond, and (5) resolve. The first two components of the cycle will fall upon the distributed constellation of system owners who may call upon the NCCIC for assistance, but it is the analysis and response portions that will need the greatest degree of attention from DHS and other government stakeholders as the United States moves forward in developing its civilian cybersecurity operations.

In the analysis phase, responders are to identify the incident in its National Cyber Risk Alert Level (NCRAL) system, which is employed to assess the impact of any cyber incident (see Table 10.2). Guidance on responses to be undertaken in responding to and resolving the incident would be based on this four-tiered system. Although the NCCIC will be able to call upon many sources of data regarding threats and vulnerabilities, it would be useful for it to develop strong capabilities in locating expertise and technical talent that can reinforce government efforts in determining the nature of cyber incidents and understanding their impact. Only by having preexisting relationships with the builders of hardware and software, as well as those experienced in mitigating vulnerability with respect to systems of high importance will the analysis portion of the NCIRP's response cycle have the opportunity to meet problems with any chance of success. In the analytical phase, the DHS will need brainpower on tap, and lots of it.

Once the analytical work begins leading to hypotheses regarding remedies, the other great challenge of cyber incident response, mentioned in the 2004 Cyber Incident Annex, emerges, the organization, management, and coordination of surge capacity to mount the response. There is language regarding what parts of an incident action plan to employ in NCIRP, but the extent of reach beyond the boundaries of the federal government envisaged by the NCIRP is unclear.

Roles and Responsibilities

Finally, NCIRP (2010, p. 27) specifies some universal roles and responsibilities regarding preparedness, incident response, and recovery. "All organizations are responsible...for preparedness activities," according to NCRIP, including engagement with NCCIC, maintenance of response plans, development of incident assignments, prepositioning of resources, training of incident responders, conduct of response exercises, and institution of evaluation mechanisms. Mandating such activity is an issue not yet decided by the U.S. Congress.

Ways Forward

Crises are crises because they are largely unexpected or do not conform to advanced planning. As a society, we are increasingly cognizant of problems produced by data breaches and the increasingly realized potential of attacks launched against real pieces of infrastructure controlled by computers. Cyber warfare, which to most seemed like science fiction not long ago, now appears real. Reports of the Stuxnet worm's impact on uranium enrichment activities by Iran and the releases of sensitive information by WikiLeaks are indicators that cyber incident response policy is needed.

A key challenge in the analytical phase, however, is sharing information, both within government and beyond. Pooling together resources to mount an effective response to a national-level incident will most likely involve questioning assumptions on how government and industry work together. For instance, most of the DHS incident responders hold U.S. government security clearances but few in the private sector do. In fact, many of those charged with running and securing the networks of the largest U.S. corporations may not even be residents of the United States.

Furthermore, the universal roles and responsibilities specified in NCIRP speak for a common situational awareness across government and the private sector, but it is unclear this can be mandated. While debate in Congress has often degenerated to disagreement regarding an Internet "kill switch," we are left to wonder how the country will marshal its resources, from the analytical talent found in universities, government labs, and industry to the legions of systems engineers that will be needed to clean up the mess that may be a major cyber incident. We have no concept of what civil defense, indeed civil security, means in cyberspace. This must change, and soon.

Then there is the fissure between civil security and military action. The Department of Defense, which has indicated tremendous interest in the topic of cybersecurity and cyber warfare, has yet to release an unclassified doctrine of either offensive or defensive cyber operations. But the United States needs a strong cyber warfare doctrine, according to a former NSA director as reported in *Defense Systems* (Jackson, 2010), an industry publication, which would be incredibly useful as it usually sets clear rules of conduct and behavior in an organizational setting. Well-crafted, cogent, and adaptive doctrine may allow those on the receiving end of cyber attacks to have a clear idea of who and where to call when a particular piece of evidence is found or type of attack is underway.

But there is the lingering question of when to call in the Pentagon. It will certainly hold significant resources for incident response, but we need to determine the point at which we want the U.S. Cyber Command to collaborate actively with the private sector, such as major Wall Street banks like Wells Fargo, JP Morgan Chase, or the Bank of America. Even though it would be useful to improve information sharing on an ongoing basis regarding incident response between the private and public sectors, this blurs the civil-military lines that will likely prompt strong reactions from corporate and national security lawyers alike, but is necessary nonetheless.

Collaboration on information security matters between government, industry, and academia largely currently rests with working groups constituted under the auspices of the Departments of Homeland Security and Defense, as well as the National Institute for Standards and Technology. These working groups, while helpful in developing relationships and providing venues for discussion are only a piece of the puzzle of developing the capacity to build government/ nongovernment response communities. A better answer may be to constitute regional cybersecurity information clearinghouses in which government is an active participant and does not hold participants at arm's length with onerous national security information control regimes. The idea is to have practitioners together to share ideas and expertise both physically and virtually in advance of a major event.

Developing the planning for and actually responding to the cyber incidents that grow in number and impact with each passing month will be the best path to being more effective responders. It is incumbent upon those charged with responding to these incidents to take good notes and share them widely.

References

Bell, D. E., and L. J. LaPadula, "Secure Computer Systems: Mathematical Foundations," MITRE, 1973.

Bush, G. W., National Response Plan, Cyber Incident Annex, 2004, p. CYB-5.

Conklin, W. A., "Why FISMA Falls Short: The Need for Security Metrics," WISP 2008, Montreal, Canada, December 7–9, 2007.

Cyberspace Policy Review, http://www.whitehouse.gov/assets/documents/ Cyberspace_Policy_Review_final.pdf, p. vi.

Davis, J., Memorandum: Suspension of Certification and Accreditation Activity, National Aeronautics and Space Administration, May 18, 2010.

Department of Homeland Security, National Response Framework, January 2008, http://www.fema.gov/pdf/emergency/nrf/nrf-core.pdf (accessed February 9, 2011), p. 1.

Department of Homeland Security (DHS), "Secretary Napolitano Opens New National Cybersecurity and Communications Integration Center," http://www.dhs.gov/ynews/releases/pr_1256914923094.shtm (accessed December 3, 2010).

Department of Homeland Security, US-CERT Monthly Activity Summary, December 2010, http://www.us-cert.gov/press_room/monthlysummary 201012.pdf (accessed February 7, 2011).

Department of Homeland Security, Homeland Security Presidential Directive 7: Critical Infrastructure Identification, Prioritization, and Protection, http:// www.dhs.gov/xabout/laws/gc_1214597989952.shtm (accessed December 6, 2010).

Federal IT Dashboard, http://it.usaspending.gov/?q=content/current-year-fy2010-enacted (accessed September 8, 2010).

FISMA U.S. Code - Title 44, Chapter 35, Subchapter III, Sec. 3544, obtained online at http://www.law.cornell.edu/uscode/usc_sec_44_00003544----000-.html (accessed October 28, 2011).

Gates, R., Department of Defense, Fiscal Year 2011 IT President's Budget Request, Department of Defense: Washington, DC, March 2010, https:// snap.pae.osd.mil/snapit/ReportOpen.aspx?SysID=PB2011_NSA (accessed July 27, 2010).

Homeland Security Presidential Directive (HSPD) Bush, G.W., Homeland Security Presidential Directive 7, Washington, D.C.: The White House, December 17, 2003, from the Federation of American Scientists' Intelligence Resource Program, http://www.fas.org/irp/offdocs/nspd/hspd-7.html. accessed October 28, 2011.

Hoover, J. N., "NSA Ready To Spend $902 Million on Informance Assurance," *Information Week Security Dark Reading*, April 14, 2010, http://darkreading.com/security/government/showArticle.jhtml?articleID=224400245 (accessed July 27, 2010).

Jackson, W. "U.S. needs strong cyberwarfare doctrine, says former NSA director," *Defense Systems*, July 30, 2010.

Lynn, W. J., "Defending a New Domain," *Foreign Affairs*, September/October 2010.

National Cyber Incident Response Plan–Interim Version (NCIRP), Department of Homeland Security, September 2010, p. 3.

Neumann, P. G., R. S. Boyer, R. J. Feiertag, K. N. Levitt, and L. Robinson, "A Provably Secure Operating System; The System, Its Applications, and Proofs." SRI International, Menlo Park, CA, February 1977.

Obama, B., Budget of the United States Government, Fiscal Year 2011, Office of Management and Budget: Washington, DC, February 1, 2010.

Ponemon Institute. 2009. Cyber Security Mega Trends: Study of IT leaders in the U.S. federal government.

Verizon 2010 Data Breach Investigations Report.

11

CYBERSECURITY HEALTH CHECK

A Framework to Enhance Organizational Security

SHIH MING PAN, CHII-WEN WU, PEI-TE CHEN, YUN TING LO, AND PEI WEN LIU

Contents

Introduction

Organizations around the world are increasingly using information technology (IT) and the Internet to offer better service to their constituents. IT is now considered a critical asset, and most organizations have implemented some form of security protection in response to cyber threats. In order to manage this risk properly, particular attention is paid to information security (IS) management, such as raising the awareness of employees, improving the skills of IT staff, introducing Information Security Management Systems (ISMSs), or applying security equipment, such as firewalls, intrusion-detection systems (IDSs), or intrusion prevention systems (IPSs) to ensure network security. All these preventive measures increase the information security budget; however, the real question is whether money is being spent on the necessary preventive measures and equipment, and whether they are really effective in protecting organizations' IT assets.

In fact, a lot of security threats are hidden in an organization due to user errors, the ineffectiveness of IS systems, or unknown external malicious acts. In order to lower these risks, many organizations have introduced ISMS based on the ISO/IEC 27001 standard, established in 2005 by the International Organization for Standardization (ISO) and the International Electrotechnical Commission (IEC). This standard provides specifications for bringing information security under management control and allows organizations to implement security control measures according to the standard's defined security policy and operational procedures, which can then be audited and certified accordingly.

In many cases, organizations would assume that they are able to identify and solve information security problems by introducing ISMS. But ISMS has two major problems. First, only security issues within its scope are audited, which means that auditors simply examine whether a policy is implemented or not; however, security issues outside of the scope are not considered. Second, ISMS results provided by auditors only provide nonconformances, not quantifiable data. Management maestro Peter Drucker once said that "what cannot be measured cannot be managed." If an organization wants to take risk control measures to reduce information security risk, it has to properly quantify information security risk and minimize the preventable risk, and the cost of loss. This is why the ISO is currently developing ISO 27004, Metrics and Measurement of Information Security Management, as announced on December 7, 2009.

To improve the problems of ISMS, the Institute for Information Industry (III), a nongovernmental organization that supports the development and applications of the information industry as well as the information society in Taiwan, set up the Information and Communication Security Technology Service Center (ICST), a task-force. The mission for ICST is to assist Research, Development, and Evaluation Commission (RDEC) of Executive Yuan (the Taiwanese Cabinet), to provide an early security warning in advance, and to recover systems after the forensic and other technical services. In this chapter, ICST introduces the Cybersecurity Health Check (CHC) framework to measure the performance of an organization's information security protection with a set of quantifiable metrics.

Because of the current lack of systematic measurement of IS performance, CHC builds on two business strategies: the theoretical perspectives of Strategy Map and Balanced Scorecard (BSC). This helps to improve security through internal and external protective mechanisms and on-site measurement. The CHC framework can assist organizations to identify their potential security threats and adopt needed protection solutions in advance. This will allow organizations to strengthen their security levels and lower the cost of loss.

Theoretical Basis of Cybersecurity Health Check (CHC)

The CHC framework measures the performance of an organization's information security protection with a set of quantifiable metrics. These metrics are created based on the management theories of Strategy Map and Balanced Scorecard (BSC) as follows.

Strategy Map

Strategy Map is a strategic planning tool proposed by Professors Robert S. Kaplan and David P. Norton (1996, 2006) of Harvard University in 1990. It includes two components: "Strategy" and "Map." Strategy is the action plan for specific objectives, and Map is the graphical representation of the strategy. That is, "Strategy Map" can be described as "an action plan road map to achieve a specific value proposition." On

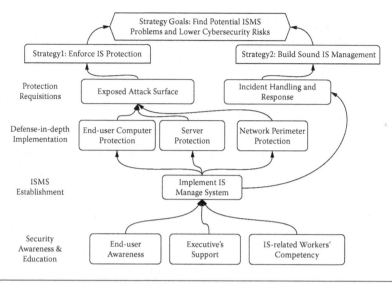

Figure 11.1   Cybersecurity Strategy Map.

the other hand, Strategy Map should clearly explain the causal and logical relationship of various strategies.

When applied to information security, the concept of Strategy Map is to emphasize the integrated resources of IS management and protection deployment. We assume the strategic goal of cybersecurity is to "find potential ISMS problems" and "lower cybersecurity risks" in an organization. In order to achieve this strategic goal, we have to find the road map and causal relationship of management and technology first, and then produce the Strategy Map of cybersecurity, as shown in Figure 11.1.

According to the casual relationship and theory of Strategy Map in Figure 11.1, four perspectives are used to reduce the risk of information security incidents, each of which will be discussed in turn: Security Awareness and Training, ISMS Establishment, Defense-in-Depth Implementation, and Protection Requisitions.

Security Awareness and Training/Education   People are the most critical factor in cybersecurity protection, but also the weakest link in the system. If an organization wants to achieve the strategic goal of reducing security risks, it should provide IT users with training. In doing so, end-users will recognize the importance of security protection to their jobs and be willing to follow the policies and regulations accordingly.

Another critical factor is whether staff members responsible for cybersecurity within the organization have enough awareness and technical competency to protect the organization from external attacks. If the IT staff members do not have the fundamental knowledge or expertise, the organization could be paralyzed when encountering security threats and make the situation worse. Last, the delegation and support of top management is also a key factor in determining the success of an action plan. After completing the fundamental training of its personnel, an organization can enact an information security policy and management system to ensure the safety of its information equipment and data.

Information Security Management System (ISMS) Establishment Considering resource limitations, an organization may base its IS management policies and procedures on ISMS to protect its IT assets. When developing ISMS, an organization has to make sure that the policy and control measures are implemented. If there are no security policies, employees have nothing to follow. If the organization has established security policies but does not implement them correctly and effectively, then ISMS will become a mere formality. It is recommended that the PDCA (Plan, Do, Check, and Act) model proposed by W. Edwards Deming could be used to examine effectiveness of ISMS at an organization.

Defense-in-Depth Implementation Once ISMS is in place, the deployment of protection equipment is needed to meet the organization's requirement in IS management criteria and control measures. The organization should focus on risk assessment. In addition, it should also keep track of the implementation of the equipment to prevent against internal or external information threats.

Protection Requisitions After tackling the above three perspectives, it does not mean an organization can just sit back and relax due to the rapid development of security attacks. In addition to well-known security issues, organizations should actively guard against unknown threats through security drills, incident reporting and response mechanisms, and so on. Organizations should continue to monitor all ISMS measures and maintain solutions for the latest information security information, and take necessary preventive measures.

Balanced Scorecard (BSC)

Balanced scorecard (BSC) is a business strategic management tool, also developed by Kaplan and Norton (1996, 2006). The concept of BSC focuses on finding the balance between the short-term and long-term goals, financial and nonfinancial measurements, lagging and leading indicators, as well as internal and external performances.

BSC can be regarded as a quantifiable indicator for organizations to review their performance on various fronts. Traditionally, a BSC system reviews the performance from four perspectives: financial, customer, internal, and learning and growth. Managers can determine different perspectives and performance measurement metrics based on different targets and strategies and match them with organizational strategy and vision to help each department to reach their objectives. BSC enables an organization to achieve its goal or mission by aligning action and vision; therefore, it can also be regarded as a performance measurement system that describes, communicates, and executes strategies.

BSC is also used to convert organizational vision and strategy into objectives and measurements. It is intended not only to develop measureable items, but to achieve the goals of management and execution in a "balanced" way. Therefore, this study designed a cybersecurity BSC (as shown in Figure 11.2) by referencing the IS protection experience. It tried to identify the vulnerabilities that exist between the ISMS strategy and IS protective operations by the indicators from different IS perspectives. It also tried to identify the performance from the key performance indicators (KPIs) and driving factors.

Definitions of Items

CHC often uses perspectives, critical activities, KPIs, and driving factors to describe the whole framework and also uses them to deduce the weak link in organizations. This section provides an overview of this terminology.

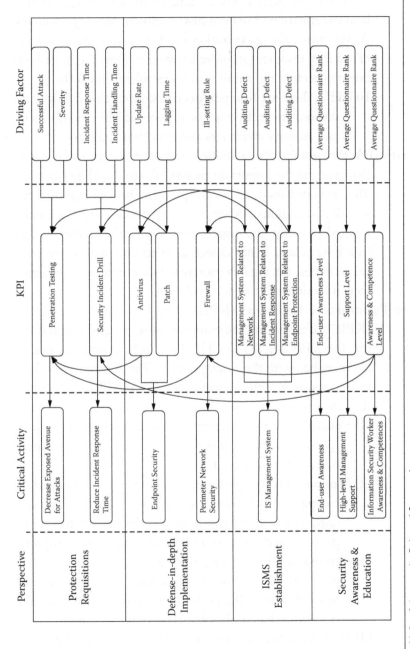

Figure 11.2 Cybersecurity Balanced Scorecard.

Perspectives: Perspectives refers to the different dimensions of IS protection in organizations. Once the performance differences in various perspectives are too large, it means the organization is in the situation of uneven distribution of security resources. At this time, the organization needs to review the allocation of security resources in order to avoid too much emphasis on one perspective and cause security problems in another.

> **In CHC, there are four perspectives:** protection requisitions, defense-in-depth implementation, ISMS establishment, and security awareness and education/training.

Critical Activities: Critical activities are possible causes of perspectives and are the important factors affecting each perspective. They are often used to view the performance of organizational security operations. When these operations are not implemented properly, the organization's critical activities will be in a lower class. If not detected, or to deal with these critical activities, the organization may face potential information security vulnerabilities and problems.

Key Performance Indicators (KPIs): Key Performance Indicators (KPIs) are significant indicators of cause in each critical activity. The KPIs defined in CHC have to be effective, efficient, and matched with the strategic goals. The indicators also have to be consistent with the principles of SMART, a way of setting targets or evaluating objectives, as follows:

> **(1) Specific:** the measurement items and results have to be specific to ensure consistent interpretation and the feasibility of measurement.
>
> **(2) Measureable:** the performance indicators will be used for comparison purpose on a yearly basis for the organization; therefore, the results need to be measurable so that the organizations would know what and how to improve.
>
> **(3) Attainable:** the consideration of the complexity of business activities, labor and financial cost concerns, and time efficiency. The performance indicators should aim at a higher but attainable performance standard.
>
> **(4) Relevant:** the performance indicators should be determined according to the proper categories and implementation data.

(5) **Time-bound:** measurement of the performance indicator should be time-bound so that people responsible for CHC would know when it can be achieved. The criteria can also be referred to as "timeliness."

Driving Factors: Driving factors are the executed "result" of present protection measures in organizations. It is the detailed contents of KPIs, reflecting the status of the most basic of all perspectives. The current performances of driving factors affect the scope and impact of potential security problems. Organizations can recognize the recent protective measures implementation through driving factors and locate security protection measures to improve the needed driving factors. This way, possible security incidents can be avoided.

Hierarchical Structure of Measurement Metrics

The metrics of CHC can be divided into six levels: overview, perspectives, critical activity, KPI, driving factor, and raw data. Each level will affect the performance of the follow-up indicators, as illustrated in Figure 11.3.

The CHC framework uses statistical analysis methods, such as the Likert scale, a measurement methodology created by Rensis Likert, which is mainly applied in the fields of social science and psychology. According to different research purposes, the Likert scale can be divided into five or seven different scales, of which each is given a specific definition. As well as actual recording or

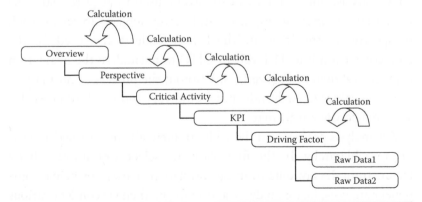

Figure 11.3 Measurement Metrics Hierarchy.

Incident Handling and Response (Critical Activity) = Security Alert Response (KPI)
+ Incident Handling (KPI)

Security Alert Response Interval (R)	Rank (R)
No alerts	11
(0, 1]	10
(1, 2]	9
(2, 3]	8
(3, 4]	7
(4, 5]	6
(5, 6]	5
(6, 7]	4
(7, 8]	3
(8, 9]	2
>9	1

Incident Handling Interval (H)	Rank (H)
No alerts	11
(0, 1]	10
(1, 2]	9
(2, 3]	8
(3, 4]	7
(4, 5]	6
(5, 6]	5
(6, 7]	4
(7, 8]	3
(8, 9]	2
>9	1

Incident Handling and Response	Rank
>20	11
19~20	10
17~18	9
15~16	8
13~14	7
11~12	6
9~10	5
7~8	4
5~6	3
3~4	2
<3	1

Figure 11.4   Key performance indicator (KPI) normalization.

data analysis, questionnaires can also be used to acquire scale values based on different responses and survey subjects to review each perspective in the IS field. The Likert Scale is also used for the data conversion into 11 levels in CHC to normalize the evaluation results, as shown in Figure 11.4. Without the process of normalization, the values of each indicator would vary too much to be evaluated in a consistent format.

All analysis processes in the CHC framework are designed according to a hierarchy. In the first place, we select a group of driving factors from the raw data by using correlation analysis, principal component analysis, factor analysis, and so forth. Then we conduct various cross-analyses to come up with the result, which are the KPIs in our framework. Layer by layer, we delve further into detail to find the critical activities and perspectives.

The values of average and standard deviation are calculated by the principle of normal distribution as the benchmark for measurement. If the measurement result is higher than the benchmark value, we may consider the IS protection performance in that specific area above average. Equally, if the measurement result is lower than the benchmark, it means that the organization's IS protection performance is below average and therefore needs to be reviewed and improved. In the CHC framework, qualitative and quantitative analyses are adopted to probe possible impacts and effects.

Detailed Infrastructure in CHC

As mentioned earlier, the four perspectives in Strategy Map are used to help organizations learn the status quo of IS protection, evaluate the protection performance, and identify possible security threats and vulnerabilities to make amendments and lower the probability of security incidents. In this section, we return to each perspective of Strategy Map and describe its detailed structure, including the characterization of driving factors, KPIs, and critical activities.

Security Awareness and Education Perspective

Figure 11.5 illustrates security awareness and training. This perspective includes three critical activities: "user awareness," "IS-related worker competency," and "executive support." Under the CHC framework, personal interviews and awareness surveys will be carried out on general users, security personnel, and chief information security officer (CISO) to see whether internal staff has basic security awareness, or the capability to deploy protection equipment for the organization. The perspective can also verify whether the internal staff of an organization is familiar with information security policy, management process, and operational procedures to evaluate the performance of an IS management system.

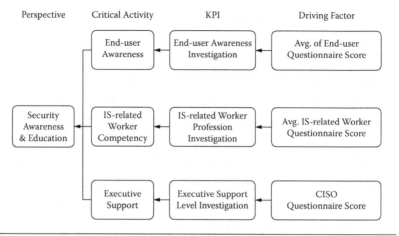

Figure 11.5   Security awareness and education structure.

ISMS Establishment Perspective

As shown in Figure 11.6, the scope of this perspective goes beyond the certification of ISO/IEC 27001 as it inspects every security management policy, process, and procedure based on the security issues identified. The purpose of CHC is not to help the organization to achieve a security certification, but to help the organization identify the vulnerabilities of IS systems in order to take preventive measures and correct issues. Further, because not all departments and

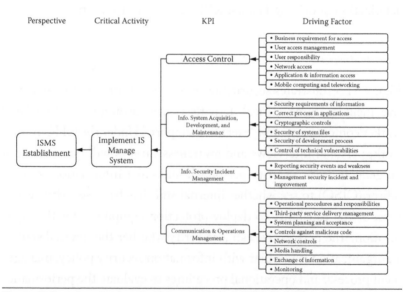

Figure 11.6   Information Security Management System (ISMS) establishment structure.

information systems are included in the scope of ISMS certification, it is essential to know how an organization would respond to security incidents that are outside of the scope of information security management certification.

The implementation of this perspective focuses on the issues of access control; IS acquisition, development, and maintenance; IS incident management; and communication and operations management. It is intended to ensure proper implementation of ISMS and the effectiveness of IS protection measures.

Defense-in-Depth Implementation Perspective

As shown in Figure 11.7, this perspective includes three critical activities: end-user computer protection, server protection, and network perimeter protection. It is implemented by conducting a host examination on user's computers and servers. End-user computer and server protection examination KPIs include the coverage and update of antivirus software, security level of user password configuration, potential risk of computer configuration, and whether malicious programs have existed in user's computer and server. KPIs of network border security include whether the firewall can filter or block malicious packets. The network architecture of the organization will also be examined to identify vulnerabilities.

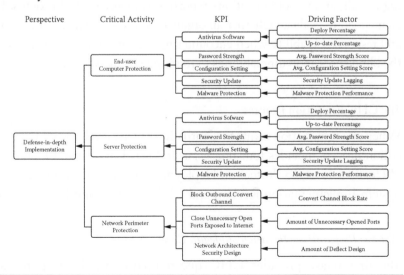

Figure 11.7 Defense-in-depth implementation structure.

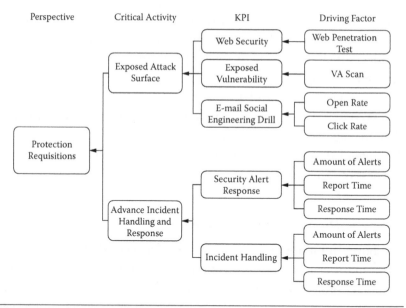

Figure 11.8 Protection requisitions structure.

Protection Requisitions Perspective

This perspective (shown in Figure 11.8) includes two critical activities: exposed attack surface and advance incident handling and response. It is implemented by evaluating the organization's website service security, external-service host vulnerability scanning, awareness of social engineering e-mail, and the organization's reporting/response on IS incidents. It is intended to evaluate whether an organization has sufficient protection and response capability when encountering security threats and identify the blind spots and vulnerabilities to minimize security incidents.

The CHC Execution Process

When an organization wants to identify its security level, the CHC execution process includes four phases, as follows: Preparative Operation of Health Check, IS Protection Deployment Testing, IS Management System Implementation Review, and CHC Analysis and Report.

Phase 1: Preparative Operation of Health Check

The first phase provides CHC questionnaires to the responsible personnel to fill out. This questionnaire is intended to capture the existing ISMS, protection deployment, and the scope of CHC for the reference of service scope definition and sampling. In addition, the responsible personnel should organize the implementation of CHC with the schedule and the necessary items, so CHC operators can perform the check operations smoothly. The output of this phase is an execution plan, including the basic information survey and execution schedule.

Phase 2: Information Security (IS) Protection Deployment Testing

CHC operators will conduct technical measurement and testing with automated tools in the second phase. These tools collect information, such as configuration, update status, antivirus status and password strength, and so forth, from a PC or server, in order to examine the end-user computer protection, server protection, and network perimeter protection. Other information on PCs or servers that cannot be gathered automatically by tools, such as malware protection, network architecture design, will be examined manually on-site by CHC operators. In addition, end-users and IT department staff will be randomly selected to fill out questionnaires designed to recognize their security awareness and education.

Moreover, two critical activities, "Exposed attack surface" and "Advance incident handling and response" are performed remotely. To examine the organization's exposed attack surface, CHC operators will do a penetration test on the organization's website and send out social engineering e-mails to employees to see the open and click rates. To check the organization's incident handling and response, CHC operators select security alert response and incident handling records from ICST database to count the amount of alerts, report time, and response time.

The output of this phase is the necessary raw data for three perspectives, Security Awareness and Education, Defense-in-Depth Implementation, and Protection Requisitions.

Phase 3: IS Management System Implementation Review

In the third phase, CHC operators will interview the ISMS managers or IT staffs based on the indicators identified in the perspectives of Protection Requisitions, Defense-in Depth Implementation, and Security Awareness and Training. The result can help CHC operators understand whether the organization has established the relevant or appropriate control measures, and determine whether an appropriate implementation of ISMS is in place based on the technical test results. By reviewing the organization's ISMS implementation, such as access control, security incident management, and communication management, CHC operators can identify deficiencies in an organization and make recommendations for improvement and preventive measures. Thus, the output of this phase are the recommendations for the ISMS Establishment perspective.

Phase 4: CHC Analysis and Report

In order to determine the protection performance and identify potential vulnerabilities, all the collected raw data will be normalized and calculated by the hierarchical structure, described earlier. The calculated results are then presented in a radar chart, as exemplified by Figure 11.9 that shows an example of a CHC analysis. As we can see most of the KPI scores are relatively high, which means the organization's security protection are above average. However, we also observe three KPI scores are relatively poor: end-user awareness, e-mail social engineering drill, and malware protection. We may conclude that in this case, the end-users may open social engineering e-mails designed by hackers because of a lack of security awareness, resulting in users' computers being infected by malicious software. Therefore, we would recommend to the organization that it should enhance end-users' security awareness education and training, thereby reducing potential security threats.

According to the calculated results, we will generate the CHC Summary Report. This report describes the relevance between each item in the radar chart and shows organizations' security performance and the most vulnerable point in the current security environment. This provides organizational CISOs with the reference they need to improve protection deployment. All the CHC data are stored in a database as a reference to see whether the organization has made corrections and improved over time.

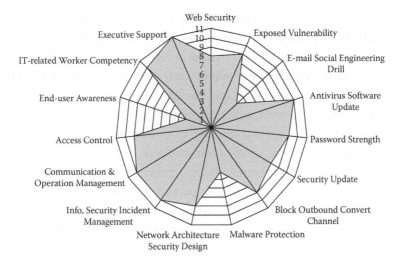

Figure 11.9 A radar chart example of Cybersecurity Health Check (CHC).

Conclusion

In this chapter, we presented the CHC framework that is based on the business concepts of Strategy Map and BSC. The framework helps to improve organizational security protection through internal and external protective mechanisms and on-site measurement. With CHC, organizations can identify their potential security threats and adopt protection solutions in advance, which in turn can strengthen their security level and lower costs.

ICST is currently using this framework in more than 10 government authorities in Taiwan. Results thus far show that in general, government agencies achieve a higher level of security in the Security Awareness and Education and ISMS Establishment perspectives due to efforts in promoting ISO/IEC 27001. Meanwhile, agencies perform less well in the Defense-in-Depth Implementation and Protection Requisitions perspectives. This shows that government agencies do not appropriately implement their defined ISMS. Specifically, we observed potential threats in three critical activities, "End-user Computer protection," "Server protection," and "Exposed attack surface." The most fundamental reason comes from the malware protection and web security KPIs. Therefore, we would recommend for these government agencies to strengthen the effectiveness of protection, such as sampling tests of the user's computer and server security, and regular vulnerability scanning or penetration testing. With CHC, we can find the information security of government agencies in the vulnerabilities and make recommendations for improvement to make the decision makers, such as CISOs, understand how information security budgets must be used effectively.

The CHC framework was designed for public sector agencies in Taiwan but can be applied broadly, to government agencies around the world or to private sector entities. Anyone who wants to examine security with this framework can define his or her own ranking values, derive the most vulnerable part of the environment with the defined driving factors, KPIs, Critical Activities, and Perspective based on Strategy Map and BSC, and make the most efficient use of budget.

References

Corporate Information Security Working Group. *Report of the Best Practices and Metrics Teams*, Subcommittee on Technology and Information Policy, Intergovernmental Relations and the Census, Government Reform Committee, U.S. House of Representatives (Rev. January 10, 2005).

Jaquith, A. *Security Metrics: Replacing Fear, Uncertainty, and Doubt*, Boston: Addison Wesley Professional. 2007.

Kaplan, R. S., and Norton, D. P., *Strategy Maps: Converting Intangible Assets into Tangible Outcomes*. Boston: Harvard Business School Publishing, 2004.

Kaplan, R. S., and Norton, D. P. *Alignment: Using the Balanced Scorecard to Create Corporate Synergies*. Boston: Harvard Business School Press, 2006.

Kaplan, R. S., and Norton, D. P. *The Balanced Scoreboard: Translating Strategy into Action*. Boston: Harvard Business School Publishing, 1996.

Kaplan, R. S., and Norton, D. P. *The Strategy-Focused Organization: How Balanced Scorecard Companies Thrive in the New Business Environment*. Boston: Harvard Business School Press, 2000.

Swanson, M., Bartol, N., Sabato, J., Hash, J., and Graffo, L. *Security Metrics Guide for Information Technology Systems*, NIST Special Publication 800-55 (Washington, DC: National Institutes of Standards and Technology, 2003).

12

BEYOND PUBLIC–PRIVATE PARTNERSHIPS

Leadership Strategies for Securing Cyberspace

DAVE SULEK AND MEGAN DOSCHER

Contents

Introduction

Around the time that Prince Henry the Navigator's (Beazley, 1894) ocean fleet ignited the Age of Exploration from the harbors of Portugal, a famous medieval map was crafted on a copper sphere, marking off *Terra Incognita,* the unexplored territories beyond the edge of the then-known world. The map, now known as the Lenox Globe, featured an inscription of a famous Latin caution, which translates as, "Here be the Dragons." The statement cloaked the unknown—both temporal and geographic—in the mantle of evil.

Aided by new technologies in ship design and navigation, explorers of the day braved the oceans and unveiled the unknown. Rather than finding dragons, they discovered a new world. Over the next 200 years, tens of thousands of people left their native lands as explorers, conquerors, and colonists with a wide range of motives, including fame, fortune, and freedom.

It was during this period that the Maritime Domain concept emerged. Those ships and technologies that permitted world travel also became channels for transferring wealth, stimulating commercial trade, and transporting raw materials and precious commodities between countries. To protect this flow of goods, naval fleets added warships to control increasingly vital sea lanes. Nations that embraced this new domain, such as England and Spain, came to rule the oceans and, as a consequence, became the world's leading military, economic, and cultural powers. The imprints of these global empires remain visible today.

To many, cyberspace appears as vast and uncharted as the oceans in the 15th century. Government, private industry, and civil society all increasingly worry about the dangers manifest in this new unknown, what the intelligence community often refers to as the "gray world." A host of bad actors—rogue states, terrorist groups, criminal syndicates, and hackers—use the murky shadows of a seemingly boundless cyberspace to continually probe for weaknesses. These are the modern-day dragons, real or imagined.

Today we are entering the era of the Cyber Domain, which bears remarkable similarities to its Maritime predecessor. Both create greater linkages and interdependencies, between continents in the historical instance and computer networks in the other, which produce greater potential rewards while also incurring new risks. Both domains represent a medium through which something of value—whether gold flowing back to the Spanish Crown or global financial information moving at the speed of light—passes from one point to another. Those seeking to control the domain face similar pressures, such as governing a vast expanse, enforcing norms of behavior, protecting vulnerable points through which value flows (whether in the form of commercial goods or bits and bytes), and dealing with rogue elements eager to exploit vulnerabilities. Even in the modern age, lawlessness and piracy remain Maritime challenges, as witnessed by continuing attacks in the Gulf of Aden on commercial shipping by Somali pirates.

Another similarity is transformative power. Like the Maritime Domain, the Cyber Domain is fundamentally changing the world around us. It is a marketplace of ideas, innovation, and competition. But it is also a black market and an emerging battlefield. It is a place where ideas flow openly, ideas are developed in collaboration regardless of physical space, ideas are stolen, and ideas are censored. The domain also involves an incredible diversity of vested actors: national governments, private industry, the academic and research communities, national and international governing and standards bodies, and individuals. As the Cyber Domain evolves, all of them have much at stake, much to gain, and much at risk.

For these reasons, collaboration among actors is essential to reap the benefits of, and to minimize the risks inherent in, the Cyber Domain. For nearly 20 years, Congressional hearings, commission reports, think-tank and consulting studies, government assessments, and research findings on security in cyberspace have pointed to a consistent conclusion: *given the role of the private sector as a predominant owner and operator of cyber infrastructure, the formation of public–private partnerships to bridge critical gaps to counter cyber threats and mitigate risks, is essential.* Yet, after nearly two decades of building these partnerships significant hurdles remain. As a 2010 General Accountability Office (GAO-10-628, p. 23) report noted, "While both private and public stakeholders report finding value in the partnership, the degree to which expectations are being met varies." The report also states that, "Without improvements in meeting private and public stakeholder expectations, the partnership will remain less than optimal, and there is a risk that owners and operators of critical infrastructure will not have the appropriate information and mechanisms to thwart sophisticated cyber attacks that could have catastrophic effects on our nation's cyber-reliant critical infrastructure."

It is time for leaders of governments, corporations, and civil society organizations to move beyond the narrow public–private partnership model of today to a more fulsome collaboration framework that integrates and includes the public sector at all levels of government, the private sector beyond Fortune 500 corporations, and—importantly— civil society. To date, the United States has focused its cyber attentions on national exposure to an external threat. Without question, this is important. But governments, corporations, and civil society should move beyond an examination of threats to identify, define, and coalesce around their overlapping vital interests.* By viewing their collective interests in the Cyber Domain more broadly, these three sectors can focus on initiatives that will improve our national security posture, enhance our prosperity and economic competitiveness, strengthen law enforcement, ensure the free flow of ideas, and improve the quality of life for all.

The first part of this chapter describes the root challenges associated with building public–private partnerships, outlines the contours of the emerging Cyber Domain, and discusses the idea of overlapping vital interests. The second part identifies five key areas where leaders in the public sector, private sector, and civil society can initiate action to strengthen collaboration in cyberspace. The hope is these leadership strategies will inspire leaders to pursue new opportunities in cyberspace with the same vision, guile, and spirit as our 15th century predecessor Prince Henry the Navigator and his contemporaries demonstrated in conquering Terra Incognita.

---

* Overlapping vital interests are present when all three sectors share a compelling reason or need to address an issue of mutual concern and importance. Gerencser, Mark, Reginald Van Lee, Fernando Napolitano, and Christopher Kelly, *Megacommunities: How Leaders of Government, Business and Non-Profits Can Tackle Today's Global Challenges Together* (St. Martin's Press, New York: 2008).

Challenges in Building a Public–Private Partnership around Cyber

Innovations in IT, coupled with globalization, transformed business models. In search of commercial efficiencies, companies automated their critical business functions and used the Internet to enhance their productivity, diversify their service offerings, reach customers globally, and rapidly prototype new products amid the drive to be the first to market. With global connectivity, the real-time exchange of information allowed multinational corporations to become 24-hour-per-day operations. However, these same technologies exposed the private sector to new risks. The drive for efficiency resulted in a more open, interconnected system that offered adversaries an avenue for exploiting computer networks. Events like the highly publicized electronic crimes of Vladimir Levin in 1995 raised awareness to the emerging hacker threat. From St. Petersburg, Russia, collaborating with members of Russian organized crime, Levin accessed CitiBank's computerized cash-management system and transferred more than $12 million to various banks worldwide, according to an Electronic Threat Intrusion Report from the U.S. government. CitiBank reported the intrusions to the Federal Bureau of Investigation, Levin was eventually apprehended, and all but $400,000 was recovered. However, the case illustrated how the global information infrastructure provided a means by which individuals or groups could access and exploit computer networks from anywhere in the world.

In 1997, President Clinton charged the Commission for Critical Infrastructure Protection with conducting an in-depth study to assess the scope and nature of infrastructure threats and vulnerabilities. In its final report, after 17 months of research, it identified seven categories of cyber threats: information warriors, national intelligence services, cyber terrorists, economic espionage, criminal organizations, institutional and recreational hackers, and insiders. It also codified an observation made by many experts—the importance of engaging the private sector in a partnership framework to mount an effective strategy to counter these threats. The recommendation to strengthen public–private partnerships has been present in nearly every study on cybersecurity since. For example, a Center for Strategic and International Studies (CSIS) report in December 2008 advised the incoming 44th President of the United States as follows: "The US government should rebuild the public-private partnership on cybersecurity to focus on key infrastructures and coordinated preventive and responsive activities." As part of its findings, it cited the need to create new bodies and organizations to help better coordinate cyber response actions across the public and private sectors.

However, the CSIS report also highlighted some critical gaps that had not been closed in the more than 20 years since cybersecurity issues first appeared on the scene in the late 1980s. Specifically, it stated:

> Despite broad recognition of the need for partnership, government and the private sector have taken separate paths. Indeed, the so-called partnership as it now exists is marked by serious shortcomings. This includes the lack of agreements on roles and responsibilities, an obsession with information sharing for its own sake, and the creation of new public-private groups each time a problem arises without any effort to eliminate redundancy. As a result, the United States has a perplexing array of advisory groups with overlapping interests, inadequate resources, varying capabilities, and a lack of clarity around roles and responsibilities. (pp. 43–44)

Upon taking office, the Barack Obama Administration initiated a comprehensive review of America's cyber policies. The resulting White House Cyberspace Policy Review, published in June 2009, echoed the findings of the CSIS report:

> Public-private partnerships have fostered information sharing and served as a foundation for U.S. critical infrastructure protection and cybersecurity policy for over a decade. …These groups perform valuable work, but the diffusion of effort has left some participants frustrated with unclear delineation of roles and responsibilities, uneven capabilities across various groups and a proliferation of plans and recommendations. As a result, government and private sector personnel, time, and resources are spread across a host of bodies engaged in sometimes duplicative or inconsistent efforts. (p. 18)

The issues outlined in the CSIS and White House reviews do, in many respects, describe the symptoms of a flawed public–private partnership model for cybersecurity. The CSIS report, for example, speaks eloquently to shortcomings in existing structures (such as duplicative advisory bodies, overlapping roles and responsibilities); but at the same time, it argues for replacing these flawed groups, organizations, and committees with new ones, albeit with more structure.

The typical public–private partnership model may not be the solution—it may be the problem. Five factors help explain why this approach has yet to work in the United States.

A History of Mistrust

In devising the American form of republican government, the Founding Fathers recognized the importance of dynamic tension between actors. By creating checks and balances between institutions, U.S. democracy would prove more resistant to Monarchial impulses. This explains why they argued for the Constitutional divisions of power between three branches of government; between two legislative bodies; across federal, state, and local authorities; between Church and State; and others. Historically, one of the most significant tensions in American society has been that between private industry and government, the counterbalancing forces that drive the U.S. economy.

Over the past 20 years, for many private sector owners and operators of critical infrastructures, working with the U.S. government has meant careful consideration of the pros and cons of sharing sensitive information with federal agencies. In many instances, this meant sharing information with agencies that also serve as their regulators. The fear was that sharing this information might expose industry to onerous regulations or unfunded mandates to meet government security requirements that might exceed realistic business needs. Exacerbating matters, the Internet and cyberspace remain today largely unregulated, and few in industry want a stronger government role in its continued development and evolution.

Realizing the tensions this creates, the U.S. government has consistently declared it would limit the use of regulation to address cybersecurity issues. For example, Presidential Decision Directive 63, signed by President Clinton on May 22, 1998, stated: "In seeking to meet our national goal to eliminate the vulnerabilities of our critical infrastructure ... we should, to the extent feasible, seek to avoid outcomes that increase government regulation or expand unfunded government mandates to the private sector." In lieu of regulation, the emphasis shifted to creating incentives that would encourage private sector protective measures. As a consequence, the existing framework includes a wide range of self-regulatory mechanisms that have, in some instances, served to improve the nation's cybersecurity posture.

But this is hardly fertile ground for the formation of a true partnership. Industry has adopted the self-regulatory position largely to stave off the potential of regulation or unfunded mandates. The private-sector argument is that industry knows these systems better than the government and, absent documented evidence of emerging threats, should assess their own levels of risk. The U.S. government meanwhile has effectively removed the threat of regulation, its primary "stick." While incentives and other carrots may compel industry to take action, the lack of a "stick" has created years of awkward maneuvering between industry and government.

Recognizing these deficiencies, Congress has assumed a more active role. More than a dozen cybersecurity bills were introduced in 2010, several of which worked to strengthen government's regulatory or policy role vis-à-vis critical infrastructure owners and operators. For example, the proposed Rockefeller-Snowe bill was popularly characterized as providing the government with an Internet "kill switch." During periods of extreme duress owing to a cyber attack of some form, the proposed policy would give the U.S. government the authority to direct U.S. critical infrastructure owners and operators to shut down their portions of the network for a period of time. But such proposals, real or hyperbole, have reignited fears by industry that government may take actions that could cause dire business consequences. Although the concept of a "kill switch" might viscerally satisfy those seeking to assume greater control of cyberspace during emergencies, such proposals raise legitimate questions for multinational corporations, who depend heavily on an Internet-enabled global supply chain and global customer base, on the effects on their bottom lines. The proposal also raised questions in the technical community, where there are significant doubts regarding the ability of any single entity to effectively shut down the vast, distributed Internet.

Lack of a Clear Business Case for Industry

Protecting computer networks against external intrusions is an expensive and complex proposition. This is especially true when one considers that commercial enterprises have benefited enormously from expanding their networks. For example, by using advanced inventory techniques combined with real-time access to sales information, Wal-Mart has automated its supply chain to gain business efficiencies. Based on buying habits, it is able to rapidly customize its stock to meet demand in certain regions of the country or even in individual stores. Inventory costs are lower, customer preferences are satisfied, and distribution networks become more efficient. These types of efficiencies make for easy return-on-investment justifications.

Compare that business case with one for improved cybersecurity. First, the majority of cyber intrusions will be largely viewed as nuisances, small dollar incidents where the costs of responding can be easily absorbed or can be passed to customers via higher fees or prices. Only when these smaller events grow to a significant number and dramatically impact the bottom line will companies begin to take more significant protective measures. Second, it can be difficult for an organization to assess the benefits of protecting a network: how does an organization quantify a return on investment for a network intrusion that never happened because a firewall or intrusion detection system prevented it from occurring? Paradoxically, the more effective the security measures, the higher the likelihood that future funding will be reduced as the aggregate number of intrusions and attacks appears to shrink. Third, the cost of IT protection is often concentrated within an organization (e.g., Chief Information Officer or Chief Information Security Officer), while the benefits of protecting networks are highly distributed. In other words, the entire organization benefits from good cybersecurity, but the bulk of the spending occurs in one cost center (and is often considered overhead), making cyber spending vulnerable to reductions. Fourth, the revelation of a cyber intrusion is not something a commercial enterprise wants. There is a business incentive for companies to refrain from sharing information about an attack out of a concern that publicity about such an event can cause bad public relations or create a negative impact on shareholder value.

One Size Does Not Fit All

Discussions of public–private partnerships to protect cyber assets often assume that one framework, model, or approach will work universally across government and assorted industries. But an examination of the 18 critical infrastructure sectors* reveals a broad array of interests and assets that are unlikely to fit a universal approach. For example, some infrastructure assets predominantly operate at the "speed of light," transmitting electrons across wires or the airwaves as the primary good or service (e.g., the Internet, ATM networks, electric power distribution). Meanwhile, "just-in-time" infrastructure assets (e.g., multimodal transportation, pipelines, and medical supplies) allow products, goods, and services to be moved via a global supply chain. But there are also immovable infrastructure assets, such as nuclear power plants, dams, hospitals, and chemical plants. Complicating matters, these disparate types of infrastructure assets:

- Typically coexist within one infrastructure sector. For example, Federal Express has a world-class information tracking system that links to a global supply chain of trucks and airplanes that connect with physical offices around the world and has at its core a critical transportation node in Memphis, Tennessee. The types of cyber and other threats each of these assets are subject to can vary greatly and require diverse solutions.
- Interact with similar assets in other infrastructures, creating interdependencies. Automated banking systems operate over a communications infrastructure that is highly dependent on electric power. Failure of those electric power systems requires the use of backup systems (diesel generators) that draw their supply from a global network, and that fuel must be refined at distinct locations before it is ready for use.
- Are regulated to various degrees and compete differently. Some sectors (e.g., oil and gas, air transportation) are dominated by a few large companies that operate in a highly regulated environment. Others are characterized by a large number of players

---

* The 18 critical infrastructures are agriculture and food; banking and finance; chemical; commercial facilities; communications; critical manufacturing; dams; defense industrial base; emergency services; energy; government facilities; health care and public health; information technology; national monuments and icons; nuclear reactors, materials and waste; postal and shipping; transportation systems; and water. http://www.dhs.gov/files/programs/gc_1189168948944.shtm (accessed October 25, 2010).

who operate in a less regulated environment (e.g., financial services). In some infrastructure sectors, collaboration is natural, whereas others operate in a more competitive environment.

- Operate with different perspectives on risk. Some sectors were developed with a "safety" or "risk" culture. Financial institutions and health care organizations, for example, are more attuned to the risks of fraud than others. Companies managing nuclear and chemical plants, meanwhile, are highly concerned with physical security of their facilities. Each infrastructure sector and subsector has developed its own cultural norms around risk and, hence, cybersecurity.

These distinctions are mirrored in the public sector. Some agencies operate in the world of national security threats and view cybersecurity from that perspective. Other agencies are predominantly regulators who are skeptical of industry actions and motives. Some come from a traditional law enforcement perspective or homeland security perspective, while others are in the civil part of the U.S. government and do not consider national or homeland security issues a top priority. For these reasons, one might question whether efforts to build "one-size-fits-all" partnership structures will ever work. Today's partnership models attempt to homogenize risks (threats, vulnerabilities, and consequences) rather than accepting and embracing the inherent diversity of the actors responsible for cybersecurity.

Tensions between Hierarchical Reporting and Horizontal Sharing

As illustrated by the CSIS report, a common assumption in the 1990s, one that perpetuates today, is the idea that only through hierarchical reporting can one create full awareness of a cyber incident. The theory holds that the growing cyber threat requires a "cyber mega-center" in which all data about network intrusions feeds into an operational center where coordinated actions can be taken to minimize the risk and damage. In response, industry developed a host of Information Sharing and Analysis Centers (ISACs) in the late 1990s that were intended to collect information and, if the proper protections were put into place, feed that data to other entities. Conceptually, these centers were designed like a "Centers for Disease Control and Prevention"-like model where State health departments and other organizations report on disease outbreaks. However, each industry adopted its own unique approach to building an ISAC, and in recent years there have been numerous attempts by the Department of Homeland Security to standardize best practices across each of these centers.

But this approach may not be desirable. Protecting the United States against a cyber attack is an enormously complex activity involving literally millions of nodes and petabytes of data. Collecting that information (even if industry were inclined to provide it), sorting through it, and finding anomalies would represent an enormous data management problem. It would also be time consuming, both in terms of lag times for data to be reported and in terms of efforts to analyze it to reveal useful patterns or trends. And once a cyber megacenter had determined an attack was underway, it would still need to possess the decision velocity and legal authority to ensure that federal agencies, state and local entities, private companies, foreign governments, universities, research institutions, and individual citizens take the steps necessary to protect themselves.

Concerns about the H1N1 virus illustrate that even established entities find such activities to be a challenge. During the flu season of 2009 to 2010, the Centers for Disease Control and Prevention (CDC) were the focal point for receiving information and making key public health determinations. The reporting process was time-consuming, involving submissions in many differing formats, and the agency faced a host of issues related to states' rights and cooperation with all parties. As a result, there was a lag time between when it needed information, received it, and disseminated it to the public. Compare that to the horizontal analysis performed by Google, which used a variety of open sources, individual entries, and algorithmic connections to quickly identify where influenza cases were happening—and also where new cases might be expected, based on predicting certain behaviors. By creating such a horizontal sharing structure ("flattening" the data requirements), Google was able to quickly discern patterns and inform the public in a timely fashion. While hardly a panacea (Google's algorithms do not possess the CDC's epidemiological expertise to coordinate national response to potential outbreaks), this instance demonstrates the challenges associated with sharing information in real time. This experience also parallels comments made in the aftermath of the 2007 distributed denial of service attacks on Estonia. In its after-action reports, the Estonian Computer Emergency Response Team (CERT) noted that only when the hierarchical government reporting requirements and assistance had faded was the CERT able to bring the cyber community together horizontally to collectively combat the attacks.

Failures to Effectively and Fully Engage Civil Society

To ignore the role of civil society, both individuals and organizations, in the emerging Cyber Domain is to fail to understand the history of the Internet and the World Wide Web. The civil part of society has always played an important role in the evolution of cyberspace. Bob Kahn (ARPANET) worked with Vint Cerf, then at Stanford University, to create the Transmission Control Protocol/Internet Protocol (TCP/IP) that enabled networks to join together through a standard interface. Marc Andreessen and Eric Bina from the National Center for Supercomputing Applications at the University of Illinois at Champaign–Urbana developed Mosaic, the first widely used web browser that allowed the web to "go global" owing to its reliability and relative ease of use. In 1995, Stewart Brand and Larry Brilliant founded The WELL, a company that many consider to be the first social networking site. The next year, Google began as a research project by Larry Page and Sergey Brin, prospective PhD candidates at Stanford University.

The magic of the Internet's evolution, development, and innovation can be traced to the values of collaboration and openness. Cyberspace is a man-made domain, its development driven by collaborations that spanned traditional public, private, and civil society. Despite this, the U.S. government continues to pursue a public–private partnership model that effectively disenfranchises many in civil society, opting instead to focus on critical infrastructure owners and operators. More specifically, civil society is often a euphemistic term for the general public, who requires greater awareness, education, training, and protection from cyber risks than it currently has. This narrow view creates a troublesome, potentially perilous blind spot. By tilting discussions of the Cyber Domain to security-related issues (e.g., concerns about an "electronic Pearl Harbor" or "cyber 9/11"), a number of potential partners and collaborators (1) are effectively excluded from the dialogue owing to the lack of security clearances or access to data, (2) become discouraged because the security lexicon may turn off those in other disciplines or fields or the discussions are dominated by Big Government and Corporate America, and (3) self-select not to participate because of perceptions that the process is not open and transparent or that their views are not welcome. The current approach also fails to recognize the importance of partnering with a number of institutions (national, regional, international) that see the future of the Internet as their core mission.

However, from a U.S. perspective, a window of opportunity may be emerging to expand discussions around cyberspace to encompass its enabling aspects. The Obama Administration has actively promoted the adoption of health information technology and electronic health records, investment in Smart Grid technologies in the electric power industry, and broadband investments. These efforts are viewed as critical enablers for future U.S. competitiveness and draw in a much wider set of organizations and individuals than traditional cybersecurity discussions. These enabling aspects of cyberspace may ultimately play as important and influential a role—if not a central role—as cybersecurity in driving the future of the Cyber Domain.

Changing the Game: The Emerging Cyber Domain

The U.S. government is recognizing the emergence and importance of the Cyber Domain. "Although cyberspace is a man-made domain, it has become just as critical to military operations as land, sea, air, and space," stated Deputy Secretary of Defense William J. Lynn in a September/October 2010 *Foreign Affairs* article (pp. 101–102). As Lynn noted, one of the three missions of the U.S. Department of Defense's new Cyber Command is to work with partners within the U.S. government, with foreign governments, and with private industry to share threat information and address shared vulnerabilities.

But as Deputy Secretary Lynn points out, the Cyber Domain is more than technology. It is a multidimensional domain, and no single entity or group can manage its complexity. In the dynamic age of cyber, government is not a sufficient proxy for the public interest. We now live in a world where users demand direct access and control over information. Government can be a useful facilitator but must use the domain construct to put effective partnerships within reach.

The Maritime Domain offers many parallels for governments today as they wrestle with new cyber challenges. At the dawn of the new Maritime Domain, partnerships were neglected by the Spanish Crown. With its "first mover" advantage, Spain staked claim to an enormous empire and quickly moved to plunder the new world for gold, silver, and other natural resources to further the wealth of the Crown. This monarchial, mercantile strategy was not sustainable. With the defeat of the Spanish Armada in 1588, Spain began its long decline while others in Europe ascended to create more sustainable global empires.

For example, the British took a more holistic approach. They sponsored corporations—such as the Massachusetts Bay Company—to manage the nation's exploration activities and the resulting resources. These new types of businesses funded the establishment of colonies and had the resources necessary to allow them to wait many years for a financial return. Rather than focusing only on gold and silver, British exploration and colonization also provided opportunities for disgruntled elements of civil society—often religious dissenters—to emigrate, undertaking the perilous journey to the New World for the opportunity to worship their chosen God. The British were able to build an empire because they understood the importance of sea lanes for commerce and national security. Once the Royal Navy's control of the seas dissipated, so did the Empire. But this was more than 300 years after the founding of the first British colonies in the New World.

Over the past 20 years, attempts by the U.S. government to navigate the emerging Cyber Domain fall somewhere between these two historical analogies. It has reached out to industry with the call for partnerships and it has invested billions in shoring up cyber defenses and devising new strategies to manage national risks. It has also created several centers of gravity in the U.S. government (e.g., U.S. Cyber Command, Department of Homeland Security) to manage cyber incidents. But these efforts do not appear sustainable over the long term for two reasons. First, current efforts have largely failed to embrace civil society, a vital player in cyberspace that has contributed many of the innovations and technological advances directly responsible for creating this new domain. Second, while engagement exists between the public and private sectors on cybersecurity, the narrow scope of the perceived national problem (i.e., limiting the partnership to countering perceived cybersecurity threats) has restricted the ability of all three elements of society—public, private, and civil society—to define the *overlapping vital interests* that will enable them to more effectively collaborate toward common outcomes.

Moving Beyond Partnerships to a Cyber Domain Megacommunity

Success in the new Cyber Domain will require the United States and other countries to navigate a problem so complex and far-reaching in its scope that no single organization or even nation can adequately address it unilaterally. Specifically, it will test the ability of governments to work with a multitude of other governments, businesses, and civil society organizations that have overlapping vital interests. The need for multisector involvement is especially great because of how seamlessly interconnected cyber systems have become with military power, with the delivery of services, and as a sociocultural phenomenon that has infiltrated every aspect of our lives. The most effective way to manage this convergence of interests is by creating partnerships across organizations, but this must occur without compromising each organization's values, mission/business imperatives, and legal responsibilities. This type of in-depth, long-term alliance has been dubbed by Booz Allen Hamilton, a consultancy, as a megacommunity. A megacommunity is a public sphere in which organizations—public, private, and civil—join together to address a compelling issue of mutual importance. Although organizations in this megacommunity may compete in other spheres, they act together to address a particular problem that none can solve on their own.

The Core Elements of a Megacommunity

A megacommunity takes advantage of pervasive information technologies (e.g., shared servers, mobile devices, satellite phones, geographic information systems, and social media) that enable people and organizations to communicate easily across national and organizational boundaries, sharing information and collaborating in ways not possible when the cybersecurity issue first emerged. In a megacommunity, five core elements are crucial to effective outcomes:

- *Three-Sector Involvement*: the public, private, and civil sectors are all engaged, involved, and invested in shared outcomes.
- *Overlapping Vital Interests*: all three sectors share a compelling reason or need (what we refer to as an "overlapping vital interest") to address an issue of mutual concern and importance.
- *Alliance*: all three sectors demonstrate their commitment by establishing an organization or organizing frameworks for working together toward shared goals.
- *Network Structure*: all three sectors participate in cross-boundary, multidisciplinary problem-solving activities that produce a social network that underpins true collaboration.
- *Adaptability*: over time, the megacommunity becomes institutionalized and capable of evolving with changing conditions.

The first two elements are preconditions for the formation of a megacommunity, whereas the last three are features of any initiative that is deliberately created to sustain a megacommunity. By its very nature, a megacommunity is horizontal rather than vertical or hierarchical, acting more as a confederation than a single authority commanding resources or directing participants. In addition, a megacommunity engages people at all levels among the participating organizations. This cross-organizational design makes the emergent social networks more dynamic and able to adapt to changing conditions, such as a new threat or unexpected consequence.

The Missing Ingredients in Cyberspace: Three-Sector
Engagement and Overlapping Vital Interests

Today's partnership structures for cybersecurity possess many of these features. But if one were to use the five core megacommunity elements to analyze shortcomings in today's cyber partnerships in the United States, two gaps are immediately clear. First, as noted previously, there is a lack of direct three-sector involvement. While some civil society groups have been engaged, the partnerships first launched in the 1990s and managed today by the Department of Homeland Security largely remain federal-centric and are almost exclusively driven in the private sector by the interests of Fortune 500 companies. This approach largely neglects important communities, such as (1) state and local governments; (2) smaller companies and subindustries that are increasingly reliant on cyber systems; (3) the academic and research communities; (4) groups responsible for creating policies and standards for the Internet and communications infrastructure, such as ICANN, the Internet Engineering Task Force, the International Telecommunication Union, and others; (5) the "white hat" community of cyber professionals that spans nearly all of these organizations but who will self-identify as members of a larger community; and (6) the more than 200 million Internet users in the United States. Only when all these parties are truly invested in a common solution will the United States see real progress toward protecting cyberspace and mastering the Cyber Domain.

Second, the failure to bring all these parties together has created another gap, namely the lack of clear overlapping vital interests that naturally draw the parties together. For 20 years, the focus of the U.S. government has centered on cyber risks. To counter potential threats and mitigate risks, the government has actively sought industry data to develop a better assessment of the Cyber Domain. But this approach is self-limiting. The Cyber Domain involves more issues than simply cybersecurity—its international dimensions that reach deep into industry, trade, intellectual property, security, diplomacy, policy, technology, and culture. And failure to open the aperture will result in the failure of public–private partnerships being a self-fulfilling prophecy.

Overlapping Vital Interests in the Cyber Domain

The Cyber Domain is inherently global. Different countries may adopt widely diverse strategies and may see the new domain as an opportunity for control rather than partnership. For example, some countries might choose to allow rampant software piracy to continue, or to turn a blind eye to widespread phishing activities or hacking rings, because of short-term financial benefits. This, too, is nothing new. In the Maritime Domain, government-sponsored "privateers" were common through the 17th and 18th centuries, but in reality they were nothing more than pirates with official blessings from their respective governments.

In a handful of countries today, such as China and Iran, government control is too strong and omnipresent on the Internet for a true partnership between the public and private sectors and civil society. In such instances a megacommunity cannot exist, because all parties will be bound to the interests of the government alone. However, the megacommunity principles can easily be applied in open societies. The 2007 cyberattacks on Estonia, and the subsequent international response, provide an example. The Baltic country is so deeply wired that when the apparent distributed-denial-of-service attacks swamped the websites of critical industries and government organizations, including the Estonian parliament, banks, and media groups, it crippled the country's economy for weeks. The attacks lasted a month and were of such scale that the Estonian government was unable to respond to them on its own. It asked the North Atlantic Treaty Organization (NATO) for assistance and worked with both the private sector and civil society throughout its response and recovery. Estonia's CERT reached out to world-renowned Internet traffic and routing experts associated with nonprofit research institutes and foundations; several of them traveled to Estonia to assist directly with the country's defense, according to an article in *Wired* magazine (Davis, 2007), an industry publication.

It took the combined efforts of the international community, industry, and civil society—the megacommunity model—to help Estonia weather the attacks. The attacks also prompted NATO to reexamine its approach to cyber defense, culminating in the establishment of NATO's Cooperative Cyber Defence (CCD) Centre of Excellence (COE) in Tallinn, Estonia. As of 2010, this international effort includes Estonia, Latvia, Lithuania, Germany, Hungary, Italy, the Slovak Republic, and Spain as sponsoring nations. The United States and Turkey have also signaled their interest to join. The center conducts research and training on cyber warfare, with the goal of helping NATO defy and successfully counter cyber threats. By focusing on the desire for an open, stable, and secure Internet, all parties have stayed true to their own values and interests, and are able to achieve common objectives.

The impact of the attacks in Estonia was significant due to the country's small size and its dependence on electronic communications; many other countries would have been able to defend against a similar attack more easily. However, the small scope of the attack should not be a reason to ignore the issue. This follows a pattern seen in existing domains: except for a few isolated battles, early warfare on the sea consisted mostly of minor skirmishes. We are now in a similar period in the Cyber Domain and a grander, decisive cyber Trafalgar may come sooner than expected, causing greater economic, physical, and logical damage than any prior event. In the international community of open societies, cooperation will be critical to defend the network as well as our common principles.

And the overlapping vital interest can expand to encompass a number of shared ideals, principles, and goals. From a U.S. perspective, all three sectors share common goals in the Cyber Domain. For example, it is in everyone's interest that the Internet remains an open environment where ideas are shared, innovation spurred, and competition promoted. From a federal government perspective, an open, innovative environment in cyberspace promotes our economic and competitiveness objectives, allows us to achieve military objectives, and deliver services to citizens. For large companies, it enables global, 24-7 operations. For small businesses, an open cyberspace provides direct access to a global customer base. For state and local governments, cyberspace continues to help deliver services to citizens in a more efficient, cost-effective manner. For civil society organizations, such as nonprofits and nongovernmental organizations, an open cyberspace provides them with a global reach and endless supply of contributors and volunteers around the world. As such, all three segments in our society can agree on an overlapping vital interest—that an open, accessible Internet is good for the country, good for business, and good for individual citizens. This broader perspective widens the discourse and can create new channels for leaders in the public sector, private sector, and civil society to collaborate.

Leadership Strategies for Securing Cyberspace

A critical element of the megacommunity concept is the notion of an "initiator," an individual (or group of individuals) who identifies the overlapping vital interests that draw the three sectors together and moves them to action. This chapter has pointed to many difficulties surrounding the creation of public–private partnerships for cybersecurity. In particular, the failure to engage civil society is a significant and systemic flaw in current partnership models. But the emergence of the Cyber Domain is creating new windows for all three sectors to engage in a broader dialogue that balances the opportunities and risks in cyberspace. This section will describe five key levers that leaders can pull as initiators for a cyber megacommunity. For each lever, we will describe how it might influence cyberspace and offer a specific example of how a leader might serve to initiate action.

Lever 1: Influencing National, Regional, and Global Policy

Cyberspace is governed by a complex, multilayered web of international organizations, national entities, and industry and volunteer associations, each with its own set of authorities, agendas, and areas of focus.* Within the U.S. government, each agency presses ahead with its own plan based on its narrow writ; in the private sector, each corporation pushes for policies that satisfy its narrow needs. Tensions between the public and private sectors over the U.S. government's proper role in cyber governance further complicate efforts to craft a comprehensive plan that ties together U.S. cyber-related activities and encourages stakeholders in the public, private, and civil sectors to work together toward common goals. This complexity is mirrored at the international level, where differing national, regional, and transnational interests shape debates about Internet policy.

Regardless of the context, effective policies in cyberspace will require a comprehensive framework that captures the dynamic interplay among its many global constituencies. However, by viewing cyberspace as a singular domain rather than a universally amorphous gray area, one can envision a more orderly development of national and international laws, policies, regulations, norms of behavior, and

---

* The Government Accountability Office (GAO) identified 19 international organizations that it regarded as the most influential in the realm of cybersecurity and governance of cyberspace. "Cyberspace: United States Faces Challenges in Addressing Global Cybersecurity and Governance," (GAO-10-606), pp. 8–9.

doctrine—or stated differently, a common context for all actors to engage globally on a level playing field. This is not theoretical: the December 2010 discussions at the United Nations about cyberspace and issues of Internet governance, policy, and regulation demonstrate a growing appetite to create such a framework. But governments alone cannot govern the Internet; all three sectors must maintain their strong roles in Internet governance policy.

Areas of potential policy collaboration across the public sector, private sector, and civil society may prove difficult, challenging, and even daunting. These include launching negotiations to harmonize electronic intrusion laws and associated extradition rules; securing international agreements to reduce cyber risks (or, as noted cyber expert Richard Clarke suggests, cyber arms control agreements); seeking common legal and policy frameworks on protecting personal privacy; determining appropriate levels of governmental regulation of cyberspace in a postconvergence environment; balancing concerns about free speech and transparency with national security needs; enforcing intellectual property rights; and preserving and protecting cyber assets viewed as critical industrial base components. It is important to note, however, that expanding the engagement of governments does not have to translate into more governmental control and regulation. Business and civil society have equally vested interests in participating in policy-making processes and carry their own weight in terms of how public policy is set. The key is creating a *common context* for those policy discussions to occur in a structured fashion, something sorely lacking today in cyberspace.

A global leader, whether from the public sphere, the private sector, or civil society, can help all the parties better understand and recognize the legitimate issues and equities of all. As noted earlier, mistrust exists between industry and government around sharing incident information. Industry fears that sharing this information will ultimately result in new regulations; from the other side, government worries that industry may expose its sources and methods for collecting cyber threat data. But this is only one part of a larger mistrust. Those in civil society may worry that governmental regulation will stifle the open qualities of the Internet, which they view as the "secret sauce" that enables it to grow exponentially and empower individuals and communities across the globe. They may also worry about perceived corporate influence over the Internet, where companies control and use vast amounts of data with limited or no oversight. For their part, governments and industry may view parts of civil society as utopian or naïve on matters of national security or economic competitiveness. This last cleavage was all-too-evident in the WikiLeaks exposures of 2010. In that instance, those in government and industry perceived parts of civil society battling against their legitimate interests, both in terms of releasing sensitive information and via hackivist attacks against corporate and government websites.

As an initiator, a global leader needs to help these parties identify where their vital interests overlap and enable them to move closer together. In government, a leader might choose to map the various jurisdictional authorities spread across the U.S. government to gain a better collective appreciation for agencies' responsibilities—and to devise a more integrated strategy. This is a complicated problem in that the legal authorities and agency roles and responsibilities have struggled to keep pace with the disruptive powers of the Internet. But failure to grasp these seams in national laws and policy will result in a Cartesian Circle of bad policy making by governments. In the commercial sector, a leader may start to work with his or her industry to better grapple with the "system of systems" challenges they collectively face when operating the Internet—to demonstrate that securing cyber networks is more than building an individual business case, but an industry resiliency issue. In civil society, a leader might work with international organizations to broaden participation in this dialogue and educate global users on the full range of security, economic, and sociocultural issues that are influencing how the Internet should be governed as a common global good.

Lever 2: Stimulating Technology Innovation

Conventional wisdom holds that government and the private sector are responsible for technology breakthroughs via large-scale research and development efforts. Perhaps the most pervasively cited model in the history of humanity for innovation is the Manhattan Project. In reality, however, innovations can come from all three sectors and take many forms, from large-scale government and corporate laboratories to the Library at Alexandria to suburban garages across the United States.

Consider, for example, the role civil society helped play in Prince Henry's great strides in exploration. The opening of the Maritime Domain could not have occurred had it not been preceded by scientific progress in the 14th century, particularly the development of geographical maps and the compass. Prince Henry also benefited from the 15th century introduction of the caravel, an improved ship with triangular sails that allowed for more maneuverability against the prevailing wind. In the 16th century, the mariner's astrolabe became widely used, giving sailors a new technology to determine latitude using the noon position of the sun or the meridian altitude of a known star. These innovations all came from individuals. As the Maritime Domain opened up in the 16th century, Prince Henry the Navigator's court quickly grew into a technological base for exploration, according to many historians. He funded a naval arsenal, an observatory, and other entities that could be seen today as research centers. As a result, his efforts laid the groundwork for the great explorers, such as Columbus, Vasco da Gama, and Magellan.

New technologies are fundamental to the exploration and development of new domains. One strategy for public sector, private sector, and civil society leaders is to initiate and champion the development of cyber regional innovation clusters. President Obama, for example, has placed a significant bet on the concept of regional innovation clusters as a competitive differentiator for the United States. The underlying belief is that regional innovation clusters produce high-value, high-paying jobs in geographic concentrations and enable greater national competitiveness. The United States is not alone in subscribing to the idea of clusters, which are prevalent across Europe and emerging in places such as India, China, and Brazil. Growing research supports the idea that cluster development is greatly enhanced through interconnections with other clusters. When a region attracts highly skilled workers, academic institutions, and associated regional cultures, other industries and clusters are more apt to follow. Geography is at the core of many cluster theories, with examples including Silicon Valley, the Research Triangle, Hollywood, and Bollywood.

To initiate the creation of a cyber megacommunity and to identify overlapping vital interests, global leaders should look at how best to increase the number of, and strengthen the interconnections between, cyber clusters around the world—to identify emerging clusters, create a community of these clusters that help drive technology innovation and development, and ensure that all three sectors are deeply invested in the success of these clusters. Take the coding of software, for example. Much of the world's software is outsourced with individual lines of code and segments of lines of code being developed in different parts of the world. A software package developed for Microsoft could theoretically include lines of code developed by individuals on every continent in the world. In the coming years, this scenario will become increasingly likely.

Lever 3: Rewarding Organizational and Management Practice Improvements

Sound management practices can play an important role by creating incentives for innovation. In 1707, more than 1,400 British sailors died when their fleet sank in stormy weather off the coast of the Isles of Scilly, far north of their intended route through the English Channel. It was one of the greatest maritime disasters in British history. The cause was the navigators' inability to accurately calculate their position. Out of this disaster arose the Longitude Act, which offered monetary awards for advancements made toward a practical way of determining a ship's longitudinal location. Funding for the program, which offered a variety of prizes based on the level of contribution to the solution, was the equivalent of approximately $5 million in today's dollars. After decades of research and development by numerous parties, in 1765, John Harrison was awarded the main prize for his work on the marine chronometer.

Based on their historical track record, award programs have proven a highly effective means by which to encourage industry interest, investment, and innovation. Successful contemporary government awards programs include the President's Quality Award, the Malcolm Baldrige National Quality Improvement Award, and the Environmental Protection Agency's ENERGYStar Program. Each possesses a different desired outcome and awards structure, but all stimulated broader industry engagement and created incentives for the private sector. In many instances, corporations viewed such awards as market and brand differentiators. Equally important, each of these awards avoided the use of what industry might view as regulatory or compliance mandates, enabling government to work with industry and civil society toward developing and implementing commonly accepted—and voluntary—best practices.

In the Cyber Domain, leaders can advocate for the creation of similar awards programs that improve core business processes and educate other leaders on how public, private, nonprofit, and other organizations can embrace cyberspace in a smart, responsible manner. Awards programs can assume many forms and functions and deliver different results. Yet, at their core, the intent is the same: motivate behaviors without resorting to regulation or other mandates. Consider the awards programs identified above. Confronted with the growing competitiveness, quality, and productivity challenges posed by Japan and the other Asian Tigers in the 1980s, the Reagan Administration created the Malcolm Baldrige National Quality Improvement Award. Averse to creating a U.S.-mandated industry policy, the award strived to take advantage of the strengths of the free market. Designed to be viewed by industry as prestigious, the award created a highly rigorous process to determine which manufacturers displayed best practices in manufacturing quality. The goal was to "raise the ceiling"—to improve U.S. quality standards. The award was crucial in helping U.S. industry regain its competitive edge, and has lived well beyond the crisis it was intended to solve. Perhaps as important, it helped create a new professional community and academic discipline—total quality management—that spans the public, private, and civil society sectors.

Conversely, the EnergySTAR program created by the U.S. Environmental Protection Agency serves to reward organizations that meet predetermined standards. The evaluation is strictly quantitative and requires a less complex application and qualification process than Baldrige. But it is also more universal, with seals going to many companies. In many respects, the goal of this program is best characterized as "raising the floor"—getting as many organizations as possible to a minimum level of performance. Although many organizations have received EnergySTAR seals, what consumers most often notice are those companies that have not. In the Cyber Domain, an award program could offer a way for government, industry, and civil society to work together on specific activities, stimulating interest, innovation, and investment into critical research areas. It could even stimulate development of a more well-defined, multidisciplinary community of experts who would ultimately become the champions for emerging technologies and best practices.

Lever 4: Developing a Cyber Workforce

The U.S. government has initiated many cybersecurity training initiatives over the years, including, most notably, the National Science Foundation's Federal Cyber Scholarship program. But none has made a significant impact in reducing the talent gap that exists between the number of Americans who already have the necessary cybersecurity skills and the number that is needed. Jim Gosler, Sandia Fellow, Visiting Scientist at the National Security Agency, and the founding Director of the CIA's Clandestine Information Technology Office, estimates that there are only about 1,000 security people in the United States with the specialized security skills needed to operate effectively in cyberspace; he puts the need at 20,000 to 30,000. This is a U.S.-specific problem; in the most recent round of the International Collegiate Programming Contest, cosponsored by IBM and the Association for Computing Machinery, four Chinese universities placed in the top 10, while there was not a single American university on the list.

In a 2010 report entitled "A Human Capital Crisis in Cybersecurity," CSIS recommended a four-pronged approach to developing a robust cybersecurity workforce: (1) promote and fund the development of more rigorous curricula in our schools; (2) support the development and adoption of technically rigorous professional certifications that include a tough educational and monitored practical component; (3) use a combination of the hiring process, the acquisition process, and training resources to raise the level of technical competence of those who build, operate, and defend governmental systems; and (4) ensure there is a career path as with other disciplines like civil engineering or medicine, rewarding and retaining those with the high-level technical skills. But this is not enough.

In the Maritime Domain, most training took place on the job. However, there were incentives for debtors to volunteer for the British navy or merchant navy; doing so protected sailors from creditors because the law forbade collecting debts accrued before enlistment.

The modern-day equivalent of this could be a job-retraining program for laid-off technology workers.

Initiatives that start in the educational system are clearly necessary and valuable, but without retraining programs for mature workers, it will take far too long for the United States to achieve the level of expertise needed to be competitive in the Cyber Domain. This is where global leaders as initiators are critical. These global leaders understand the human capital demands on their organizations, their industries, their regions, and their professional disciplines. They often direct resources and investments around education, training, and awareness programs. But perhaps most importantly, they are dependent upon having a workforce that can deliver against their mission (whether public service, for profit, or nonprofit)—and building a culture that attracts and retains this workforce.

Global leaders can promote greater cyber education and training. One innovative example, as reported by Nextgov.com (Sternstein, 2010), an online industry source, is a public–private consortium, supported by the National Institute of Standards and Technology's National Initiative for Cybersecurity Education, that is opening a research institute to retrain up to 1,000 National Aeronautics and Space Administration (NASA) contractors who are set to be laid off as the space shuttle program winds down. The institute supports a range of educational opportunities, including noncredit courses and academic degrees, for periods of time from 6 months to 4 years, depending on the skill and experience level of the workers. Only by using mature workers as well as seeding the educational system will the United States close the technology talent gap.

Booz Allen's own corporate experience as an initiator bears this out. We have launched three initiatives designed to strengthen our own cyber workforce, which we deploy against U.S. government needs in the cyber arena. First, we worked closely with the University of Maryland (University College) to develop the first-ever master's degree program in cybersecurity. This program is designed to not just teach cybersecurity, but to thrive in cyberspace through distance learning. The University of Maryland–University College is the largest distance learning program in the country with more than 90,000 students. As a firm with a national and global footprint, having this span was critical. Second, we launched our own internal Cyber

University training program. The intent was to offer a blend of internal and external courses that enabled us to retrain our existing workforce and quickly inform new employees of our best practices. To accomplish this, we designed multiple potential career tracks (more than just technically focused) and tailored programs around those tracks. Finally, we sponsored an extensive internship program that included contests and special projects, with some of those projects turning into actual capabilities and services the firm has subsequently delivered to clients.

Lever 5: Delivering Operational Excellence

Perhaps the Holy Grail in cyberspace to date has been attaining situational awareness—a real-time wide-ranging understanding of the constantly changing threat environment. Tracking electrons at the speed of light is a challenge, but situational awareness is made more difficult by three factors. First, the disruptive nature of Internet technologies and associated applications make for a volatile environment where trends are often outdated within months. Second, the lack of attribution in cyberspace makes attaining situational awareness nearly impossible. Without matching actor and intent to a series of electrons, a malignancy could be quickly identified as benign and vice versa. Third, there is little integration across the public and private sectors; between differing sectors in industry; between government agencies; and within industry sectors. For example, companies have little access to classified information about cyber threats, and there is no single, authoritative government source for cybersecurity information. At the same time, the private sector shares little with government. Input from civil society and academia is not always widely distributed to industry and government entities who could benefit from it. And there is no overarching strategy to encourage civil society to take part in addressing the most pressing cyber issues.

Industry, government, and civil society have made numerous attempts to improve cyber information sharing, but it has never been attempted within the construct of a megacommunity. Past efforts have failed to succeed for numerous reasons, with a "lack of trust" often cited as a culprit. Some have urged that an enormous cyber watch center be built and staffed around the clock with representatives from industry, government, and civil society. Only through such expensive, hierarchical, labor-intensive efforts, some say, can true collaboration exist.

However, the need for trust is something of a red herring and has become a distraction that threatens to undermine information-sharing efforts across the domain. In an article in the *American Journal of Sociology*, Stanford University's Dr. Mark Granovetter (1973) offers evidence that a strong relationship is not necessary to productive exchange of information. Instead, he finds that one can reach a much larger and better informed audience through "weak ties." Even though weak ties can be perceived as alienating, in reality they facilitate relationships between small groups, allowing for small-scale interaction to be translated into large-scale patterns. Weak ties are indispensable to individuals' integration into communities. Strong ties, while they account for cohesion within small groups, actually lead to overall fragmentation. The Cyber Domain has already seen some measure of success through organic operations based on weak ties. In the fight against Conficker, a virulent self-updating worm that has infected tens of millions of computers around the world since November 2008, cybersecurity experts reached out to one another to form a loosely knit group through which they shared information and built on one another's discoveries. While the Conficker worm is still propagating through unpatched machines, this group allowed participating experts to build on one another's discoveries and protect their systems accordingly.

Global leaders can expand their own networks, and encourage their teams to do so as well, reaching out to colleagues across the three sectors. This improves information sharing in both directions— a team with a wide network of weak ties will be better positioned to disseminate its own research or information and will receive critical updates from other groups faster and more efficiently. This requires a bit of a change in perspective—the fear of sharing based on issues such as intellectual property or bad publicity often dampens any urge to share. But a team with a wide network is situated well to move forward at the cutting edge.

Conclusion

By viewing cyberspace as a Domain as opposed to a perpetually uncharted ocean, we open up possibilities for improved partnering. What is lacking today, however, is a common policy context for the diverse cyber constituencies to productively engage, the lack of which explains why public–private partnerships have not effectively worked and why vital elements of civil society seem excluded from the dialogue. We advocate a different approach:

- Recognize that the Cyber Domain is a global opportunity. As with the land, sea, air, and space domains, the Cyber Domain will be at once a social gathering place, a mode to accumulate and move wealth, and potentially a military and economic battlefield between rivals.
- Strategies in the Cyber Domain must mirror the technological convergence that has inspired the growth of the Internet and its influence. Our laws, policies, and even cultures are struggling to keep pace with the disruptive nature of cyberspace. This requires a partnership that expands beyond U.S. government agencies and Fortune 500 companies. Only by launching a more holistic, inclusive process that brings all governments, the private sector, and civil society together can we hope to master the Cyber Domain.
- Engaging these parties means finding common ground in the form of overlapping vital interests that draw them together. Consider, for example, the idea of an open Internet. While there are certainly national security and economic considerations to factor into the meaning of an open Internet, a reality confronts all parties: openness has been the "secret sauce" of the Internet, driving its technological innovation, its explosive growth to all regions of the globe, and its remarkable pace of social adoption. Efforts to limit this openness will only serve to kill the Golden Goose.
- Global leaders are essential as initiators, experimenters, and explorers. Whether helping to devise a more holistic policy framework, stimulating the development of global cyber innovation clusters, creating national or global awards programs to improve management practices, investing in education

programs, or striving to improve our ability to understand what is happening in cyberspace, leaders must step forward and bring these three sectors together.

In most societies, an open Internet remains in the best interest of all. Government leaders must work with their colleagues in industry and the previously marginalized civil society on their overlapping vital interests. The emerging Cyber Domain presents a window of opportunity to change the course of history by nurturing true partnerships across all three sectors based on this and other yet-to-be-defined overlapping vital interests. As with all domains before it, there are numerous challenges and opportunities facing leaders. The United States and the world are at an important maturation point as the Cyber Domain replaces the Terra Incognita of the early days of the Internet with a new order. This presents all three sectors with the opportunity to define their overlapping vital interests and build collaborative, productive, and enduring partnerships that at once significantly reduce global, national, and organizational cyber risks while also recognizing the significance of the cyberspace as a global good.

References

Beazley, C. R. *Prince Henry the Navigator, the Hero of Portugal and of Modern Discovery; 1394–1460 A.D.: With an Account of Geographical Progress Throughout the Middle Ages As the Preparation for His Work.* (London: G. P. Putnam's Sons, 1898) (accessed via http://www.archive.org/details/princehenrythena18757gut).

Center for Strategic and International Studies. December 2008. Securing Cyberspace for the 44th Presidency. csis.org/files/media/csis/pubs/081208_securingcyberspace_44.pdf.

Center for Strategic and International Studies. November 2010. A Human Capital Crisis in Cybersecurity. http://csis.org/publication/prepublication-a-human-capital-crisis-in-cybersecurity.

Davis, J., "Hackers Take Down the Most Wired Country in Europe," *Wired*, August 21, 2007.

Gerencser, M., R. Van Lee, F. Napolitano, and C. Kelly, *Megacommunities: How Leaders of Government, Business and Non-Profits Can Tackle Today's Global Challenges Together* (St. Martin's Press, New York: 2008).

Government Accountability Office. "Critical Infrastructure Protection: Key Public and Private Cyber Expectations Need to Be Consistently Addressed" (GAO-10-628), p. 23.

Government Accountability Office. "Cyberspace: United States Faces Challenges in Addressing Global Cybersecurity and Governance" (GAO-10-606), pp. 8–9.

Granovetter, M. S., "The Strength of Weak Ties," *American Journal of Sociology* 78 (6): 1360–1380, May 1973.

http://ia361308.us.archive.org/10/items/princehenrythena18757gut/18757-h/18757-h.htm#Page_308.

Lynn III, W. J. "Defending a New Domain," *Foreign Affairs*, September/October 2010, pp. 101–102.

Presidential Decision Directive 63, Critical Infrastructure Protection, May 22, 1998.

Sternstein, A. October 9, 2010. NIST to help retrain NASA employees as cyber specialists. Nextgov.com. http://www.nextgov.com/nextgov/ng_20100910_7598.php.

The President's Commission on Critical Infrastructure Protection, Critical Foundations: Protecting America's Infrastructures (Government Printing Office, Washington, DC: 1997), p. 20.

White House. June 2009. Cyberspace Policy Review: Assuring a Trusted and Resiliant Information and Communications Infrastructure. http://www.whitehouse.gov/assets/documents/Cyberspace_Policy_Review_final.pdf.

13

IS THERE A CONCLUSION TO CYBERSECURITY?

KIM ANDREASSON

Contents

Introduction

Cybersecurity is a moving target that evolves with such speed that it is difficult to capture an up-to-date picture of it. New threats, or variations of old ones, emerge every day as do strategies to defend against them. Parts of this volume may be out of date by the time it is published, but that is a chance worth taking if other parts can contribute to our understanding of the topic. Cybersecurity is a challenge at all levels of government: from municipalities handling online transactions to federal agencies dealing with matters of national security. It is also a challenge that is unlikely to go away and, as such, there does not seem to be a conclusion to cybersecurity. Instead, it has to continuously evolve to defend against emerging threats.

The first part of this chapter highlights some practical organizational considerations when building, or improving, cybersecurity from a policy perspective. The second part of the chapter provides an overview of two broad emerging trends that are likely to increasingly affect the public sector and hence its cybersecurity efforts: the movement to mobility and cyber warfare.

Part I: Organizational Cybersecurity

To simply build virtual walls, so called firewalls, to keep out intruders is not possible. As illustrated in the physical world, in the cases of the Great Wall of China and the Berlin Wall, such an approach is not always effective. The size or strength of these walls were useless when people eventually found ingenious ideas to get around them, by flying over them, digging under them, masquerading as someone else to get through them, or continuously attacking them. Like its physical counterparts, the most important aspect of cybersecurity, therefore, is not the technical building blocks but rather human behavior. People are users, implicit or explicit perpetrators, and the first line of defense. Because human behavior is fundamental to cybersecurity, it also means we can all do something to improve it.

The Role of Information

There is lots of available information to help improve organizational cybersecurity at all levels. International organizations, such as the ITU, offer several guidelines and toolkits. Public sector organizations, such as the U.S. Multi-State Information Sharing and Analysis Center (MS-ISAC), which describes itself as "a collaborative organization with participation from all 50 States, the District of Columbia, local governments, and U.S. Territories," provide numerous awareness resources, including an annual toolkit. Private sector organizations, such as the IBM Center for The Business of Government, provide practical advice, such as their 2011 "A Best Practices Guide to Information Security" report. Nonprofit organizations, such as the U.S. National Cyber Security Alliance, provide detailed guidelines, such as StaySafeOnline.org, an initiative with a comprehensive resource section targeting specific audience groups. Similar initiatives are also created all over the world.

The problem is that more work is needed to create and maintain comprehensive and clearly communicated cybersecurity policies that are followed. As trivial as this seems, according to the 2010 Data Breach Investigations Report from Verizon, an American telecommunications firm, 85% of confirmed cyber breaches were not considered very difficult, and 96% of them were avoidable by simple or intermediate controls. Similarly, "a high percentage of security breaches occur because internal users are careless or fail to follow procedures" (p. 8), according to an annual survey of Federal Chief Information Officers (CIO) in the United States in March 2010, by TechAmerica, an IT trade association.

Significant improvements have been made since the early days of the Internet, but more awareness is needed. The public and private sectors, nongovernmental organizations (NGOs) and civil society all have a role to play in this effort. Cybersecurity is too often left to IT specialists with little understanding of larger organizational issues or policy making while senior management members do not understand the technical issues involved. In this effort, a major challenge is to translate the latest technical terms and threats into something senior management, employees, and society at large can understand. In a 2010 study that compares the views of 320 IT security staff (employees) in various U.S. federal agencies to one of 217 federal IT executives, the Ponemon Institute, a consultancy, found that employees are more likely than executives to appreciate awareness and training initiatives.

Closing the gap between IT professionals and public sector executives and policy makers is fundamental to improving cybersecurity. As such, organizational leaders need to ask themselves what the technical risks are and how they are being met from a policy perspective in order to provide people with practical guidelines that can be followed, the governance aspect.

It is important to begin by understanding an organization's target state for cybersecurity, which is the maximum amount of risk that management can live with. In this effort an organization should account for both known and emerging cyber threats as well as the unknown. This must be balanced against public sector limitations, such as the tension between transparency and privacy, as well as cost optimization and the potential implications of breach. Once the proper balance has been determined, a culture of cybersecurity must be developed and maintained by establishing policies and clearly communicating them up and down, especially as technologies and risks evolve over time.

A common problem at the organizational level is that public sector agencies only seek to meet minimum standards or levels of security, often due to cost or lack of awareness. This is similar to the issue of corruption where many enterprises establish baseline policy and hope that people follow it. But there, as with cybersecurity, organizations must be proactive in pushing internal guidelines and raising awareness.

Organizations can also develop a stronger cyber defense by building closer relationships and collaborate with others, including the private sector, to share experiences, mistakes, lessons learned, and other information and research. The willingness to collect, analyze, and share information, including about cyber incidents, is crucial to improve security for everyone.

Trust But Verify

Every organization has a responsibility to be proactive and establish policies that improve trust and confidence. In this effort, an objective system of performance assessments is needed and information security professionals can help by identifying key performance indicators (KPIs) and translating technical terms into language that can be understood by management and senior policy makers. Cybersecurity, therefore, becomes an area in which one needs to "trust but verify," to borrow a phrase from former president Ronald Reagan.

But complete deterrence and prevention is hard to maintain as new threats constantly emerge. The second line of cybersecurity, therefore, is to limit the scope of an attack if it happens by protecting data and minimizing damage, in regard to infrastructure as well as information. Despite large sums of cybersecurity spending and improved policies, attacks occur against even the best defended systems, such as those of technology companies like Google or military agencies.

When it comes to the more technical aspects of protection, organizations need to again ask themselves what the risks are, and how they can respond if their data are compromised. For example, where does the data reside, who has access to this data, and how does the data enter and leave the organization?

According to the TechAmerica survey, efforts to proactively monitor and protect networks can have a positive effect. For example, many CIOs say they do not allow removable storage devices, such as USB drives, and also do not support local storage. Instead, they store everything remotely on protected servers. Even though a cloud computing environment, an emerging trend, may complicate internal efforts to secure the transmission of data, moving information to a centrally managed location can also increase security as responsibility moves from an individual to the central provider.

But, as discussed in the next section, the ability to secure and monitor computer systems, the web environment, and any devices connected to network(s) is increasingly complex due to the rise of mobility.

Part II: Emerging Trends

As external and internal public sector efficiency can vastly improve through use of new information and communication technologies (ICTs), e-government is at an exciting crossroads; however, emerging trends can also lead to new challenges or fresh problems in old areas. A host of issues are often mentioned in this regard, including mobile devices and a mobile workforce, cloud computing, outsourcing, virtualization, and Web 2.0 tools such as social networking. For example, "CIOs say they are challenged and frustrated by the difficulty in establishing the right balance between security and improved access to information" (p. 8), according to the annual survey by TechAmerica.

According to a survey of 217 senior-level IT executives across U.S. federal organizations conducted by the Ponemon Institute (2009), a consultancy, the leading security risks within their organization resulting from various trends were the rise in unstructured data (cited by 79% of respondents), cyber terrorism (71%), mobility (63%), and Web 2.0 (52%).

Because this volume has already discussed several broad trends, such as the rise in data and Web 2.0 (Gov 2.0), this chapter seeks to supplement rather than duplicate those efforts. As such, the next section delves into more detail regarding the potential ramifications of the move to mobility, a certain short-term trend, and the inevitable rise of some form of cyber warfare and cyber terrorism, which are likely to have profound affects on the public sector over the long term.

Mobility: From E-Government to M-Government and from Spam to Spim

At a global level, the biggest current trend is undoubtedly the move from stationary to mobile computing, including the ability to browse the web on various devices, such as smart phones and tablets. And as many observers, including *The Economist* (Lucas, 2008), have noted, it is an especially exciting development because countries without a comprehensive ICT infrastructure can leapfrog. At the end of 2010, there were more than five billion mobile subscriptions in the world, according to the ITU, including an estimated mobile penetration in developing countries of about 68%. By about 2014 the number of mobile Internet users will surpass the number of desktop users, according to Morgan Stanley Research estimates (2010).

A key development in mobility is the convergence of 3G networks with greater bandwidth and the rise of smart phones (and other devices) with full-fledged operating systems and browsers that make mobile Internet access seamless. According to the Organization for Economic Cooperation and Development (OECD), Japan and Sweden both boost 100% 3G population coverage and others are catching up, including emerging markets. According to the ITU, about one-fifth (940 million) of all mobile subscriptions have 3G services and 143 countries were offering such services commercially in 2010, an increase from only 95 in 2007. The rise in mobile access is coupled with a decrease in cost and improved efficiency and convenience for all. As such, future e- and m-government development will rely greatly on mobile devices.

Unsurprisingly, public sector administrators around the world are jumping at the opportunity to add m-government to their portfolios. The Singapore government portal lists more than 100 services that can be conducted specifically over mobile phones and countries from South Korea to the United States are supplementing their national website portals with customized mobile access points.

But mobility, broadly defined, goes beyond simply the use of mobile devices to also mean the ability to work remotely and, in a larger societal context, the ability to be online whenever and wherever, a mobile lifestyle of sorts. The private sector, for example, has largely embraced remote work and the public sector is following, albeit at a slower pace.

The worldwide growth in mobile devices (phones, but also tablets and other devices capable of connecting to the Internet wirelessly) offer great opportunities but simultaneously also expose organizations to new threats, such as insecure wireless connections and various new forms of data loss.

Further, a particular problem with mobile devices is that they are "always on," meaning they can connect, or stay connected, to the Internet at all times through 3G/4G networks or WiFi connections. Conversely this means someone can also attack them at any time.

Any mobile device with an Internet browser is, of course, subject to distributed denial of service attacks and Internet Protocol (IP) reputation schemes, but there are also particular threats developed specifically for the mobile platform, such as mobile malware, phishing, spam (spim), and credit attacks.

Although mobile malware has been around for some time, it is becoming increasingly common. According to McAfee (2010), a security company, there was a 46% increase in mobile malware in 2010 compared with 2009. A particular problem with malware is also the rise in third-party mobile apps, which can contain malicious code. When users download a game, for example, they do not know whether or not it contains malicious code, such as a trojan. A recent development in this area is the emergence of advanced forms of mobile malware, such as Zeus MitMo, which received a lot of attention in 2010 as this sophisticated trojan could access the banking information of its unsuspecting users. Similarly, there are specific phishing attempts targeting mobile banking, and there is now spam on instant messaging for mobile phones, also known as spim.

Telecommunications providers push security updates to many mobile devices, but users are relatively unaware of the ongoing battle and the organizations they work for are often not part of the process. Because of the large, and growing, numbers of mobile users, many of whom are unprotected or unaware of the security issues that come with their device, this is an area of interest to cyber criminals. As reported in Cisco's 2010 Annual Security Report, as security products for computers continue to improve another problem is that criminals are likely to shift their focus to mobile devices. Further, according to a February 2011 report from AdaptiveMobile, an industry source, mobile device information is increasingly at risk due to an increase in the sophistication of attacks.

Although mobile users can put themselves and their data at risk, it is also an organizational problem as public sector agencies must extend its cybersecurity strategy to include mobile devices in order to protect the information that can be accessed through such appliances. Like their stationary counterparts, such organizational initiatives should include comprehensive and clearly communicated policies that are enforced in areas such as the establishment of secure transmissions, implementation of security on the devices themselves, awareness and training, preparedness, providing a list of approved apps, data loss prevention (DLP), and a central backup of data.

But the complexity of extending cybersecurity to various mobile devices is likely to increase as the implications of the rise of mobility for the public sector are greater than simply protecting individual handsets and managing back-up procedures. The move to mobility will ultimately mean that we are all connected all the time and, as illustrated by the ITU figures, increasingly so globally. From a broader perspective then, the public sector needs to work with network and service operators to develop a secure architecture and enable monitoring and filtering of traffic, as well as continuously enhancing governance policies and guidelines within the organization.

Cyber Warfare Is Coming to a Device Near You

Coming back to where we started the volume: Because of its benefits, ICTs are embraced by the public sector in the form of e-government. But with our increasing reliance on the Internet, fueled by global interconnectivity, the rise of mobility and the development of "The Internet of Things," tech speak for connecting everything to the Internet, including everyday objects, it is only a matter of time before we are completely dependent on the Internet and, as such, the risks rise exponentially.

It does not matter if it is a device designed to browse the Internet, such as a computer, tablet, or mobile phone, a gadget converted into a browsing machine, such as InternetTV (IPTV) or a video game console, or an everyday object that is now being connected through

"The Internet of Things," they are all susceptible to attack and in case of disruption, can negatively affect productivity.

As President-elect Barack Obama noted at a Summit on Confronting New Threats, in West Lafayette, Indiana, on July 16, 2008, "Every American depends—directly or indirectly—on our system of information networks. They are increasingly the backbone of our economy and our infrastructure; our national security and our personal well-being. But it's no secret that terrorists could use our computer networks to deal us a crippling blow."

Carl von Clausewitz, the German military strategist, remarked that "[w]ar is merely the continuation of policy by other means" (p. 87). So too, has cyberspace, or the fifth domain as it is known in policy circles, increasingly become the platform for policy, which will eventually translate into some form of cyber warfare. Because cyberspace is unregulated and provides anonymity, the "fog of war," as the unpredictability of war is known, has taken a new turn.

The International Institute for Strategic Studies, the London-based think tank that is the world's leading authority on global security, explained in the press statement for the 2010 Military Balance, an annual assessment of global military activities:

> The IISS agrees with the growing consensus that future state on state conflict may be characterised by the use of so-called asymmetric techniques. Chief among these may be the use of cyber-warfare to disable a country's infrastructure, meddle with the integrity of another country's internal military data, try to confuse its financial transactions or to accomplish any number of other possibly crippling aims. Despite evidence of cyber attacks in recent political conflicts, there is little appreciation internationally of how properly to assess cyber-conflict.

Everyone is at risk: from democracies, who generally want to keep information open (WikiLeaks being one obvious exception), to authoritarian regimes, who generally want to keep information under lid. According to Jim Lewis, Director and Senior Fellow, Technology and Public Policy Program at the Center for Strategic and International Studies (CSIS), there is a delicate balance between the benefits of participating in the online global network and the risks of increasing access to information, which can create offline political pressures.

For example, while some say the cyber domain is "borderless," as Lewis points out, there are borders in cyberspace too as the online environment is dependent on physical infrastructure, operated by various business entities that can support, or disrupt, the network. It is an important point because, as demonstrated by Egypt during the uprisings there, a country does have some ability to shut down parts of the Internet within its territory, hence the idea behind the U.S. "kill switch" proposal that would enable it to stop incoming traffic during attack. But the argument of our economic and social reliance on the Internet, stressed by industry executives and libertarians alike, won out and the idea never materialized, though it shows the potential importance of innovation in resilience.

In another example, as illustrated by a 2009 article in *The New York Times*, some, such as Nick McKeown, a Stanford engineer, have proposed another radical suggestion: to scrap the current Internet and build a new version. This is, of course, highly unlikely, and even if it happens, other negative cyber consequences could arise (or return in new forms). Until otherwise announced, therefore, it is likely we will have to adjust to cybersecurity.

Stuxnet may have been the first instance of a cyber attack with physical consequences but it certainly will not be the last. Governments around the world will respond by establishing cybersecurity operations and participating in international dialogue. In regard to the former, defensive measures have been only one side of the equation as many countries race to establish also offensive capabilities as illustrated by, among others, China and the United States. In part because of the proliferation of offensive capabilities, there is growing agreement about the need for online rules of conduct to reduce the risk of cyber warfare and establish norms for when it occurs.

As reported in the *Financial Times* in early 2011, the foreign secretary in the United Kingdom, William Hague, explained the growing importance for doing so by pointing to three attacks against British interests, including one targeting his office, which is set to host a conference on the topic in 2011 "to lay the basis for a set of standards on how countries should act in cyberspace."

Broad international agreement and cooperation will help in mitigating nonpolitical threats (typically financially motivated, such as cyber crime, intellectual property theft, and fraud, but also hacking for fun or retribution; for example, from a disgruntled employee). It will be a lot harder to deal with politically motivated threats that are state organized or state supported (such as cyber warfare, cyber terrorism, espionage, and hacktivism, the hacking for political purposes).

In this battle, Gopai Khanna, a senior fellow at the Technology Leadership Institute (TLI) at the University of Minnesota and formerly the CIO for the State of Minnesota, argues that open societies are in a better position to tackle the challenge than their adversaries because of their innovation. For example, many countries and organizations are setting up cyber competitions that seek to raise awareness around cybersecurity and stimulate interest in such careers, the U.S. Cyber Challenge being one example. But if organizations are to meet the politically motivated cybersecrutiy challenge, more innovation at all levels is still needed.

The Conclusion That Wasn't

It is likely that cyber attacks will increase in both frequency and scope. Malware, insider jobs, botnets, and DDoS attacks will rise in sophistication and continue to cause financial and reputational damage in addition to being disruptive.

But the real threat is coming from highly advanced forms of cyber espionage, terrorism, and ultimately warfare with both online and offline consequences.

Advanced persistent threat (APT), for example, as implied by its name, is a highly advanced form of threat, typically an act of espionage or attack, that is distinguished by the resources, intent, and engineering aspects behind it that make it likely to be the work of a state or state-sponsored entity, and that have recently evolved into a concern for the private and public sectors alike, as illustrated by Stuxnet.

Cybersecurity is a global problem that requires a global response; but it is also a local problem that requires a local response. Governments and public sector organizations around the world must meet the cybersecurity challenge, including, as illustrated above, across three key areas: at the organizational level, in regard to mobility, and in preparation for cyber warfare.

References

AdaptiveMobile. Global Security Insight for Mobile (GSIM) report February 2011.

Author's interview with Jim Lewis, Director and Senior Fellow, Technology and Public Policy Program at the Center for Strategic and International Studies (CSIS), March 25, 2011.

Author's interview with Gopal Khanna, a Senior Fellow at the Technological Leadership Institute (TLI) at the University of Minnesota and formerly the chief information officer (CIO) for the State of Minnesota, March 25, 2011.

Barker, A., and J. Blitz. February 3, 2011. UK Seeks Global Accord on Cyber Behavior. *Financial Times*.

CISCO, 2010. Annual Security Report.

von Clausewitz, C., trans. M. Howard and P. Paret. *On War*. New Jersey: Princeton University Press, 1976.

http://www.cfr.org/us-election-2008/barack-obamas-speech-university-purdue/p16807.

IBM Center for the Business of Government. 2011. A Best Practices Guide to Information Security.

International Institute for Strategic Studies. Military Balance 2010, Press Statement. http://www.iiss.org/publications/military-balance/the-military-balance-2010/military-balance-2010-press-statement/.

International Telecommunications Union. The World in 2010: ICT Facts and Figures. October 2010.

Lucas, E. *The Economist*. February, 16, 2008. The electronic bureaucrat.

Markoff, J. February 14, 2009. Do We Need a New Internet? *The New York Times*.

McAfee Threats Report: Fourth Quarter, 2010.

Morgan Stanley. Internet Trends, April 12, 2010.

Multi-State Information Sharing and Analysis Center (MS-ISAC). http://www.msisac.org/awareness/index.cfm.

National Cyber Security Alliance. http://www.staysafeonline.org/tools-resources/resource-documents.

Ponemon Institute. 2009. Cyber Security Mega Trends: Study of IT leaders in the U.S. federal government.

Ponemon Institute. 2010. Security in the Trenches: Comparative study of IT practitioners and executives in the U.S. federal government.

Singapore government portal. http://www.gov.sg.

TechAmerica's Twentieth Annual Survey of Federal Chief Information Officers (CIO). March 2010.

Verizon 2010 Data Breach Investigations Report.

Index

T - #0085 - 101024 - C0 - 234/156/21 [23] - CB - 9781439846636 - Gloss Lamination